A Passion for Books

A Passion for Books

A Book Lover's Treasury of Stories, Essays,
Humor, Lore, and Lists on Collecting,
Reading, Borrowing, Lending, Caring
for, and Appreciating Books

Edited by

Harold Rabinowitz and Rob Kaplan

with a Foreword by

Ray Bradbury

THREE RIVERS PRESS • NEW YORK

Published by Three Rivers Press, New York, New York. Member of the Crown Publishing Group.

Originally published in hardcover in 1999 by Times Books.

Random House, Inc. New York, Toronto, London, Sydney, Auckland
www.randomhouse.com

THREE RIVERS PRESS is a registered trademark and the Three Rivers Press colophon is a trademark of Random House, Inc.

Printed in the United States of America
Design by Debbie Glasserman

Library of Congress Cataloging-in-Publication Data is available on request.

ISBN 0-8129-3113-0

10 9 8 7 6 5 4 3 2 1

First Paperback Edition

TO THE MEMORY OF CHAIM GRADE,
Great Soul, Great Poet, Great Jew, and Great Friend
HR

TO JOSHUA,
*who is just beginning to appreciate
the joys of reading and books*
RAK

Without books, God is silent, justice dormant, natural science at a stand, philosophy lame, letters dumb, and all things involved in darkness.

THOMAS V. BARTHOLIN

Disparage no book, for it is also a part of the world.

RABBI NACHMAN OF BRATZLAV

Foreword

BY RAY BRADBURY

Back in 1953 when I had finished a longer version of my novel *Fahrenheit 451,* I sought a metaphor for my artist friend Joe Mugnaini that would be appropriate to the text. Glancing through his sketches, I fused a combined metaphor: a neo–Don Quixote armored in newspaper print standing on a pyre of burning books. That chap isn't really a faux Don Quixote, it's me. My history is all books, and rarely anything else, which is why I am up front here, as preface.

The women in my life have all been librarians, English teachers, or booksellers. If they couldn't speak pidgin Tolstoy, articulate Henry James, or give me directions to Usher and Ox, it was no go. I have always longed for education, and pillow talk's the best.

I found my wife, Marguerite (Maggie), in Fowler Bros. marvelous bookshop across from San Francisco's Pershing Square in the happy spring of 1946. She took a vow of poverty to marry me in 1947. Church-mice-poor, we lived in Venice before it was a funny-farm, surviving on hot dogs, pizza, and bad wine while I constructed literary rockets that missed the Moon but somehow reached Mars.

Along the way I increased my library with ten-cent and quarter purchases of much needed books at the Goodwill. Shakespeare, Steinbeck, and Shaw marked down seemed to me as one of life's unbelievable bargains.

I believed in books so much that when I graduated from L.A. High with no hope for college, I carried with me the memory of my short-story teacher, Jannet Johnson, and my Yeats/Keats/Shelley/Lady Snow Longley Housh volume. My second novel, *Something Wicked This Way Comes,* is dedicated to them.

The library as raving influence is best summed in my first novel, *Fahrenheit 451.* Trying to write in my carless garage was impossible. My daughters knocked on the back window, yelling for Dad to come play. I did so, with a diminution of stories and funds.

Wandering around the UCLA campus, I heard the clatter of type-writers under the library, went down, and discovered a typing room where I could hammer out my breathless prose for ten cents a half hour. There was a device under each typewriter, a slot machine in which to shove dimes against the clock. You typed madly until the machine froze, then ran to fetch more cash. In nine days I wrote *Fahrenheit 451.* It cost me nine dollars and eighty cents to write what I later described as my dime novel.

But the important aspect here was the wonderfully crushing weight of the library above. Between stints at my rented Royal I dashed upstairs to grope, blindly, along various shelves to seize strange books and make friends. When I found apt sentences I ran back downstairs to pop them in the mouths of Montag, my flame-throwing book burner and his equally inflammatory chief. Hyper-ventilation, then, was my lifestyle, plunging down to hammer my novel into shape. The library turned out to be the best damn mater-nity hospital in my entire life. My child, born in semipoverty (I was still writing short stories that sold for one or two cents a word), has survived McCarthy, Stalin, and Mao and their fear of information. It now lodges in schools, thank God, around the country.

Along the way I have written more stories, poems, essays, and novels about other writers than any others in our time. I have claimed in one poem that Emily Dickinson was my mother and Poe my father, with H. G. Wells and Verne crazed uncles up-attic. The title of one poem was "Emily Dickinson Where Are You, Herman Melville Called You Last Night in His Sleep." My story, "Any Friend of Nicholas Nickleby's Is a Friend of Mine," told how, age twelve, I helped Charles Dickens finish *A Tale of Two Cities* upstairs in my grandparents' boarding house in 1932.

Finally, not so long ago with "Last Rites," I invented a time machine so I could travel back to save my favorite authors on their deathbeds, offering them hope for their literary futures. Arriving in Melville's last hour, I laid out new editions of his books published in 1930, 1954, and 1999 so that this old man, long abandoned, could see his immortality guaranteed. Herman, I whispered, open your eyes. Read the first line of your book, republished in 1939. Herman did so and murmured: "Call me Ishmael." And died.

I then visited Poe and left copies of his *Tales of Mystery and Imagination*. Finally to Paris to bid farewell to Wilde.

So there you have it, a lifetime of first *smelling* the books, they all smell wonderful, *reading* the books, *loving* the books, and *remembering* the books.

The Egyptians often, in death, had their favorite cats embalmed, to cozen their feet. If things go well, my special pets will pace me into eternity, Shakespeare as pillow, Pope at one elbow, Yeats at the other, and Shaw to warm my toes. Good company for far-traveling.

Meanwhile, I stand here with my hopeless prejudices, to preface these loves.

Please, to begin.

Contents

Introduction:
A Passion for Books

In February 1998 Sotheby's in New York held a series of auctions of a rather unique collection of books. The collection, some three thousand volumes, had belonged to the late duke of Windsor—the former King Edward VIII of England—who had collected them since childhood and had taken the collection with him when he abdicated the throne in 1936. After the duke died in 1972, the books, along with the rest of his possessions, had remained in the hands of his duchess—the former Wallis Warfield Simpson—the woman for whom he had forsaken his family, his country, and his crown.

On the duchess's death in 1986, their mansion near the Bois de Boulogne in Paris, and its contents, were purchased by Mohamed al-Fayed, the Egyptian businessman perhaps best known as the father of the man who died in an automobile accident with Diana, the princess of Wales, the estranged wife of the duke's grandnephew Prince Charles. Some ten years later, Mr. al-Fayed decided to sell the duke and duchess's possessions, and thus they found their way to Sotheby's.

There were three things that made these auctions of particular interest to bibliophiles. First, many of the books were inscribed by famous and/or wealthy individuals. They included, for example, a copy of John F. Kennedy's *Profiles in Courage,* inscribed "To the

Duke and Duchess of Windsor with the highest respects," as well as a Book of Common Prayer inscribed "For My Darling little David [Edward] on his 7th birthday, when he went to Church for the first time, from his loving old Granny," by Queen Alexandra, wife of Edward VII.

Second, these auctions represented the first time in history that books from a British royal library had ever been offered for sale. Although the royal family, as would be expected, made no comment about the auctions, one doubts that they were happy about these books being placed on the market, the sale of such items being, at the very least, unseemly.

But the third—and perhaps most remarkable—aspect of the auctions was that they were proof that although the duke of Windsor had been willing to give up his throne "for the woman I love," he had not been willing to give up his books. Such is the mark of a bibliophile.

We count ourselves among those who share the duke's passion—at least his passion for books. We are among those for whom there is no such thing as too many books and, as a consequence, have become inured, of necessity, to that ridiculous question we all face from time to time from those who do not share our passion: "Have you *read* all these books?"

We are the people who can spend hours browsing through the shelves of a bookstore, completely oblivious not only to the passage of time, but to everything else around us. One of the editors of this book, in fact, was once so engrossed in browsing through the shelves of the old Brentano's on Fifth Avenue in New York that it took him some moments to recognize that the man standing in front of him was his father.

We are the people for whom buying books is not a luxury but a necessity, those who can understand what Thomas Jefferson meant when he said, "I cannot live without books," and how Desiderius Erasmus could write, "When I have a little money I buy books. And if any is left, I buy food and clothing."

While making the decision to buy a book may be an easy one, deciding which pieces to include in a collection such as this is not. In fact, we read and discussed—sometimes at great length—more than five times as many selections as we ultimately decided to use. It wasn't that those we put aside were necessarily less valuable than those we chose, but, rather, that were we to include everything we would originally have liked to, this book would have been several times its present size.

At the outset, we established two rather simple criteria. The first was that the pieces should be well written, entertaining, and informative. The second was that each should exemplify the extraordinary ardor those who love books have for those curious bundles of paper bound together between hard or soft covers. After reading all the material we had gathered and began discussing it, we reluctantly added a third criterion that we would use no more than one piece by any single author.

To be honest, we have cheated a little here. There are two short, although related, pieces by Umberto Eco ("How to Justify a Private Library" and "How to Organize a Public Library"), two pieces by Christopher Morley ("In a Second-Hand Bookshop" and "On the Return of a Book Lent to a Friend"), and two pieces by A. Edward Newton ("What Is the Matter with the Bookshop?" and "The Last of His Race"), the last such a loving and lovely portrait of a book collector of the old school that we simply couldn't resist including it.

In making the selections, however, we also endeavored to include pieces that represented several aspects of bibliophilia. One of these, for example, concerns the eternal question of whether or not to borrow and/or lend books. We have accordingly included Anatole Broyard's "Lending Books," the anonymous poem "Welcome Home Borrowed Book," and a selection from Roger Rosenblatt's appropriately named one-man show, *Bibliomania.*

Bibliomania itself—the ultimate form of bibliophilia—was another of the aspects we wished to explore, to which end we've included Gustave Flaubert's classic short story "Bibliomania" (the title of which was an early coinage of the word), a selection from Nicholas Basbanes's *A Gentle Madness* on Samuel Pepys's unique disposition of his library, and a selection from Susan Sontag's novel *The Volcano Lover,* as trenchant a portrait of a collector as we have ever seen.

Nor have we otherwise slighted the collector. Although the passion for collecting is an undercurrent running through the entire book, it is particularly exemplified by such selections as Robertson Davies's "Book Collecting," Petrarch's "My Friends," William Targ's

"The Collector," and the above-mentioned A. Edward Newton's "The Last of His Race," among others. Because we thought the history of the book was important as well, you'll also find here William Dana Orcutt's "Aldus Manutius," on the founder of the Aldine Press, and Ben Zevin's "The Bible Through the Ages," a history of the Bible as a printed book rather than as Holy Scripture.

Just to show, though, that while we take our book collecting seriously we don't necessarily take ourselves that seriously, we've also included several humorous pieces, including those mentioned above by Umberto Eco and Roger Rosenblatt, John Updike's "The Invasion of the Book Envelopes," and Robert Benchley's "Why Does Nobody Collect Me?" in which he questions why first editions of books by his friend Ernest Hemingway are valuable while his are not, when "I am older than Hemingway, and have written more books than he has."

There are several other aspects of bibliophilia represented here as well. Among these are the particular pleasures to be found in old books (A. S. W. Rosenbach's "Talking of Old Books"), the founding of Book-of-the-Month Club (Al Silverman's "A Good Time to Start a Book Club"), the joys of reading in bed (Clifton Fadiman's "Pillow Books"), and the future of books (Anna Quindlen's "How Reading Changed My Life").

Finally, to reflect the eclectic nature of book collectors and book collecting, we have also scattered among the longer pieces a number of book lists (by such people as Norman Mailer, Jonathan Yardley, Anna Quindlen, and Clifton Fadiman), entertaining anecdotes, cartoons, poems, and quotations from such literary luminaries as John Milton, Michel de Montaigne, and many others.

We do have to admit, though, that we have our personal favorites among the selections. One of these is Leo Rosten's "Potch," the first reading of which, some years ago, marked the entry of one of the editors into the world of words, ideas, and books. The other is George Hamlin Fitch's "Comfort Found in Good Old Books," an extraordinarily touching piece in which the author writes of the comfort he found in reading after the death of his son.

In all we have included nearly sixty selections for all those who, like us, have a "A Passion for Books." We regret the necessary omission of many other excellent pieces and hope someday to compile another collection to remedy that situation. For now, though, our only hope is that you find as much pleasure in reading this collection as we found in compiling it.

—The Editors
Riverdale, N.Y., January 1999
Cortlandt Manor, N.Y., January 1999

A Passion for Books

In a Second-Hand Bookshop

BY CHRISTOPHER MORLEY

What waits me on the shelves? I cannot guess,
But feel the sure foreboding; there will cry
A voice of human laughter and distress,
A word that no one needs as much as I.

For always where old books are sold and bought
There comes that twinge of dreadful subtlety—
These words were actual, and they were thought
By someone who was once alive, like me.

Unpacking My Library

A Talk About Book Collecting

BY WALTER BENJAMIN

*With almost every passing year, it seems, more serious students of litera-
ture discover the work and sensitive writing of Walter Benjamin, a
critic who approached the loftiest ideas and pursuits with his feet planted
firmly on the ground. His suicide in 1940 was brought on by his fear of
capture by the Nazis, from whom he was fleeing. In this essay from his
1955 collection,* Illuminations, *Benjamin applies his critical approach
to the simple pleasure of unpacking books.*

I am unpacking my library. Yes, I am. The books are not yet on the
shelves, not yet touched by the mild boredom of order. I cannot
march up and down their ranks to pass them in review before a
friendly audience. You need not fear any of that. Instead, I must ask
you to join me in the disorder of crates that have been wrenched
open, the air saturated with the dust of wood, the floor covered with
torn paper, to join me among piles of volumes that are seeing day-
light again after two years of darkness, so that you may be ready to
share with me a bit of the mood—it is certainly not an elegiac mood
but, rather, one of anticipation—which these books arouse in a genuine collector. For such a man is speaking to you, and on closer
scrutiny he proves to be speaking only about himself. Would it not
be presumptuous of me if, in order to appear convincingly objective

and down-to-earth, I enumerated for you the main sections or prize pieces of a library, if I presented you with their history or even their usefulness to a writer? I, for one, have in mind something less obscure, something more palpable than that; what I am really concerned with is giving you some insight into the relationship of a book collector to his possessions, into collecting rather than a collection. If I do this by elaborating on the various ways of acquiring books, this is something entirely arbitrary. This or any other procedure is merely a dam against the spring tide of memories which surges toward any collector as he contemplates his possessions. Every passion borders on the chaotic, but the collector's passion borders on the chaos of memories. More than that: the chance, the fate, that suffuse the past before my eyes are conspicuously present in the accustomed confusion of these books. For what else is this collection but a disorder to which habit has accommodated itself to such an extent that it can appear as order? You have all heard of people whom the loss of their books has turned into invalids, or of those who in order to acquire them became criminals. These are the very areas in which any order is a balancing act of extreme precariousness. "The only exact knowledge there is," said Anatole France, "is the knowledge of the date of publication and the format of books." And indeed, if there is a counterpart to the confusion of a library, it is the order of its catalogue.

Thus there is in the life of a collector a dialectical tension between the poles of disorder and order. Naturally, his existence is tied to many other things as well: to a very mysterious relationship to ownership, something about which we shall have more to say later; also, to a relationship to objects which does not emphasize their functional, utilitarian value—that is, their usefulness—but studies and loves them as the scene, the stage, of their fate. The most profound enchantment for the collector is the locking of individual items within a magic circle in which they are fixed as the final thrill, the thrill of acquisition, passes over them. Everything remembered and thought, everything conscious, becomes the pedestal, the frame, the base, the lock of his property. The period, the region, the craftsmanship, the former ownership—for a true collector the whole background of an item adds up to a magic encyclopedia whose quintessence is the fate of his object. In this circumscribed area, then, it may be surmised how the great physiognomists—and collectors are the physiognomists of the world of objects—turn into interpreters of fate. One has only to watch a collector handle the objects in his glass case. As he holds them in his hands, he seems to be seeing through them into their distant past as though inspired. So much for the magical side of the collector—his old-age image, I might call it.

Habent sua fata libelli: these words may have been intended as a general statement about books. So books like *The Divine Comedy,* Spinoza's *Ethics,* and *The Origin of Species* have their fates. A collector, however, interprets this Latin saying differently. For him, not only books but also copies of books have their fates. And in this sense, the most important fate of a copy is its encounter with him, with his own collection. I am not exaggerating when I say that to a true collector the acquisition of an old book is its rebirth. This is the childlike element which in a collector mingles with the element of old age. For children can accomplish the renewal of existence in a hundred unfailing ways. Among children, collecting is only one process of renewal; other processes are the painting of objects, the cutting out of figures, the application of decals—the whole range of childlike modes of acquisition, from touching things to giving them names. To renew the old world—that is the collector's deepest desire when he is driven to acquire new things, and that is why a collector of older books is closer to the wellsprings of collecting than the acquirer of luxury editions. How do books cross the threshold of a collection and become the property of a collector? The history of their acquisition is the subject of the following remarks.

Of all the ways of acquiring books, writing them oneself is regarded as the most praiseworthy method. At this point many of you will remember with pleasure the large library which Jean Paul's poor little schoolmaster Wutz gradually acquired by writing himself, all the works whose titles interested him in bookfair catalogues; after all, he could not afford to buy them. Writers are really people who write books not because they are poor, but because they are dissatisfied with the books which they could buy but do not like. You, ladies and gentlemen, may regard this as a whimsical definition of a writer. But everything said from the angle of a real collector is whimsical. Of the customary modes of acquisition, the one most appropriate to a collector would be the borrowing of a book with its attendant non-returning. The book borrower of real stature whom we envisage here proves himself to be an inveterate collector of books not so much by the fervor with which he guards his borrowed treasures and by the deaf ear which he turns to all reminders from the everyday world of legality as by his failure to read these books. If my experience may serve as evidence, a man is more likely to return a borrowed book upon occasion than to read it. And the nonreading of books, you will object, should be characteristic of collectors? This is news to me, you may say. It is not news at all. Experts will bear me out when I say that it is the oldest thing in the world. Suffice it to quote the answer which Anatole France gave to a philistine who admired his library and then finished with the standard question, "And you have read all these books, Monsieur France?" "Not one-tenth of them. I don't suppose you use your Sèvres china every day?"

Incidentally, I have put the right to such an attitude to the test. For years, for at least the first third of its existence, my library consisted of no more than two or three shelves which increased only by inches each year. This was its militant age, when no book was allowed to enter it without the certification that I had not read it. Thus I might never have acquired a library extensive enough to be worthy of the name if there had not been an inflation. Suddenly the emphasis shifted; books acquired real value or, at any rate, were difficult to obtain. At least this is how it seemed in Switzerland. At the eleventh hour I sent my first major book orders from there and in this way was able to secure such irreplaceable items as *Der blaue Reiter* and Bachofen's *Sage von Tanaquil,* which could still be obtained from the publishers at that time.

Well—so you may say—after exploring all these byways we should finally reach the wide highway of book acquisition, namely, the purchasing of books. This is indeed a wide highway, but not a comfortable one. The purchasing done by a book collector has very little in common with that done in a bookshop by a student getting a textbook, a man of the world buying a present for his lady, or a businessman intending to while away his next train journey. I have made my most memorable purchases on trips, as a transient. Property and possession belong to the tactical sphere. Collectors are people with a tactical instinct; their experience teaches them that when they capture a strange city, the smallest antique shop can be a fortress, the most remote stationery store a key position. How many cities have revealed themselves to me in the marches I undertook in the pursuit of books!

By no means all of the most important purchases are made on the premises of a dealer. Catalogues play a far greater part. And even though the purchaser may be thoroughly acquainted with the book ordered from a catalogue, the individual copy always remains a surprise and the order always a bit of a gamble. There are grievous disappointments, but also happy finds. I remember, for instance, that I once ordered a book with colored illustrations for my old collection of children's books only because it contained fairy tales by Albert Ludwig Grimm and was published at Grimma, Thuringia. Grimma was also the place of publication of a book of fables edited by the same Albert Ludwig Grimm. With its sixteen illustrations my copy of this book of fables was the only extant example of the early work of the great German book illustrator Lyser, who lived in Hamburg around the middle of the last century. Well, my reaction to the consonance of the names had been correct. In this case too I discovered the work of Lyser, namely *Linas Marchenbuch,* a work which has remained unknown to his bibliographers and which deserves a more detailed reference than this first one I am introducing here.

The acquisition of books is by no means a matter of money or expert knowledge alone. Not even both factors together suffice for the establishment of a real library, which is always somewhat impenetrable and at the same time uniquely itself. Anyone who buys from catalogues must have flair in addition to the qualities I have mentioned. Dates, place names, formats, previous owners, bindings, and the like: all these details must tell him something—not as dry, isolated facts, but as a harmonious whole; from the quality and intensity of this harmony he must be able to recognize whether a book is for him or not. An auction requires yet another set of qualities in a collector. To the reader of a catalogue the book itself must speak, or possibly its previous ownership if the provenance of the copy has been established. A man who wishes to participate at an auction must pay equal attention to the book and to his competitors, in addition to keeping a cool enough head to avoid being carried away in the competition. It is a frequent occurrence that someone gets stuck with a high purchase price because he kept raising his bid—more to assert himself than to acquire the book. On the other hand, one of the finest memories of a collector is the moment when he rescued a book to which he might never have given a thought, much less a wishful look, because he found it lonely and abandoned on the marketplace and bought it to give it its freedom—the way the prince bought a beautiful slave girl in *The Arabian Nights*. To a book collector, you see, the true freedom of all books is somewhere on his shelves.

To this day, Balzac's *Peau de chagrin* stands out from long rows of French volumes in my library as a memento of my most exciting experience at an auction. This happened in 1915 at the Rumann auction put up by Emil Hirsch, one of the greatest of book experts and most distinguished of dealers. The edition in question appeared in 1838 in Paris, Place de la Bourse. As I pick up my copy, I see not only its number in the Rumann collection, but even the label of the shop in which the first owner bought the book over ninety years ago for one-eightieth of today's price. "Papeterie I. Flanneau," it says. A fine age in which it was still possible to buy such a deluxe edition at a stationery dealer's! The steel engravings of this book were designed by the foremost French graphic artist and executed by the foremost engravers. But I was going to tell you how I acquired this book. I had gone to Emil Hirsch's for an advance inspection and had handled forty or fifty volumes; that particular volume had inspired in me the ardent desire to hold on to it forever. The day of the auction came. As chance would have it, in the sequence of the auction this copy of *La Peau de chagrin* was preceded by a complete set of its illustrations printed separately on India paper. The bidders sat at a long table; diagonally across from me sat the man who was the focus of all eyes at the first bid, the famous Munich collector Baron von Simolin. He was greatly interested in this set, but he had rival bidders; in short, there was a spirited contest which resulted in the highest bid of the entire auction—far in excess of three thousand marks. No one seemed to have expected such a high figure, and all those present were quite excited. Emil Hirsch remained unconcerned, and whether he wanted to save time or was guided by some other consideration, he proceeded to the next item, with no one really paying attention. He called out the price, and with my heart pounding and with the full realization that I was unable to compete with any of those big collectors I bid a somewhat higher amount. Without arousing the bidders' attention, the auctioneer went through the usual routine—"Do I hear more?" and three bangs of his gavel, with an eternity seeming to separate each from the next—and proceeded to add the auctioneer's charge. For a student like me the sum was still considerable. The following morning at the pawnshop is no longer part of this story, and I prefer to speak about another incident which I should like to call the negative of an auction. It happened last year at a Berlin auction. The collection of books that was offered was a miscellany in quality and subject matter, and only a number of rare works on occultism and natural philosophy were worthy of note. I bid for a number of them, but each time I noticed a gentleman in the front row who seemed only to have waited for my bid to counter with his own, evidently prepared to top any offer. After this had been repeated several times, I gave up all hope of acquiring the book which I was most interested in that day. It was the rare *Fragmente ausdem Nachlass eines jungen Physikers* (*Posthumous Fragments of a Young Physicist*), which Johann Wilhelm Ritter published in two volumes at Heidelberg in 1810. This work has never been reprinted, but I have always considered its preface, in which the author-editor tells the story of his life in the guise of an obituary for his supposedly deceased unnamed friend—with whom he is really identical—as the most important sample of personal prose of German Romanticism. Just as the item came up I had a brain wave. It was simple enough: since my bid was bound to give the item to the other man, I must not bid at all. I controlled myself and remained silent. What I had hoped for came about: no interest, no bid, and the book was put aside. I deemed it wise to let several days go by, and when I appeared on the premises after a week, I found the book in the secondhand department and benefited by the lack of interest when I acquired it.

Once you have approached the mountains of cases in order to mine the books from them and bring them to the light of day—or, rather, of night—what memories crowd in upon you! Nothing highlights the fascination of unpacking more clearly than the difficulty of stopping this activity. I had started at noon, and it was midnight before I had worked my way to the last cases. Now I put my hands on two volumes bound in faded boards which, strictly speaking, do not belong in a bookcase at all: two albums with stick-in pictures which my mother pasted in as a child and which I inherited. They are the seeds of a collection of children's books which is growing steadily even today, though no longer in my garden. There is no living library that does not harbor a number of booklike creations from fringe areas. They need not be stick-in albums or family albums, autograph books or portfolios containing pamphlets or religious tracts; some people become attached to leaflets and prospectuses, others to handwriting facsimiles or typewritten copies of unobtainable books; and certainly periodicals can form the prismatic fringes of a library. But to get back to those albums: Actually, inheritance is the soundest way of acquiring a collection. For a collector's attitude toward his possessions stems from an owner's feeling of responsibility toward his property. Thus it is, in the highest sense, the attitude of an heir, and the most distinguished trait of a collection will always be its transmissibility. You should know that in saying this I fully realize that my discussion of the mental climate of collecting will confirm many of you in your conviction that this passion is behind the times, in your distrust of the collector type. Nothing is further from my mind than to shake either your conviction or your distrust. But one thing should be noted: the phenomenon of collecting loses its meaning as it loses its personal owner. Even though public collections may be less objectionable socially and more useful academically than private collections, the objects get their due only in the latter. I do know that time is running out for the type that I am discussing here and have been representing before you a bit ex officio. But, as Hegel put it, only when it is dark does the owl of Minerva begin its flight. Only in extinction is the collector comprehended.

Now I am on the last half-emptied case and it is way past midnight. Other thoughts fill me than the ones I am talking about—not thoughts but images, memories. Memories of the cities in which I found so many things: Riga, Naples, Munich, Danzig, Moscow, Florence, Basel, Paris; memories of Rosenthal's sumptuous rooms in Munich, of the Danzig Stockturm, where the late Hans Rhaue was domiciled, of Sussengut's musty book cellar in North Berlin; memories of the rooms where these books had been housed, of my student's den in Munich, of my room in Bern, of the solitude of Iseltwald on the Lake of Brienz, and finally of my boyhood room, the former location of only four or five of the several thousand volumes that are piled up around me. O bliss of the collector, bliss of the man of leisure! Of no one has less been expected, and no one has had a greater sense of well-being than the man who has been able to carry on his disreputable existence in the mask of Spitzweg's "Bookworm." For inside him there are spirits, or at least little genii, which have seen to it that for a collector—and I mean a real collector, a collector as he ought to be—ownership is the most intimate relationship that one can have to objects. Not that they come alive in him; it is he who lives in them. So I have erected one of his dwellings, with books as the building stones, before you, and now he is going to disappear inside, as is only fitting.

The Ritual

BY ROB KAPLAN

Everyone, of course, has their little eccentricities, but book collectors may have more than their fair share. Here editor Rob Kaplan explains, in considerable detail, the procedure by which he incorporates new books into his library—and his life.

Although I consider myself a reader rather than a book collector per se, the fact is that I have in effect been collecting books for almost forty years and now count nearly 4,000 volumes in my library. To be sure, there are others with larger collections—I recently read of a woman whose more than 10,000 books fill every nook and cranny of her New York City apartment—but even so, my books are without doubt my most important possessions.

Having purchased 4,000 books over forty years means I've brought home, on average, almost two books every week, year in and year out, for most of my life. And over all this time I've developed—albeit unwittingly and to some extent unintentionally—a procedure, a ritual by which I make each of those books mine and incorporate each into my library. Although the ritual has changed in subtle ways over the years, it has remained essentially the same for as long as I can remember.

The first step, of course, is walking into a bookstore. (I also purchase books through the numerous mail-order catalogs I receive on a regular basis, but when I do the procedure is somewhat different.) As many hundreds or thousands of times as I've done it, I still feel a thrill at stepping through the doors of such an establishment, something akin to the feeling I get stepping out from under the stands at Giants Stadium and seeing the broad, green playing field before the start of a game. There's an expectation of discovery, a sense of journeying into the unknown, that always excites me.

For some time now I've kept an ongoing list of books I want to buy, and when I go on serious buying expeditions—as opposed to simply dropping into a bookstore—I always bring the list with me. This does not, of course, mean I buy only what's on the list—or even that I necessarily do buy what's on the list—but it's a starting point. Even so, I always allow myself a little time to simply browse, taking in the "New Arrivals" section as well as a number of other subject categories that I habitually peruse.

Eventually, though, I find the appropriate section and look for the title I'm after. Of course, the book I'm looking for may not actually be there, but when I do find it I again feel that sense of embarking on a journey. So with restrained excitement, I gently take the book from the shelf and hold it for a moment, checking the front cover to make sure it is, in fact, the book I want.

Since I generally buy books on the basis of familiarity with the author, reviews, and/or recommendations from friends, it is not, strictly speaking, necessary for me to read the flap copy of hardcovers or the back panels of paperbacks, but I always do. I do it, I think, out of a sense of responsibility, because, as a former book editor myself, I know what an effort editors go through to accurately and—even more important—invitingly describe the contents of each title. But since I generally already know what the book is about, and am already inclined to buy it, it is a cursory reading at best.

The next step is to open the book itself, carefully lifting the front cover and, with brand-new books (as opposed to used ones), quietly thrilling at the slight resistance offered by a cover that's never been opened before. Gingerly turning the pages, I read the half-title page, the title page, and, in a nonfiction book, the table of contents, savoring each step, until I come to the first page of text. This is the real test, the point at which I will decide to buy or not to buy, elect to

make this book part of my life or place it back on the shelf. And so
I read the first paragraph, only the first paragraph, never more. If I
find myself sufficiently disinterested as to not be able to finish reading the first paragraph, I close the book and put it back where it
came from. But if those first hundred words are to my liking—and
I have no idea what specific criteria I apply—then the decision has
been made.

But even now I'm not ready to bring the book up to the cashier
with my money in hand. Before doing so I always inspect the book,
to make sure it's flawless, to be sure that this is the copy I want to
bring home with me. So I look carefully at the dust jacket to make
sure it's neither torn nor soiled in any way, then gently remove it and
inspect the binding, both front and back. If I find flaws, I take another copy from the shelf and go through the same procedure until
I find one I'm satisfied with, and then, and only then, do I proceed
to the cashier. (To be honest, since I rarely buy one book at a time it
can take anywhere from half an hour to an hour before I actually
stroll over to the cashier.)

At the earliest opportunity thereafter, usually later in the evening,
in the quiet of my home office after my wife and children have gone
to sleep, I proceed to the next step of the ritual. I must admit here
that I am not only a confirmed bibliophile but also an inveterate list
maker, and it's at this point that these two inclinations dovetail into
each other. Because for years I've not only kept a running list of
those books I've purchased—as well as those I've read, incidentally—but also an index card file, such as used to be found in libraries, of all the books in my collection. I started all this, I believe,
when I was ten or eleven years old, beginning with a simple handwritten list of titles and authors before graduating to handwritten,
then typed, index cards, and finally to a computer database program. But I'm getting a bit ahead of myself.

Having seated myself at my desk, I gently remove my new books
from the bag I've carried them home in—or from the package in
which they've arrived from the catalog dealer—and bring up the acquisitions list on my computer. Each new title is assigned an acquisitions number—a consecutive number, beginning with number
one for the first purchase of each year—and the list includes, in addition to this number, the book's author and title as well as the subject matter of the book. None of this, I've long since admitted to

myself, serves any truly useful purpose, other than the psychological one of making the book mine, of incorporating it not only into my library, but into my mind.

Then I bring up the database program. This is the second such program I've had—the first, an old one by computer standards, was ultimately not sufficiently sophisticated—and it's become an extremely important part of the ritual. The database contains a template—a "form," in Microsoft's language—for each book record, each of which includes a number of fields that I faithfully fill in for each purchase. These fields contain the kind of bibliographic information one would expect in such a record—the author, title, city of publication, publisher, and year of publication. In addition, however, they include the subject matter, to three levels of specification, such as History, American, 20th Century, as well as the book's format (cloth, trade paperback, mass market paperback, and so forth), the date on which I purchased the book, the acquisitions number, and other miscellaneous information about the book. Finally, there's a field for the book's "status," which I record as "To Be Read," "Reference," or "Reserve," the last of which is used for those books that I may read at some point in the future but are not on the primary list. Of course, as a book's status changes—for example, once I've read it—I go back into the database to change the information.

Again, none of this serves any obvious practical purpose, yet I find the process of cataloging new books to be one of the greatest pleasures of my life. It provides a kind of closure. It's a means of taking possession and a way of putting things into order in an otherwise disordered and disorderly world. Although there have been times I've felt that perhaps my systems were overwhelming me, I take heart from the fact that Thomas Jefferson, surely one of the greatest of all American minds, similarly devised such systems. Of Jefferson's penchant for doing so, Jack McLaughlin wrote in his excellent book, *Jefferson and Monticello,* that "Assembling data of this sort had to be an end in itself for Jefferson, just as his collection of books was more than a convenient library of knowledge. Collecting odd pieces of data and fitting these meaningless bits into a rational system was a way of structuring and ordering his personal universe." And so it is with me—my catalog serves as a kind of safety net, a means of feeling that, at least to some extent, I have control over my life.

(There is, to be honest, at least one practical use of all of this. Purchasing more books than I have time to read, I'm constantly falling behind and, at any given time, have several hundreds books I intend to read but haven't yet had the opportunity to. The "status" field in my database enables me, once I've finished reading a book, to immediately call up a list of all those books I haven't yet read, thus giving me a choice from which I can select the next one.)

While I have to admit that I derive a certain amount of satisfaction from cataloging a book (or books, as is frequently the case), there is nevertheless something a little depressing about it as well. It is, perhaps, a little like sex: once it's done, while one (hopefully) feels satisfied, it's also tinged with a little sadness, as if one were sorry it was over.

The ritual is now almost over. Having recorded all the pertinent data into my computer, having officially accessioned my new books, I now open the book from the back and, in pencil, write the purchase date in the upper right hand corner of the back cover. In all the years I've been doing this—and it's now close to thirty—I've never had any reason to want to know specifically when I purchased a book. So this too serves no meaningful purpose, except as part of the ritual.

Now, at last, I'm ready to place my new book on my shelves. After waiting for more years than I like to remember, I recently bought a large number of seven-foot-high bookcases, fulfilling a lifelong dream of filling an entire room with books, and finally having the opportunity to display all my books rather than having half hidden away in cardboard boxes. My library is now divided according to subject area, the books in each area arranged alphabetically by author, so there is a place for everything. And in the final step of my ritual, I find the appropriate section, make a space for the new book between whichever authors it belongs, and slowly slide it into place, making sure that the spine is lined up with all the other books on the shelves, because anything less would offend my sense of order.

(This last, incidentally, has for years driven my wife to distraction, and she's threatened on more than one occasion to sneak into the library one night and pull some of the books out just enough so they're no longer perfectly lined up. I can't really blame her—it's the only complaint I ever hear from her about the books—but she restrains herself because she knows if she were to do it, I'd only line them all up again.)

The chances are, of course, that I may never pull that book from its shelf again, may never feel a sufficiently strong desire to read it or a need to consult it. But it doesn't matter. It's there whether I read it or not, whether I need it or not: it's mine.

When we are collecting books,
we are collecting happiness.

—VINCENT STARRETT

How to Get Started in the Book Business

BY STUART BRENT

For nearly half a century, Stuart Brent was one of America's premier book dealers, a champion of literature and fine bookmaking. His store was Chicago's mecca for the great writers of the Midwest—or those just passing through. We once spent five glorious hours talking with him about currents in contemporary literature and publishing—in both areas Mr. Brent was a prophet who should have been listened to more carefully. This selection is from his marvelous 1962 memoir, The Seven Stairs.

I had decided to become a bookseller because I loved good books. I assumed there must be many others who shared a love for reading and that I could minister to their needs. I thought of this as a calling. It never occurred to me to investigate bookselling as a business.

Had I done so, I should have learned that eighty percent of all the hardcover books purchased across the counter in America are sold by twenty booksellers. If I had been given the facts and sat down with pencil and paper, I could have discovered that to earn a living and continue to build the kind of inventory that would make it possible to go on selling, I would need to have an annual gross in the neighborhood of $100,000!

Even if I had had the facts in hand, they would not have deterred me. If vows of poverty were necessary, I was ready to take them. And

I refused to be distressed by the expressions on people's faces when I confided that I was about to make a living selling books. Sell freight, yes. Sell bonds or stocks or insurance, certainly. Sell pots and pans. But books!

And I was not only going to sell books—I was going to sell *real* books: those that dealt seriously and truly with the spirit of man.

I had finished cleaning and decorating my little shop before it dawned on me that I did not know how to go about the next step: getting a stock of books and records to sell. A study of the classified telephone directory revealed the names of very few publishers that sounded at all familiar. Was it possible there were no publishers in Chicago? If that were the case, would I have to go to New York?

There was a telephone listing for Little, Brown and Company, so I called them. The lady there said she would be glad to see me. She proved to be very kind, and very disillusioning.

"No," she said, "the book business is not easy, and your location is bad. No, the big publishers will not sell to you direct because your account is too small. No, we at Little, Brown won't either. If I were you, I'd forget the whole idea and go back to teaching."

Everything was No. But she did tell me where I could buy books of all publishers wholesale, and that was the information I wanted. I hastened to A. C. McClurg's and presented myself to the credit manager.

The fact that I had a shop, nicely decorated, did not seem to qualify me for instant credit. First I would have to fill out an application and await the results of an investigation. In the meantime if I wanted books, I could buy them for cash.

"All right," I said. "I want to buy three hundred dollars' worth of books."

"That isn't very much," the man said. "How big is your store?"

"Well," I said, "it's fifteen feet long and nine feet wide, and I'm going to carry records, too."

He shook his head and, with a sidewise glance, asked, "What did you say your name was?" Then, still apparently somewhat shattered, he directed me to a salesman.

I launched into my buying terribly, terribly happy, yet filled with all sorts of misgivings. Was I selecting the right books? And whom would I sell them to? But I had only to touch their brand-new shiny jackets to restore my confidence. I remember buying Jules Romain's

Men of Good Will. In fifteen years, I never sold a copy. I'm still trying. I bought Knut Hamsun, Thomas Mann, Sigrid Undset, Joseph Hergesheimer, Willa Cather, Henry James—as much good reading as I could obtain for $298.49. I was promised delivery as soon as the check cleared.

When the books arrived on a Saturday morning, it was like a first love affair. I waited breathlessly as the truck drew up, full of books for my shop. It wasn't full at all, of course—not for me, anyway. My books were contained in a few modest boxes. And I had built shelves all the way up to the ceiling!

Again, a moment of panic. Enough, my heart said. Stay in the dream! What's next?

The next step was to get recordings. In this field, at least, I found that all the major companies had branch offices in Chicago. I called Columbia Records and was told they'd send me a salesman.

He arrived a few days later, blue eyed and blond haired, an interesting man with a sad message. "No, we can't open you up," he said. "It's out of the question. Your store is in direct conflict with Lyon and Healy on the Avenue. So there's no question about it, we can't give you a franchise. We won't. Decca won't. And I'm sure RCA won't."

I was overcome with rage. Didn't he know I had fought to keep this country free? Wasn't there such a thing as free enterprise? Didn't I have a right to compete in a decent and honorable manner? If I couldn't get records one way, I'd get them another, I assured him. Strangely enough, he seemed to like my reaction. Later he was able to help me.

But for the present, I was reduced to borrowing more money from my brother-in-law with which to buy offbeat recordings from an independent distributor. I brought my own phonograph from home and my typewriter and settled down to the long wait for the first customer.

How do you get going in a business of which you have no practical knowledge and which inherently is a doomed undertaking to begin with? The only answer is that you must be favored with guardian angels.

The first one to bring a flutter of hope into my life came into it on a September afternoon at a luncheon affair, under I do not know what auspices, for Chicago authors. There I encountered a distinguished-looking white-haired gentleman, tall but with the sloping back of a literary man, standing mildly in a corner. I introduced myself to Vincent Starrett, bibliophile and Sherlock Holmes scholar.

He listened attentively to my account of myself and took my phone number. A few days later he called to ask for more information about my idea of combining the sale of books and records.

I pointed out that it was easy, for example, to sell a copy of Ibsen's *Peer Gynt* if the customer was familiar with Grieg's incidental music for the play. Besides, reading and listening were closely allied activities. Anyone with literary tastes could or should have equivalent tastes in music. It was logical to sell a record at the same time you sold a book. Mr. Starrett thought this was a fine idea and, to my shocked surprise, wrote a paragraph about me in his column in the "Books" section of the *Chicago Sunday Tribune.*

The Monday after the write-up appeared, I could hardly wait to get to the shop. I expected it would be flooded with people. It wasn't. The phone didn't even ring. I was disappointed but still felt that hidden forces were working in the direction of my success. Mr. Starrett's kind words were a turning point for me—I no longer felt anonymous.

Some people did see the write-up—intelligent, charming, good people, such as I had imagined gathering in my tiny premises. Among them were two young women who were commercial artists. One day they complained that there was nothing in the store to sit on, and after I had stumbled for excuses, they presented me with a bench decorated on either side with the inscriptions "Words and Music by Stuart Brent," and "Time Is Well Spent with Stuart Brent." Now I felt sure things were looking up.

My next good genie and an important influence in my life was a short, bald gentleman with horn-rimmed spectacles who stood uncertainly in the doorway and asked, "Where's the shop?"

He was Ben Kartman, then associate editor of *Coronet* magazine, a man as kind and thoughtful as he is witty and urbane. He came in and looked around, studied the empty shelves, and shook his head. He shook his head often that afternoon. He wondered if I was seriously trying to be a bookseller—or was I just a dreamer with a hideout?

Surely I wanted to survive, didn't I? Surely I wanted to sell books. Well, in that case, he assured me, I was going about it all wrong. For one thing, I had no sign. For another, I had no books in the windows. And most important of all, I had no stock. How can you do business without inventory? You can't sell apples out of an empty barrel.

I took all his comments without a sound.

Then Ben said, "Sunday, come out to the house. I've got a lot of review copies as well as old but saleable books. Even if you don't sell them, put them on the shelves. The store will look more prosperous."

He gave me several hundred books from his library, which we hauled to the store in his car. The Seven Stairs began to look like a real bookshop.

Ben Kartman also decided that I needed publicity. Not long afterward, my name appeared in a daily gossip column in one of the Chicago newspapers. Ben said that these daily puffers could be important to me, and this proved to be the case.

Meshing with my association with Kartman was another significant influence—a man who certainly altered my life and might have changed it still more had he lived. He was Ric Riccardo, owner of a famous restaurant a quarter of a mile down the street from my shop and one of the most extraordinary and magnetic personalities I have ever encountered. He was an accomplished artist, but it was his fire, his avid love of life, his utterly unfettered speech and manner, his infatuation both with physical being and ideas that drew the famous and the somewhat famous and the plain hangers-on constantly to his presence. He is the only great romantic character I have known.

He first came into my store one day before Christmas. He wore a Cossack fur hat and a coat with a huge mink collar and held a pair of Great Danes on a leash. He had the physique of Ezio Pinza and the profile (not to mention more than a hint of the bags beneath the eyes) of his friend the late John Barrymore. He was tremendous. He told me all he wanted was some light reading to get his mind off his troubles.

Later when Riccardo and the Danes entered the shop, virtually filling it, I would stand on a chair to converse with him. He was very tall, and it gave me a better chance to observe him. Although his language was often coarse, he shunned small talk or fake expressions. The only time he ever reprimanded me was the day I used the phrase "I've got news for you." As our friendship became firm, I would often join him after closing the store for a bowl of green noodles (still a great specialty of the restaurant, which is now managed by his son).

Now if, as Ben said, I did everything wrong, there was at least one thing I certainly did not neglect to do. I talked to people. I knew my books, and I knew what I was talking about. Ideas were and are living things to me and objects of total enthusiasm. It hurt me terribly if someone came in and asked for a book without letting me talk with him about it. The whole joy of selling a book was in talking about the ideas in it. It was a matter of sharing my life and my thought and my very bloodstream with others. *That* was why I had been impelled into this mad venture—unrelated to any practical consideration beyond enthusiasm for the only things that seemed to me to be meaningful. Ric was one of those who responded to this enthusiasm.

One very cold February morning, a cab stopped outside the shop. I saw two men and a woman get out and come up the stairs. There was a good fire going in the fireplace, and it was quiet and warm inside.

Ric was the only member of the trio I recognized, although the other man looked at me as though I should know him. But the woman! She wore the longest, most magnificent mink coat I had ever seen, the collar partially turned up about her head. When she spoke I backed away, but she stepped in and extended her hand to me. It was Katharine Hepburn.

"Oh, yes, that's Katie," the unidentified man said, and all of them laughed at my obvious confusion. Miss Hepburn sat on my decorated bench and held out her hands to the fire.

Ric said, "Stuart, my boy, this is Luther Adler."

I was too nervous to say anything as we shook hands.

I could only keep staring at Katharine Hepburn. I adored her. I loved her accent and those cheekbones and that highly charged voice. I wanted so much to do something for her, but I couldn't think of anything to do.

Suddenly Ric said, "Let's buy some books."

Mr. Adler looked about and said, "Do you have a book for a Lost Woman?"

I said, "Yes," and handed him a copy of Ferdinand Lundberg's new book, *Modern Woman: The Lost Sex.* He gave it to Miss Hepburn, saying, "Here, Katie, this is for you."

Without a pause she turned and said, "Do you have a good book for a Lost Jew?"

"Yes," I said, and produced a Sholem Asch volume.

She gave it to Mr. Adler, saying, "Here, Luther, this is for you."

They bought many books that morning, and I was swept away in wonder and exhilaration at the possibility of bringing happiness to Lost Women, Lost Jews, the Beautiful, and the Great, alike in their needs with all of us for the strength and joy of the spirit. It was wonderful—but it was awful when I had to take their money.

A world very much like that of my dreams began to open up. People came. Authors began to congregate around the fireplace. The shop was visited by newspaper writers like Martha King of the *Chicago Sun-Times,* who wrote a charming article, for which I was deeply grateful. I was beginning to do business, although still without a cash register. The rent was paid promptly, and McClurg's permitted me to have a charge account. One or two eastern publishers even let me have some books on open account. And the man from Columbia Records kept dropping by, leading me to believe that they might be thinking about me in spite of their presumed obligations to Lyon and Healy.

Why did people come, often far out of their way and at considerable inconvenience? I was too busy to reflect upon the matter at the time. There was nothing there but the books and me—and a great deal of talk. But some need must have been filled—by moving people to take notice of themselves, forcing them to think about what they were reading or what they were listening to. We talked a lot of small talk, too, but it was small talk with heart in it. And the effect was contagious. Those who came told others, and they came, too.

*Where is human nature so weak as
in the bookstore?*

—HENRY WARD BEECHER, *STAR PAPERS* (1855)

Ten Best-Selling Books
Rejected by Publishers Twenty
or More Times

1. *Dubliners* by James Joyce
2. *M*A*S*H* by Richard Hooker
3. *Heaven Knows, Mr. Allison* by Charles Shaw
4. *Kon-Tiki* by Thor Heyerdahl
5. *Jonathan Livingston Seagull* by Richard Bach
6. *The Postman Always Rings Twice* by James M. Cain
7. *Lorna Doone* by Richard Doddridge Blackmore
8. *Auntie Mame* by Patrick Dennis
9. *The Peter Principle* by Laurence Peter
10. *Dune* by Frank Herbert

Lending Books

BY ANATOLE BROYARD

A longtime book critic, book review editor, and essayist for The New York Times, *Anatole Broyard was also the author or editor of several books himself, including* Aroused by Books, Kafka Was the Rage: A Greenwich Village Memoir, *and* Intoxicated by My Illness and Other Writings on Life and Death. *In this piece, which originally appeared in* The New York Times Book Review *in 1981, Broyard explains the agonies he goes through when asked to lend a book to a friend, noting, "I feel about lending a book the way most fathers feel about their daughters living with a man out of wedlock."*

Summer vacation is a time for reading, and my friends come to me to borrow books because I have more than most people. In their innocence, they have no idea what I go through in lending a book. They don't understand that I think of myself as offering them love, truth, beauty, wisdom, and consolation against death. Nor do they suspect that I feel about lending a book the way most fathers feel about their daughters living with a man out of wedlock.

This is not to say that there is no pleasure in lending. Each man has a bit of the evangelist in him, and when a book moves me I want to put it into everyone's pocket. If such a book were widely read, the world would be a better, lovelier place. But it is not these books that people ask to borrow. How many friends have asked for *The Collected Poems of Elizabeth Bishop,* or Johan Huizinga's *The Waning of the Middle Ages?*

A less noble motive for lending books is a simple curiosity to see what will happen, a throwback to the child who makes his toys collide. To press a potent book on someone is like giving a dinner guest a strong drink that may cause him to act either foolish or exalted. Some readers even "pass out" after imbibing such a book: they dismiss the experience because they can't handle it.

Occasionally I'm asked, as if I were a doctor, to prescribe a book for a particular condition—for a recently divorced person or one who is suffering from depression. What kind of book a divorced or depressed person might want to read is a nice question: Should it be comforting or a confirmation of their conviction that things fall apart and the center cannot hold? Why doesn't anyone ask me to suggest a book for someone who has just fallen in love?

It is irritating to think that others consider reading a leisurely, holiday activity. They enjoy a fling with books while I'm married to them. In their restless promiscuity, they ask only for new books, while I feel that they have no right to the latest Leonard Michaels until they have gone through Chaucer and Rabelais. They are nostalgic about everything but books.

The thought of people reading in the sun, on a beach, tempts me to recommend dark books, written in the shadow of loneliness, despair, and death. Let these revelers feel a chill as they loll on their towels. Let Baudelaire's "wing of madness" pass over them like a scavenging seagull.

There are times when someone will ask for a particular book, and I'll try to turn them away from it out of a fear that they won't do it justice.

Helen Vendler said that I. A. Richards, one of the great poetry critics, was always trying to protect his favorites against the misinterpretations of a careless world. Mallarmé had a severe attitude toward the same issue. He said that "if a person of ordinary intelligence and insufficient literary preparation happens by accident to open one of my books and pretends to enjoy it, there has been a mistake. Things must be returned to their places."

Not many of my friends are poor, and thus the question arises: If you truly wish to read this book, if you are serious, why don't you go out and buy it? Why don't you make the same offering to literature that you make to other good causes? In *Loitering with Intent,* Muriel Spark's heroine observes that otherwise worldly people often act as if books were mysteriously difficult to procure. To the doting book lover, the idea of reading a borrowed book is disgusting, an unclean habit akin to voyeurism.

Occasionally I come across a book so extraordinary that I want to keep the experience to myself. Such a book seems to confer an immense advantage, to make the reader more desirable, witty, or profound than those who have not read it. To lend such a book, to give up such a precious edge in this furiously competitive world, would be foolish. The secrets in a book like this ought to be saved for a rainy day, for an exquisite emergency.

The moment a book is lent, I begin to miss it. According to T. S. Eliot, each new book that is written alters every previous one. In the same way, each absent book alters those that remain on my shelves. The complexion of my library, the delicate gestalt, is spoiled. My mind goes to the gap as one's tongue goes to a cavity. My security is

For him that stealeth, or borroweth and returneth not, this book from its owner, let it change into a serpent in his hand and rend him. Let him be struck with palsy, and all his members blasted. Let him languish in pain, crying aloud for mercy, and let there be no surcease to this agony till he sing in dissolution. Let bookworms gnaw his entrails . . . and when at last he goeth to his final punishment, let the flames of Hell consume him forever.

—ANONYMOUS "CURSE" ON BOOK THIEVES FROM THE MONASTERY OF SAN PEDRO, BARCELONA, SPAIN breached, my balance tipped, my affections confused, my barricades against chaos diminished. Until the book is returned, I feel like a parent waiting up in the small hours for a teenage son or daughter to come home from the dubious party. In *Zuckerman Unbound,* Zuckerman's brother marries a girl as the only way to repossess a book he lent her. Some bibliomaniacs would sooner give away a book than suffer the anxiety of lending it.

The most dangerous part of lending books lies in the returning. At such times, friendships hang by a thread. I look for agony or ecstasy, for tears, transfiguration, trembling hands, a broken voice— but what the borrower usually says is, "I enjoyed it."

I enjoyed it—as if that were what books were for.

On the Return of a
Book Lent to a Friend

BY CHRISTOPHER MORLEY

I give hearty and humble thanks for the safe return of this book, which having endured the perils of my friend's bookcase and the bookcases of my friend's friends, now returns to me in reasonably good condition. I give hearty and humble thanks that my friend did not see fit to give this book to his infant for a plaything, nor use it as an ashtray for his burning cigar, nor as a teething-ring for his mastiff. When I loaned this book, I deemed it as lost; I was resigned to the business of the long parting; I never thought to look upon its pages again. But now that my book has come back to me, I rejoice and am exceedingly glad! Bring hither the fatted morocco and let us rebind the volume and set it on the shelf of honor, for this my book was lent and is returned again. Presently, therefore, I may return some of the books I myself have borrowed.

Welcome Home Borrowed Book

ANONYMOUS

I really am obliged to you for bringing back my book,
It moves me much to look whereon I thought no more to look;
It reminds me of the early time when it was lent to you,
When life was young and hope was fair, and this old book was new.

How well does memory recall the gilt that on it shone
The day I saw it, coveted, and bought it for my own;
And vividly I recollect you called around that day,
Admired it, then borrowed it, and carried it away!

And now it comes to me again across the lapse of time,
Wearing the somewhat battered look of those beyond their prime.
Old book, you need a rest—but ere you're laid upon the shelf,
Just try and hang together till I read you through myself.

I cannot comfortably read a book belonging to
another person because I feel all the time afraid
of spoiling it. —LAFCADIO HEARN

How to Justify a Private Library

BY UMBERTO ECO

Umberto Eco is a professor of semiotics at the University of Bologna and the author of the best-selling novels The Name of the Rose *and* Foucault's Pendulum. *In the first of these two short essays, both of which appeared in his 1994 collection,* How to Travel with a Salmon & Other Essays, *Eco deals with the question everyone with a sizable library inevitably encounters—"Have you read all these books?" In the second, he vents the frustration he has felt as a user of public and institutional libraries.*

Generally speaking, from my childhood on, I have been always subjected to two (and only two) kinds of jokes: "You're the one who always answers" and "You resound in valleys." All through my early years I believed that, by some strange chance, all the people I met were stupid. Then, having reached maturity, I was forced to conclude that there are two laws no human being can escape: the first idea that comes into a person's mind will be the most obvious one; and, having had an obvious idea, nobody ever thinks that others may have had the same idea before.

I possess a collection of review headlines, in all the languages of the Indo-European family, going all the way from "The Echo of Eco" to "A Book with Echoes." In the latter case I suspect the printed headline wasn't the first idea that came into the subeditor's mind. What probably happened was this: The editorial staff met, they debated some twenty possible titles, and finally the managing editor's face lighted up and he said, "Hey, guys, I've had a fantastic idea!" And the others responded, "Boss, you're a devil! Where do you get them?" "It's a gift," he must have replied.

I'm not saying people are banal. Taking as divine inspiration, as a flash of originality, something that is obvious reveals a certain freshness of spirit, an enthusiasm for life and its unpredictability, a love of ideas—small as they may be. I will always remember my first meeting with that great man Erving Goffman, whom I admired and loved for the genius and penetration with which he could identify infinitesimal aspects of behavior that had previously eluded everyone else. We were sitting at an outdoor café when, looking at the street after a while, he said, "You know something? I believe there are too many automobiles in circulation in our cities." Maybe he had never thought this before because he had had far more important things to think about; he had just had a sudden epiphany and still had the mental freshness to express it. I, a little snob infected by the *Unzeitgemasse Betrachtungen* of Nietzsche, would have hesitated to say it, even if I thought it.

A second shock of banality occurs to many people in my condition—that is, people who possess a fairly sizable library (large enough in my case that someone entering our house can't help but notice it; actually, it takes up the whole place). The visitor enters and says, "What a lot of books! Have you read them all?" At first I thought that the question characterized only people who had scant familiarity with books, people accustomed to seeing a couple of shelves with five paperback mysteries and a children's encyclopedia bought in installments. But experience has taught me that the same words can be uttered also by people above suspicion. It could be said that they are still people who consider a bookshelf as a mere storage place for already read books and do not think of the library as a working tool. But there is more to it than that. I believe that, confronted by a vast array of books, *anyone* will be seized by the anguish of learning and will inevitably lapse into asking the question that expresses his torment and his remorse.

The problem is that when someone says, "Eco? You're the one who always answers," you can reply with a little laugh and, at most, if you want to be polite, with, "That's a good one!" But the question about your books has to be answered, while your jaw stiffens and rivulets of cold sweat trickle down your spine. In the past I adopted a tone of contemptuous sarcasm. "I haven't read any of them; otherwise, why would I keep them here?" But this is a dangerous answer because it invites the obvious follow-up: "And where do you put them after you've read them?" The best answer is the one always used by Roberto Leydi: "And more, dear sir, many more," which freezes the adversary and plunges him into a state of awed admiration. But I find it merciless and angst-generating. Now I have fallen back on the riposte: "No, these are the ones I have to read by the end of the month. I keep the others in my office," a reply that on the one hand suggests a sublime ergonomic strategy and on the other leads the visitor to hasten the moment of his departure.

The contents of someone's bookcase are part of his history, like an ancestral portrait.

—ANATOLE BROYARD

How to Organize a Public Library

BY UMBERTO ECO

1. The various catalogues must be housed as far apart as possible from one another. All care must be taken to separate the catalogue of books from that of periodicals, and these two from the catalogue by subject; similarly, the recent acquisitions must be kept well away from older collections. If possible, the spelling in the two catalogues (recent acquisitions and older collections) must be different. In the recent acquisitions, for example, *pajama* should be spelled with an *a,* in the older, *pyjama* with a *y. Chaikovskii* in recent acquisitions will follow the Library of Congress system; in the older catalogue the name will be spelled in the old-fashioned way, with *Tch.*
2. The subjects must be determined by the librarian. On their copyright pages the books must bear no indication of the subjects under which they are to be listed.
3. Call numbers should be impossible to decipher and, if possible, very complex, so that anyone filling out a call slip will never have room to include the last line of numbers and will assume they are irrelevant. Then the desk attendant will hand the slip back to him with the admonition to fill it out properly.
4. The time between request and delivery must be as long as possible.

5. Only one book should be released at a time.

6. The books distributed by the attendant after the request form has been properly submitted cannot be taken into the reference room, so the scholars must divide their working life into two fundamental aspects: reading on the one hand and reference consultation on the other. The library must discourage, as conducive to strabismus, any crossover tendencies or attempts at the simultaneous reading of several books.

7. Insofar as possible, no photocopier should be available; if such a machine does exist, access to it must be made very time-consuming and toilsome, fees should be higher than those in any neighborhood copy shop, and the maximum number of copied pages permitted should not exceed two or three.

8. The librarian must consider the reader an enemy, a waster of time (otherwise he or she would be at work), and a potential thief.

9. The reference librarian's office must be impregnable.

10. Loans must be discouraged.

11. Interlibrary loans must be impossible or, at best, must require months. The ideal course, in any event, is to ensure the impossibility of discovering the contents of other libraries.

12. Given this policy, theft must be very easy.

13. Opening hours must coincide precisely with local office hours, determined by foresighted discussions with trade union officials and the Chamber of Commerce; total closing on Saturday, Sunday, evenings, and mealtimes goes without saying. The library's worst enemy is the employed student; its best friend is Thomas Jefferson, someone who has a large personal library and therefore no need to visit the public library (to which he may nevertheless bequeath his books at his death).

14. It must be impossible to find any refreshment inside the library, under any circumstances; and it must also be impossible to leave the library to seek sustenance elsewhere without first returning all books in use, so that, after having a cup of coffee, the student must fill out requests for them again.

15. It must be impossible on a given day to find the book one had been using the day before.

16. It must be impossible to learn who has a book that is currently out on loan.

17. If possible, no rest rooms.

18. Ideally, the reader should be unable to enter the library. If he does actually enter, exploiting with tedious insistence a right, granted on the basis of the principles of 1789, that has nevertheless not been assimilated by the collective sensibility, he must never, ever—with the exception of rapid visits to the reference shelves—be allowed access to the sanctum of the stacks.

CONFIDENTIAL NOTE: All staff must be affected by physical defects, as it is the duty of a public institution to offer job opportunities to handicapped citizens (the fire department is considering an extension of this rule to its ranks). In particular, the ideal librarian should limp, in order to lengthen the time devoted to receiving the call slip, descending into the basement, and returning. For personnel expected to use ladders to reach the shelves more than eight meters above the ground, it is required that missing arms be replaced by prosthetic hooks, for security reasons. Personnel lacking both upper limbs will deliver the requested volume by gripping it in their teeth (library regulations tend to prevent the delivery of volumes in a format larger than octavo).

Samuel Pepys's Library

BY NICHOLAS BASBANES

Nicholas Basbanes's 1995 book, A Gentle Madness, *is a richly anecdotal study of bibliomania through the ages. In this excerpt he discusses the innovative arrangements Samuel Pepys made to guarantee that his library would survive—intact—after his demise.*

When the incomparable journal maintained for nine and a half years by Samuel Pepys (1633–1703) during the reign of King Charles II was "discovered" in the nineteenth century, the prevailing assumption was that the diarist wrote his entries out in code because he did not want anybody to read his private thoughts. Eventually it was shown that Pepys used a form of forgotten shorthand called tachygraphy, yet the vexing question remained: Why? Did this indomitable perfectionist take steps to ensure that his candid insights into Restoration life would be read by future generations, or did he wish them to remain concealed?

Because diaries were not published in the seventeenth century, it is unlikely that Pepys envisioned a printed book emerging from the million and a quarter words he wrote between January 1, 1660, and May 31, 1669. But Pepys did insist that his journal be part of the great private library he took ingenious steps to preserve intact, leaving little doubt that the six volumes were pieces of the bequest he emphatically stated was "for the benefit of posterity."

Three centuries after it was formed, the library endures as a time capsule from another era. With seven exceptions, every book that the former secretary of the admiralty chose to include is present, and every one is shelved not only in the precise order he indicated, but in the same glazed book "presses" that had been built to his specifications by British navy shipwrights. Since 1724 the library has been housed behind a graceful courtyard at Magdalene College in Cambridge on the northeastern bank of the River Cam. There is nothing else quite like it—and presumably this was part of the collector's plan as well.

Barely a fortnight before his death on May 31, 1703, Pepys specified the future of his library in two codicils to his will. A widower for thirty-four years with no children of his own, Pepys directed that his sister's son John Jackson be given "full and sole possession of all my collection of books and papers" and that the young man enjoy full use of the library for the "terme of his natural Life." He further stipulated that "all possible provision should be made" to assure "unalterable preservation and perpetual security" of his wishes and that upon his nephew's death, the library should "be placed and for ever settled in one of our universities and rather in that of Cambridge than Oxford."

Pepys was inclined to see the library placed in the "new building" he had helped finance at his alma mater, Magdalene College, in the 1660s, but he also mentioned Trinity College as an alternative. He insisted that the library remain "in its present form" with no "other books mixt therewith." To ensure that this would be the case, he proposed a further security arrangement that would require the two

I have always imagined that Paradise will be a kind of library.

—JORGE LUIS BORGES

colleges to conduct "a reciprocal check upon one another." Whichever institution accepted the books would have to allow annual visitations from its counterpart, and if "any breach" in "said covenants" were discovered, the library would go over to the other school immediately. Trinity has not exercised its right of inspection within the last century, but there has been no need; the terms have been observed for more than 265 years.

Pillow Books

BY CLIFTON FADIMAN

Clifton Fadiman (1904–1999) was one of America's most respected writers and editors. A member of the board of editors of the Encyclopaedia Britannica *and an active member of the editorial board of the Book-of-the-Month Club until shortly before his death, he was also the author or editor of numerous other books. "Pillow Books," his essay on the art of reading in bed, first appeared in* Holiday *magazine and was later included in the 1955 selection of his writings,* Party of One.

Reading in bed, like other gentle customs of the pre–Tension Age, may be on the way out. Yet it is a minor art we should not willingly let die.

There are three schools. At one extreme are those who say, with Sir J. C. Squire, "The bedside book for me is the book that will longest keep me awake." I suspect such literary night owls of being less avid of reading than fearful of sleeping, like the student Lia Hsun, who, according to Giles's *Chinese Biographical Dictionary,* had "a lighted twist of hemp arranged in such a way as to bum his hair if he began to nod from drowsiness." They would do as well to stuff the pillow with a pair of spurs.

At a far remove from those who misuse books to keep themselves awake are those who misuse books to put themselves to sleep. When laudanum failed, the poet Coleridge was forced to administer something stronger—the blank-verse odes of his friend Southey. We have no Southeys today, but a dose of current historical romance might do as well, or a bitter ounce of novel by any of our young men who have reached the land of despair without bothering to pass through the intervening country of reflection.

I hold with neither the Benzedrine nor the Seconal school. As for the first, to read the whole night through is to trespass upon nature. The dark hours belong to the unconscious, which has its own rights and privileges. To use the literary lockout against the unconscious is unfair to the dreamers' union. Hence the wise bed-reader, rendering unto Morpheus the things that are Morpheus', will shun any book that appears too interesting.

Nor, in my view, should a book be used merely as an opiate. Indeed, I do not understand how it *can* be. Dull books soothe only dull brains—a moderately healthy mind will be irritated rather than rested by a dull book. (This irritation is of a special kind; it is known as boredom, and no one need blush for it. He who boasts that he is never bored confesses himself half-dead, irritability being one of the marks of all living tissue.) But is this capacity to irritate through ennui really what we seek in a pillow book? I doubt it. Books that bore you into a kind of dull paralysis are committing mayhem on your mind. I avoid them as I do the man with total recall of his morning paper, the woman with total recall of her shopping day.

As a middle-of-the-roader I have found (nothing surprising about it) that the ideal book to read before sleep should neither bore nor excite.

Take newspapers, which tend to do both. Charles Lamb said, "Newspapers always excite curiosity. No one ever lays one down without a feeling of disappointment." I do not urge upon anyone my own reactionary notion, which is that the proper time to read a newspaper is when passing the newsstand. For me much daily journalism might as well be condensed to skywriting.

But even if this extreme position be disallowed, there is something to be urged against the habit of reading newspapers before sleep—apart from the legacy of smudge they leave upon sheets, pillows, and fingers. Preslumber reading should be a kind of small private devotion during which we beat a quiet retreat from the practical. Now the newspaper is but the daily reiteration of the practical. It is the enemy of the settled mind, which is the province of those truly important concerns that are not practical at all, but speculative. The newspaper, with its unkillable obsession with the actual, is the systematic generator of worry. All newspaper readers furrow their brows. This may be a good thing during the active day, but to read the paper in bed is to open Pandora's box at the very moment when we are least able to deal with its contents. It is to fall asleep with a gadfly inside your skull.

There is a famous essay, "Mr. Bennett and Mrs. Brown." In this essay Virginia Woolf attacked novelists like Wells, Bennett, and Galsworthy on the grounds that reading their books left one feeling incomplete, even frustrated. Such novels, she said, seemed to call for action on your part: reform the economic system, improve education, divorce your wife. I think Virginia Woolf thought up this pretty theory to camouflage the fact that she just didn't like novels so different from her own. However, applied more narrowly to bedside books, it makes fair sense.

The man of Wall Street should not take to bed the stock market quotations; the quiet counterpane is no proper field for raging bulls and bears. Problem novels (usually produced by problem children) should never companion your pillow; midnight is no hour to worry about the time being out of joint. Avoid political arguments that step upon your toes, whether the toes be Republican or Democratic. Await a more fitting hour than bedtime to scare yourself stiff with the latest volume on the atom bomb. Above all, put from you all reading matter that aims (like this essay) to persuade you of something or change you into a finer and more alert citizen. The state of a man comfortably tucked in bed is already kingly; it will not brook improvement. All books too close to our worn and fretted daily lives make dubious bedtime reading. Avoid the call to action.

In my own case I can think of two seeming exceptions to this rule. The first is travel books. The normal human being is made restless by such reading, and quite properly so. But I am of such rooted and stationary nature that I can enjoy the most seductive tales of gypsying without feeling any impulse to kick away the blanket and phone for reservations on the next plane to Rio. However, if I owned an itching foot, I would confine such unsettling reading to the non-horizontal hours.

The second exception concerns my favorite bedtime pabulum, books about food and drink. For me there are few nobler experiences than to read myself almost to sleep over a classic like P. Morton Shand's *A Book of Food* or André Simon's *Concise Encyclopaedia of Gastronomy* or M. F. K. Fisher's *Here Let Us Feast.* I say *almost* to sleep, for of course such reading can have but one outcome—a 2 A.M. invasion of refrigerator and cellar. This would appear a flat contradiction of my rule: No calls to action. Yet the contradiction is apparent, not real. Such reading, it is true, maketh a full man, but a full man is a better sleeper, and so books on food and wine lead roundabout to sweet slumber.

In sum, for me the best bed books are those that deny the existence of tomorrow. To read in bed is to draw around us invisible, noiseless curtains. Then at last we are in a room of our own and are ready to burrow back, back, back to that private life of the imagination we all led as children and to whose secret satisfactions so many of us have mislaid the key. Not that the book need be "good." Indeed, like another bedtime favorite of mine, science fiction (some of it), it can be pleasant trash. But, "good" or "bad," it should act as a bridge, a middle term between the sharp fact of daily existence and the cloudy fact of the dream life. It must commit me to nothing, least of all to assent or contradiction. All the better if it be removed in some degree from my current time, my current place—life is too short for us to spend more than a few hours a day being up-to-date. Finally, it should not be in any way excessive, whether in humor or depth or even originality.

Nevertheless, if for you the *World Almanac* satisfies these conditions, then by all means bed yourself with the *World Almanac.* The books that do the job for me may quite well bore you to a catalepsy or infuriate you to a raging insomnia. The following paragraphs may therefore be of no use to you. On the other hand, they may.

Most intelligent bed-readers will get a not too stimulating pleasure from any well-conceived general anthology, such as Huntington Cairns's *The Limits of Art* or Somerset Maugham's more conventional *Traveller's Library.* Maugham's own tales, published complete in two stout volumes, *The World Over* and *East and West,* are perfect for the alcove. I like detective stories, if good, but must confess that most of the current crop read as if they had been punched out on an IBM machine. Sound collections, like those by Dorothy Sayers, of short whodunits are most satisfactory. E. C. Bentley's two detective novels and his handful of short stories have recently been put into a single volume, *Trent's Case Book:* a superior affair; and there is also available a Josephine Tey omnibus. Otherworldly tales (but they must stop just short of the gruesome) do nicely. The contrast between their shudders and one's own snug safety supplies a childish pleasure whose roots lie too deep for us to scorn them. Of anthologies of the weird there are dozens—Alexander Laing's *The Haunted Omnibus* and the Modern Library's *Great Tales of Terror and the Supernatural* are among the better ones.

I like also to roam around in the General Catalogue of the Oxford University Press, a publication that costs you nothing and is rich with peculiar treasures. There is nothing quite like these endless book titles and brief descriptions to produce in the reader a gentle, serene amazement at the quantity of extraordinary matters, from *Acrocephaly* and *Acrocephalosyndactyly* to the *Zla-ba-Bsam-'grub,* that have engaged the minds of our fellow human beings. Here we find Galen's *On Medical Experience,* with this bit of useful information: "Since the original Greek text of this work was lost, except for two small fragments, this ninth-century Arabic translation is the earliest known complete version." Who follows Galen? Why, no others than Gall, Alice and Crew, Fleming, whose *Flat Tail* is described as "The story of a beaver during the second and most interesting year of his life, told with imagination and accuracy." What a brave and perennially new world this is that can contain cheek to cheek such creatures as Galen and Flat Tail!

Books about people who lived lives fantastically different from my own I have found excellent for the bedside. I like to read about the Middle Ages; you may prefer Polynesia or even more alien climes, such as William Faulkner's Southland. Books of popular science please me, but there are few writers today who have the liveliness and wit of Eddington, Jeans, and H. G. Wells. (Rachel Carson's *The Sea Around Us* and Guy Murchie's *Song of the Sky* are delightful exceptions.) Nonacademic books about words and language are first-rate for me, but this may be a narrow professional interest.

As for novels, give me no profound Russians, no overlucid Frenchmen, no opaque Germans. Give me solid Englishmen of the nineteenth century or early twentieth—William De Morgan, Wilkie Collins, George Borrow, Charles Reade. (I omit Dickens and

Thackeray as too obvious.) Above all give me Trollope, from whom I have received so much pleasure that I would willingly call him another St. Anthony; Trollope, who breaks through the time barrier and teleports the horizontal reader instantly to a divinely settled, comfortable, income-taxless vanished world. His half a hundred novels are good for five years of bedside reading. Of those who minister to the tired, night-welcoming mind, Trollope is king. He never fails to interest, but not too much; to soothe, but not too much. Trollope is the perfect novelist for the bedside.

The New Lifetime Reading Plan

BY CLIFTON FADIMAN AND JOHN S. MAJOR

Clifton Fadiman's The Lifetime Reading Plan *was first published in 1960, with revised editions in 1978 and 1986. It was but one gem in a lustrous career promoting reading and the joy of the printed word. The* New Lifetime Reading Plan, *written with John S. Major, the bare list of which is presented here, was published by HarperCollins in 1997. What is so interesting about the entire enterprise is the assertion, made with Fadiman's customary confidence born of many decades of immersion in literature, that even in an age in which books are published in avalanche-like numbers, only a few endure and deserve special attention. The list is enlightening and enjoyable, but the comments on each title by the authors are even more joyous to anyone who loves books.*

1. Anonymous, ca. 200 B.C.E. (Scribe Sin-Leqi-Unninni, ca. 700 B.C.E.), *The Epic of Gilgamesh*
2. Homer, ca. 800 B.C.E., *The Iliad*
3. Homer, ca. 800 B.C.E., *The Odyssey*
4. Confucius, 551–479 B.C.E., *The Analects*
5. Aeschylus, 525–456/5 B.C.E., *The Oresteia*
6. Sophocles, 496–406 B.C.E., *Oedipus Rex; Oedipus at Colonus; Antigone*

7. Euripides, 484–406 B.C.E., *Alcestis; Medea; Hippolytus; The Trojan Women; Electra; The Bacchae*

8. Herodotus, ca. 484–425 B.C.E., *The Histories*

9. Thucydides, ca. 470/460–ca. 400 B.C.E., *The History of the Peloponnesian War*

10. Sun-tzu, ca. 450–380 B.C.E., *The Art of War*

11. Aristophanes, 448–388 B.C.E., *Lysistrata; The Clouds; The Birds*

12. Plato, 428–348 B.C.E., Selected Works

13. Aristotle, 384–322 B.C.E., *Ethics; Politics; Poetics*

14. Mencius, ca. 400–320 B.C.E., *The Book of Mencius*

15. Attributed to Valmiki, ca. 300 B.C.E., *The Ramayana*

16. Attributed to Vyasa, ca. 200 B.C.E., *The Mahabharata*

17. Anonymous, ca. 200 B.C.E., *The Bhagavad Gita*

18. Ssu-ma Ch'ien, 145–86 B.C.E., *Records of the Grand Historian*

19. Lucretius, ca. 100–ca. 50 B.C.E., *Of the Nature of Things*

20. Virgil, 70–19 B.C.E., *The Aeneid*

21. Marcus Aurelius, 121–180, *Meditations*

22. Saint Augustine, 354–430, *The Confessions*

23. Kalidasa, ca. 400, *The Cloud Messenger* and *Sakuntala*

24. Revealed to Muhammad, completed 650, The Koran

25. Hui-neng, 638–713, *The Platform Sutra of the Sixth Patriarch*

26. Firdausi, ca. 940–1020, *Shah Nameh*

27. Sei Shonagon, ca. 965–1035, *The Pillow-Book*

28. Lady Murasaki, ca. 976–1015, *The Tale of Genji*

29. Omar Khayyám, 1048– ?, *The Rubaiyat*

30. Dante Alighieri, 1265–1321, *The Divine Comedy*

31. Luo Kuan-chung, ca. 1330–1400, *The Romance of the Three Kingdoms*

32. Geoffrey Chaucer, 1342–1400, *The Canterbury Tales*

33. Anonymous, ca. 1500, *The Thousand and One Nights*

34. Niccolò Machiavelli, 1469–1527, *The Prince*

35. François Rabelais, 1483–1553, *Gargantua and Pantagruel*

36. Attributed to Wu Ch'eng-en, 1500–1582, *Journey to the West*

37. Michel Eyquem de Montaigne, 1533–1592, Selected Essays

38. Miguel de Cervantes Saavedra, 1547–1616, *Don Quixote*

39. William Shakespeare, 1564–1616, Complete Works

40. John Donne, 1573–1631, Selected Works

41. Anonymous, published 1618, *The Plum in the Golden Vase* (*Chin P'ing Mei*)

42. Galileo Galilei, 1574–1642, *Dialogue Concerning the Two Chief World Systems*

43. Thomas Hobbes, 1588–1679, *Leviathan*

44. René Descartes, 1596–1650, *Discourse on Method*

45. John Milton, 1608–1674, *Paradise Lost;* "Lycidas"; "On the Morning of Christ's Nativity"; *Sonnets; Areopagitica*

46. Molière, 1622–1673, Selected Plays

47. Blaise Pascal, 1623–1662, *Thoughts* (*Pensées*)

48. John Bunyan, 1628–1688, *Pilgrim's Progress*

49. John Locke, 1632–1704, *Second Treatise of Government*

50. Matsuo Basho, 1644–1694, *The Narrow Road to the Deep North*

51. Daniel Defoe, 1660–1731, *Robinson Crusoe*

52. Jonathan Swift, 1667–1745, *Gulliver's Travels*

53. Voltaire, 1694–1778, *Candide* and other works

54. David Hume, 1711–1776, *An Enquiry Concerning Human Understanding*

55. Henry Fielding, 1707–1754, *Tom Jones*

56. Ts'ao Hsüeh-ch'in, 1715–1763, *The Dream of the Red Chamber* (also called *The Story of the Stone*)

57. Jean-Jacques Rousseau, 1712–1778, *Confessions*

58. Laurence Sterne, 1713–1768, *Tristram Shandy*

59. James Boswell, 1740–1795, *The Life of Samuel Johnson*

60. Thomas Jefferson and others, *Basic Documents in American History,* edited by Richard B. Morris

61. Hamilton, Madison, and Jay, *The Federalist Papers,* 1787, edited by Clinton Rossiter

62. Johann Wolfgang von Goethe, 1749–1832, *Faust*

63. William Blake, 1757–1827, Selected Works

64. William Wordsworth, 1770–1850, *The Prelude*; Selected Shorter Poems; Preface to *Lyrical Ballads* (1800)

65. Samuel Taylor Coleridge, 1772–1834, "The Rime of the Ancient Mariner"; "Christabel"; "Kubla Khan"*; Biographia Literaria;* Writings on Shakespeare

66. Jane Austen, 1775–1817, *Pride and Prejudice; Emma*

67. Stendhal, 1783–1842, *The Red and the Black*

68. Honoré de Balzac, 1799–1850, *Père Goriot; Eugénie Grandet; Cousin Bette*

69. Ralph Waldo Emerson, 1803–1882, Selected Works

70. Nathaniel Hawthorne, 1804–1864, *The Scarlet Letter;* Selected Tales
71. Alexis de Tocqueville, 1805–1859, *Democracy in America*
72. John Stuart Mill, 1806–1873, *On Liberty; The Subjection of Women*
73. Charles Darwin, 1809–1882, *The Voyage of the Beagle; The Origin of Species*
74. Nikolai Vasilievich Gogol, 1809–1852, *Dead Souls*
75. Edgar Allan Poe, 1809–1849, Short Stories and Other Works
76. William Makepeace Thackeray, 1811–1863, *Vanity Fair*
77. Charles Dickens, 1812–1870, *Pickwick Papers; David Copperfield; Great Expectations; Hard Times; Our Mutual Friend; The Old Curiosity Shop; Little Dorrit*
78. Anthony Trollope, 1815–1882, *The Warden; The Last Chronicle of Barset; The Eustace Diamonds; The Way We Live Now; Autobiography*
79. The Brontë Sisters
    79A. Charlotte Brontë, 1816–1855, *Jane Eyre*
    79B. Emily Brontë, 1818–1848, *Wuthering Heights*
80. Henry David Thoreau, 1817–1862, *Walden;* "Civil Disobedience"
81. Ivan Sergeyevich Turgenev, 1818–1883, *Fathers and Sons*
82. Karl Marx, 1818–1883, and Friedrich Engels, 1820–1895, *The Communist Manifesto*
83. Herman Melville, 1819–1891, *Moby Dick; Bartleby the Scrivener*
84. George Eliot, 1819–1880, *The Mill on the Floss; Middlemarch*
85. Walt Whitman, 1819–1892, Selected Poems; *Democratic Vistas;* Preface to the first issue of *Leaves of Grass; A Backward Glance O'er Travelled Roads*
86. Gustave Flaubert, 1821–1880, *Madame Bovary*
87. Feodor Mikhailovich Dostoyevsky, 1821–1881, *Crime and Punishment; The Brothers Karamazov*
88. Leo Nikolayevich Tolstoy, 1828–1906, *War and Peace*
89. Henrick Ibsen, 1828–1906, Selected Plays
90. Emily Dickinson, 1830–1886, Collected Poems
91. Lewis Carroll, 1832–1898, *Alice's Adventures in Wonderland; Through the Looking Glass*
92. Mark Twain, 1835–1910, *Huckleberry Finn*
93. Henry Adams, 1838–1918, *The Education of Henry Adams*

94. Thomas Hardy, 1840–1928, *The Mayor of Casterbridge*
95. William James, 1842–1910, *The Principles of Psychology; Pragmatism;* four essays from *The Meaning of Truth; The Varieties of Religious Experience*
96. Henry James, 1843–1916, *The Ambassadors*
97. Friedrich Wilhelm Nietzsche, 1844–1900, *Thus Spake Zarathustra; The Genealogy of Morals; Beyond Good and Evil;* other works
98. Sigmund Freud, 1856–1939, Selected Works, including *The Interpretation of Dreams; Three Essays on the Theory of Sexuality; Civilization and Its Discontents*
99. George Bernard Shaw, 1856–1939, Selected Plays and Prefaces
100. Joseph Conrad, 1857–1924, *Nostromo*
101. Anton Chekhov, 1860–1904, *Uncle Vanya; Three Sisters; The Cherry Orchard;* Selected Short Stories
102. Edith Wharton, 1862–1937, *The Custom of the Country; The Age of Innocence; The House of Mirth*
103. William Butler Yeats, 1865–1939, Collected Poems; Collected Plays; *Autobiography*
104. Natsume Soseki, 1867–1916, *Kokoro*
105. Marcel Proust, 1871–1922, *Remembrance of Things Past*
106. Robert Frost, 1874–1963, Collected Poems
107. Thomas Mann, 1875–1955, *The Magic Mountain*
108. E. M. Forster, 1879–1970, *A Passage to India*
109. Lu Hsün, 1881–1936, Collected Short Stories
110. James Joyce, 1882–1941, *Ulysses*
111. Virginia Woolf, 1882–1941, *Mrs. Dalloway; To the Lighthouse; Orlando; The Waves*
112. Franz Kafka, 1883–1924, *The Trial; The Castle;* Selected Short Stories
113. D. H. Lawrence, 1885–1930, *Sons and Lovers; Women in Love*
114. Tanizaki Junichiro, 1886–1965, *The Makioka Sisters*
115. Eugene O'Neill, 1888–1953, *Mourning Becomes Electra; The Iceman Cometh; Long Day's Journey into Night*
116. T. S. Eliot, 1888–1965, Collected Poems; Collected Plays
117. Aldous Huxley, 1894–1963, *Brave New World*
118. William Faulkner, 1897–1962, *The Sound and the Fury; As I Lay Dying*
119. Ernest Hemingway, 1899–1961, Short Stories
120. Kawabata Yasunari, 1899–1972, *Beauty and Sadness*

121. Jorge Luis Borges, 1899–1986, *Labyrinths; Dreamtigers*
122. Vladimir Nabokov, 1899–1977, *Lolita; Pale Fire; Speak, Memory*
123. George Orwell, 1903–1950, *Animal Farm; 1984; Burmese Days*
124. R. K. Narayan, 1906– , *The English Teacher; The Vendor of Sweets*
125. Samuel Beckett, 1906–1989, *Waiting for Godot; Endgame; Krapp's Last Tape*
126. W. H. Auden, 1907–1973, Collected Poems
127. Albert Camus, 1913–1960, *The Plague; The Stranger*
128. Saul Bellow, 1915– , *The Adventures of Augie March; Herzog; Humboldt's Gift*
129. Aleksander Isayevich Solzhenitsyn, 1918– , *The First Circle; Cancer Ward*
130. Thomas Kuhn, 1922–1996, *The Structure of Scientific Revolutions*
131. Mishima Yukio, 1925–1970, *Confessions of a Mask; The Temple of the Golden Pavilion*
132. Gabriel García Márquéz, 1928– , *One Hundred Years of Solitude*
133. Chinua Achebe, 1930– , *Things Fall Apart*

*An ordinary man can . . . surround himself
with two thousand books . . . and thenceforward
have at least one place in the world in which it
is possible to be happy.*

—AUGUSTINE BIRRELL

Comfort Found in
Good Old Books

BY GEORGE HAMLIN FITCH

For more than thirty years, in the late nineteenth and early twentieth centuries, George Hamlin Fitch wrote a weekly column for the Sunday book page of the San Francisco Chronicle. *In this extraordinarily touching piece—first published in the* Chronicle *and later collected in Fitch's 1911 book,* Comfort Found in Good Old Books—*he writes of the comfort he found in reading after the death of his son and of why it is so important to have favorite books: "So may you come into the true Kingdom of Culture . . . and may you be armed against the worst blows that fate can deal you in this world."*

Nothing Soothes Grief Like Sterling Old Books— How the Sudden Death of an Only Son Proved the Value of the Reading Habit

For the thirty years that I have spoken weekly to readers of the *Chronicle* through its book review columns, it has been my constant aim to preach the doctrine of the importance of cultivating the habit of reading good books, as the chief resource in time of trouble and sickness. This doctrine I enforced, because for many years reading has been my principal recreation, and I have proved its usefulness in broadening one's view of life and in storing up material from the world's greatest writers which can be recalled at will. But it never occurred to me that this habit would finally come to mean the only thing that makes life worth living. When one passes the age of forty he begins to build a certain scheme for the years to come. That scheme may involve many things—domestic life, money-getting, public office, charity, education. With me it included mainly literary work, in which I was deeply interested, and close companionship with an only son, a boy of such lovable personal qualities that he had endeared himself to me from his early childhood. My relations with my son, Harold, were not those of the stern parent and the timid son, as Edmond Gosse has depicted with so much unconscious pathos in his "Father and Son." Rather it was the relation of elder brother and younger brother.

Hence, when only ten days ago this close and tender association of many years was broken by death—swift and wholly unexpected, as a bolt from cloudless skies—it seemed to me for a few hours as if the keystone of the arch of my life had fallen and everything lay heaped in ugly ruin. I had waited for him on that Friday afternoon until six o'clock. Friday is my day off, my one holiday in a week of hard work, when my son always dined with me and then accompanied me to the theater or other entertainment. When he did not appear at six o'clock in the evening I left a note saying I had gone to our usual restaurant. That dinner I ate alone. When I returned in an hour it was to be met with the news that Harold lay cold in death at the very time I wrote the note that his eyes would never see.

When the first shock had passed came the review of what was left of life to me. Most of the things which I had valued highly for the sake of my son now had little or no worth for me; but to take up again the old round of work, without the vivid, joyous presence of a companion dearer than life itself, one must have some great compensations; and the chief of these compensations lay in the few feet of books in my library case—in those old favorites of all ages that can still beguile me, though my head is bowed in the dust with grief and my heart is as sore as an open wound touched by a careless hand.

For more than a dozen years in the school vacations and in my midsummer holidays my son and I were accustomed to take long tramps in the country. For five of these years the boy lived entirely in the country to gain health and strength. Both he and his older sister,

Mary, narrowly escaped death by pneumonia in this city, so I transferred them to Angwin's on Howell Mountain, an ideal place in a grove of pines—a ranch in the winter and a summer resort from May to November. There the air was soft with the balsam of pine, and the children throve wonderfully. Edwin Angwin was a second father to them both, and his wife was as fond as a real mother. For five years they remained on the mountain. Mary developed into an athletic girl, who became a fearless rider, an expert tennis player, and a swimmer, who once swam two miles at Catalina Island on a foolish wager. She proved to be a happy, wholesome girl, an ideal daughter, but marriage took her from me and placed half the continent between us. Harold was still slight and fragile when he left the country, but his health was firmly established, and he soon became a youth of exceptional strength and energy.

Many memories come to me now of visits paid to Angwin's in those five years. Coming home at three o'clock on winter mornings after a night of hard work and severe nervous strain, I would snatch two or three hours' sleep, get up in the chill winter darkness, and make the tedious five-hour journey from this city to the upper Napa Valley, in order to spend one day with my boy and his sister. The little fellow kept a record on a calendar of the dates of these prospective visits and always had some dainty for me—some bird or game or choice fruit which he knew I relished.

Then came the preparatory school and the college days, when the boy looked forward to his vacations and spent them with me in single-minded enjoyment that warmed my heart like old wine. By means of constant talks and much reading of good books, I labored patiently to develop his mind and at the same time to keep his tastes simple and unspoiled. In this manner he came to be a curious mixture of the shrewd man of the world and the joyous, carefree boy. In judgment and in mental grasp he was like a man of thirty before he was eighteen, yet at the same time he was the spontaneous, fun-loving boy whose greatest charm lay in the fact that he was wholly unconscious of his many gifts. He drew love from all he met, and he gave out affection as unconsciously as a flower yields its perfume.

In college he tided scores of boys over financial straits; his room at Stanford University was open house for the waifs and strays who had no abiding-place. In fact, so generous was his hospitality that the manager of the college dormitory warned him one day in sarcastic vein that the renting of a room for a term did not include the privilege of taking in lodgers. His friends were of all classes. He never joined a Greek letter fraternity because he did not like a certain clannishness that marked the members; but among fraternity men as well as among Barbarians he counted his close associates by the score. He finished his college course amid trying circumstances, as he was called upon to voice the opinion of the great body of students in regard to an unjust ruling of the faculty that involved the suspension of many of the best students of the college. And through arbitrary action of the college authorities his degree was withheld for six months, although he had passed all his examinations and had had no warnings of any condemnation of his independent and manly course as an editor of the student paper. Few boys of his age have ever shown more courage and tact than he exhibited during that trying time, when a single violent editorial from his pen would have resulted in the walking out of more than half of the university students.

Then came his short business life, full of eager, enthusiastic work for the former college associate who had offered him a position on the Board of Fire Underwriters. Even in this role he did not work so much for himself as to "make good" and thus justify the confidence of the dear friend who stood sponsor for him. Among athletes of the Olympic Club he numbered many warm friends; hundreds of young men in the professional and business life greeted him by the nickname "Mike," which clung to him from his early freshman days at Stanford. The workers and the idlers, the studious and the joy-chasers, all gave him the welcome hand, for his smile and his gay speech were the password to all hearts. And yet so unspoiled was he that he would leave all the gaiety and excitement of club life to spend hours with me, taking keen zest in rallying me if depressed or in sharing my delight in a good play, a fine concert, a fierce boxing bout, or a spirited field day. Our tastes were of wide range, for we enjoyed with equal relish Mascagni's *Cavalleria Rusticana,* led by the composer himself, or a championship prizefight; Margaret Anglin's somber but appealing *Antigone* or a funny "stunt" at the Orpheum.

Harold's full young life was also strongly colored by his close newspaper associations. The newspaper life, like the theatrical, puts its stamp on those who love it, and Harold loved it as the child who has been cradled in the wings loves the stage and its folk. Ever since he wore knickerbockers he was a familiar figure in the *Chronicle* editorial rooms. He knew the work of all departments of the paper, and he was a keen critic of that work. He would have made a success in this field, but he felt the work was too exacting and the reward too small for the confinement, the isolation, and the nervous strain. After the fire he rendered good service when competent men were scarce, and in the sporting columns his work was always valued, because he was an expert in many kinds of sport and he was scrupulously fair and never lost his head in any excitement. The news of his death caused as deep sorrow in the *Chronicle* office as would the passing away of one of the oldest men on the force.

Now that this perennial spirit of youth is gone out of my life, the beauty of it stands revealed more clearly. Gone forever are the dear, the fond-remembered holidays, when the long summer days were far too short for the pleasure that we crowded into them. Gone are the winter walks in the teeth of the blustering ocean breezes, when we "took the wind into our pulses" and strode like Berserkers along the gray dunes, tasting the rarest spirit of life in the open air. Gone, clean gone, those happy days, leaving only the precious memory that wets my eyes that are not used to tears.

And so, in this roundabout way, I come back to my literary shelves, to urge upon you who are wrapped warm in domestic life and love to provide against the time when you may be cut off in a day from the companionship that makes life precious. Take heed and guard against the hour that may find you forlorn and unprotected against death's malignant hand. Cultivate the great worthies of literature, even if this means the neglect of the latest magazine or of the newest sensational romance. Be content to confess ignorance of the ephemeral books that will be forgotten in a single half year, so that you may spend your leisure hours in genial converse with the great writers of all time. Dr. Eliot of Harvard recently aroused much discussion of his "five feet of books." Personally, I would willingly dispense with two-thirds of the books he regards as indispensable. But the vital thing is that you have your own favorites—books that are real and genuine, each one brimful of the inspiration of a great soul. Keep these books on a shelf convenient for use, and read them again and again until you have saturated your mind with their wisdom and their beauty. So may you come into the true Kingdom of Culture, whose gates never swing open to the pedant or the bigot. So may you be armed against the worst blows that fate can deal you in this world.

Who turns in time of affliction to the magazines or to those books of clever short stories which so amuse us when the mind is at peace and all goes well? No literary skill can bind up the brokenhearted; no beauty of phrase satisfy the soul that is torn by grief. No, when our house is in mourning, we turn to the Bible first—that font of wisdom and comfort which never fails him who comes to it with clean hands and a contrite heart. It is the medicine of life. And after it come the great books written by those who have walked through the Valley of the Shadow, yet have come out sweet and wholesome, with words of wisdom and counsel for the afflicted. One book through which beats the great heart of a man who suffered yet grew strong under the lash of fate is worth more than a thousand books that teach no real lesson of life, that are as broken cisterns holding no water, when the soul is athirst and cries out for refreshment.

This personal heart-to-heart talk with you, my patient readers of many years, is the first in which I have indulged since the great fire swept away all my precious books—the hoarded treasures of forty years. Against my will it has been forced from me, for I am like a sorely wounded animal and would fain nurse my pain alone. It is written in the first bitterness of a crushing sorrow; but it is also written in the spirit of hope and confidence—the spirit which I hope will strengthen me to spend time and effort in helping to make life easier for some poor boys in memory of the one dearest boy who has gone before me into that "undiscovered country," where I hope someday to meet him, with the old bright smile on his face and the old firm grip of the hand that always meant love and tenderness and steadfast loyalty.

Build yourself a book-nest to forget the world without.

—ABRAHAM COWLEY

Among men of New England strain like myself it is easy to labor long hours, to endure nervous strain, to sacrifice comfort and ease for the sake of their dear ones; but men of Puritan strain, with natures as hard as the flinty granite of their hillsides, cannot tell their loved ones how dear they are to them, until Death lays his grim hand upon the shoulder of the beloved one and closes his ears forever to the words of passionate love that now come pouring in a flood from our trembling lips.

SAN FRANCISCO, OCTOBER 9, 1910

The Collector

BY SUSAN SONTAG

Susan Sontag's 1992 novel, The Volcano Lover, *is based on the lives of Sir William Hamilton, his wife, Emma, and Lord Nelson. Sir William was a collector of paintings, but Sontag's comments on the collector's obsession are equally applicable to those who collect books.*

That tremor when you spot it. But you don't say anything. You don't want to make the present owner aware of its value to you; you don't want to drive up the price, or make him decide not to sell at all. So you keep cool, you examine something else, you move on or you go out, saying you'll be back. You perform a whole theatre of being a little interested, but not immoderately; intrigued, yes, even tempted; but not seduced, bewitched. Not ready to pay even more than is being asked, because you must have it. So the collector is a dissembler, someone whose joys are never unalloyed with anxiety. Because there is always more. Or something better.

You must have it because it is one step toward an ideal completing of your collection. But this ideal completion for which every collector hungers is a delusive goal. A complete set of something is not the completeness the collector craves. The entire production of some notable dead painter could conceivably, improbably, end up in someone's palace or cellar or yacht. (Every last canvas? Could you, imperious acquirer, be sure there was not one more?) But even if you could be sure that you had every last item, the satisfaction of having it all would eventually, inevitably, decay. A complete collection is a dead collection. It has no posterity. After having built it, you would love it less each year. Before long, you would want to sell or donate it, and embark on a new chase.

The great collections are vast, not complete. Incomplete: motivated by the desire for completeness. There is always one more. And even if you have everything—whatever that might be—then you will perhaps want a better copy (version, edition) of what you have; or with mass-produced objects (pottery, books, artifacts), simply an extra copy, in case the one you possess is lost or stolen or broken or damaged. A backup copy. A shadow collection. A great private collection is a material concentrate that continually stimulates, that overexcites. Not only because it can always be added to, but because it is already too much. The collector's need is precisely for excess, for surfeit, for profusion. It's too much—and it's just enough for me. Someone who hesitates, who asks, Do I need this? Is this really necessary? is not a collector. A collection is always more than is necessary.

Without disparaging the other forms of collecting, I confess a conviction that the human impulse to collect reaches one of its highest levels in the domain of books.

—THEODORE C. BLEGEN

Bibliomania

BY GUSTAVE FLAUBERT

Gustave Flaubert's "Bibliomania" was written in 1836, when he was fourteen years old, and became his first published work when it appeared the following year in Le Colibri, *a small literary magazine published in Rouen. It is a slightly fictionalized version of the true story of Don Vincente, a Spanish monk who was, literally, willing to kill to possess a book he wanted for his collection. It still stands as a classic example of bibliophilia taken to extremes.*

There once lived in a narrow and sunless street of Barcelona, one of those men with a pale face, dull and sunken eye, one of those satanic and bizarre beings such as Hoffmann dug up in his dreams.

He was Giacomo the bookseller.

Though but thirty years of age, he passed already for old and worn out. His figure was tall, but bent like that of an old man. His hair was long, but white. His hands were strong and sinewy, but dried up and covered with wrinkles. His costume was miserable and ragged. He had an awkward and embarrassed air; his face was pale, sad, ugly, and even insignificant. People rarely saw him in the streets, except on the days when they sold rare and curious books at auction. Then he was no longer the same indolent and ridiculous man; his eyes were animated, he ran, walked, stamped his feet; he had difficulty in moderating his joy, his uneasiness, his anguish, and his grief. He came home panting, gasping, out of breath; he took the cherished book, devoured it with his eyes, and looked at it and loved it as a miser does his treasure, a father his daughter, a king his crown.

This man had never spoken to anyone, unless it were to the *bouquinistes* and to the second-hand dealers. He was taciturn and a dreamer, sombre and sad. He had but one idea, but one love, but one passion: books. And this love, this passion, burned within him, used up his days, devoured his existence.

Often, in the night, the neighbours saw through the windows of the bookshop a light which wavered, then advanced, retreated, mounted, then sometimes went out. Then they heard a knocking at their door and it was Giacomo coming to relight his candle, which a gust of wind had blown out.

These feverish and burning nights he passed among his books. He ran through the storerooms, he ran through the galleries of his library with ecstasy and delight. Then he stopped, his hair in disorder, his eyes fixed and sparkling. His hands, warm and damp, trembled on touching the wood of the shelves.

He took a book, turned over the leaves, felt the paper, examined the gilding, the cover, the letters, the ink, the folds, and the arrangement of drawings for the word *Finis*. Then he changed its place, put it on a higher shelf, and remained for entire hours looking at its tide and form.

He went next to the manuscripts, for they were his cherished children. He took one of them, the oldest, the most used, the dirtiest; he looked at its parchment with love and happiness; he smelt its holy and venerable dust; then his nostrils filled with joy and pride, and a smile came upon his lips.

Oh! he was happy, this man, happy in the midst of all that learning of which he scarcely understood the moral import and the literary value. He was happy, seated among all these books, letting his eyes roam over the lettered backs, the worn pages, the yellowed parchment. He loved knowledge as a blind man loves the day. No! it was not learning that he loved; it was its expression. He loved a book because it was a book; he loved its odour, its form, its tide. What he loved in a manuscript was its old illegible date, the bizarre and strange Gothic characters, the heavy gilding which loaded its drawings. It was its pages covered with dust, dust of which he breathed the sweet and tender perfume with delight. It was this pretty word *Finis,* surrounded with two cupids, carried on a ribbon, supporting themselves on a fountain engraved on a tomb or reposing in a basket of flowers between the roses, the golden apples, and the blue bouquets.

This passion had entirely absorbed him. He scarcely ate, he no longer slept, but he dreamed whole days and nights of his fixed idea: books. He dreamed of all that a royal library should have of the divine, the sublime, and the beautiful, and he dreamed of making for himself as big a library as that of the King. How freely he breathed, how proud and strong he felt, when he cast his eye into the immense galleries where the view was lost in books! He raised his head? Books! He lowered it? Books! To the right, to the left, still more books!

In Barcelona he passed for a strange and infernal man, for a savant or a sorcerer.

Yet he scarcely knew how to read.

Nobody dared speak to him, so severe and pale was his face. He had a wicked and treacherous air, and yet he never touched a child to hurt it. It is true that he never gave anything to charity.

He saved all his money, all his goods, all his emotions, for books. He had been a monk, and for books he had abandoned God. Later he sacrificed for them that which men hold dearest after their God: money. Then he gave to books that which people treasure next to money: his soul.

For some time now his vigils were longer; people saw still later in the night his lamp which burned on his books, meaning that he had a new treasure, a manuscript.

One morning, there came into his shop a young student of Salamanca. He seemed to be rich, for two footmen held his mule at Giacomo's door. He had a toque of red velvet, and rings shone on his fingers.

He did not have, however, that air of sufficiency and of nullity usual with people who have bedecked valets, fine clothes, and an empty head. No, this man was a savant, but a rich savant. That is to say a man who, at Paris, writes on a mahogany desk, has books gilded on the edges, embroidered slippers, a dressing gown, Chinese curiosities, a gilt clock, a cat that sleeps on a rug, and two or three women who make him read his verses, his prose, and his tales, who say to him: "You have ability," and who find him only a fop.

The manners of this gentleman were polished. On entering, he saluted the bookseller, made a profound bow, and said to him in affable tone:

"Do you not have here some manuscripts?"

The bookseller became embarrassed and replied stammering:

"Why, sir, who told you that?"

"Nobody, but I imagine it."

And he put down on the desk of the bookseller a purse full of gold, which he made resound, smiling as does everyone who touches gold of which he is the owner.

"Sir," replied Giacomo, "it is true that I have some, but I do not sell them. I keep them."

"And why? What do you do with them?"

"Why, my lord?" And he became red with anger. "You ask what I do with them? Oh, no, you do not know what a manuscript is!"

"Pardon, Master Giacomo, I am posted on it and to give you the proof of it I will tell you that you have here the *Chronicle of Turkey*!"

"I? Oh, they have deceived you, my lord!"

"No, Giacomo," replied the gentleman. "Reassure yourself, I do not at all want to rob you, but to buy it from you."

"Never!"

"Oh, you will sell it to me," replied the scholar, "for you have it here. It was sold at Ricciami's the day of his death."

"Well, then, yes, sir, I have it. It is my treasure: it is my life. Oh! you will not snatch it from me! Listen! I am going to confide a secret in you: Baptisto, you know Baptisto, the bookseller, my rival and my enemy, who lives in the Palace Square? Well, then, he does not have it, not he, but I do have it!"

"At how much do you value it?"

Giacomo stopped a long time and replied with a proud air:

"Two hundred pistoles, my lord."

He looked at the young man with a triumphant air, as if he were saying to him: "You are going to leave; it's too high, and yet I will not give it for less."

He was mistaken, for the other man, showing his purse, said:

"There are three hundred."

Giacomo turned pale and almost fainted.

"Three hundred pistoles?" he repeated. "But I am a fool, my lord, I will not sell it for four hundred."

The student began to laugh, fumbling in his pocket, from which he drew out two other purses.

"Well, then, Giacomo, here are five hundred. Oh, no, you do not want to sell it, Giacomo, but I will have it. I will have it to-day, this instant. I need it. If I had to sell this ring given with a kiss, if I had to sell my sword studded with diamonds, my houses, and my palaces, if I had to sell my soul, I must have this book. Yes, I must have it at all costs, at any price. In a week I am defending a thesis at Salamanca. I need this book to become a doctor. I must be a doctor to be an archbishop. I need the purple gown before I can have the tiara on my forehead."

Giacomo approached him with admiration and respect as the only man whom he had understood.

"Listen, Giacomo," interrupted the nobleman. "I am going to tell you a secret which is going to make your fortune and your happiness. There is a man here who lives at the Arabs' Gate. He has a book: it is *The Mystery of Saint Michael.*"

"*The Mystery of Saint Michael?*" said Giacomo, raising a cry of joy. "Oh, thanks! You have saved my life!"

"Quick! Give me the *Chronicle of Turkey.*"

Giacomo ran to a shelf. There he suddenly stopped, turned pale, and said with an astonished air:

"But, my lord, I do not have it."

"Oh, Giacomo, that is a very clumsy trick, and your looks belie your words."

"Oh, my lord, I swear to you, I do not have it."

"Why, you are an old fool, Giacomo. Look, here are six hundred pistoles."

Giacomo took the manuscript and gave it to the young man.

"Take care of it," said he when the other man went off laughing and said to his valets as he mounted his mule:

"You know that your master is a fool, but he has just deceived an imbecile. The idiot of a churlish monk!" he repeated, laughing. "He believes that I am going to be Pope!"

And the poor Giacomo remained sad and disconsolate, leaning his burning forehead on the windowpanes of his shop, weeping with rage and regarding with bitterness and grief his manuscript, the object of his care and of his affection, which the gross footmen of the nobleman were carrying away.

"Oh, accursed man of hell! Accursed, a hundred times accursed are you who have robbed me of all that I love on earth! Oh, I cannot live now! I know that he has deceived me, the infamous one, he has deceived me! If this be so, I shall avenge myself. Let us go quickly to the Arabs' Gate. If this man were to ask me a sum larger than I have, what to do then? Oh, it is enough to kill one!"

He took the money which the student had left on the desk and went out running.

While he was going through the streets he saw nothing of all that surrounded him. Everything passed before him like a nightmare, of which he did not understand the enigma. He heard neither the feet of the passersby nor the noise of the wheels on the paving. He did not think, he did not dream, he did not see anything but books. He was thinking of *The Mystery of Saint Michael.* He fashioned it to himself, in his imagination, large and thin, with parchment ornamented with gold letters. He tried to guess the number of pages which it must contain. His heart beat with violence like that of a man who awaits his death sentence.

At last he arrived. The student had not deceived him. On an old Persian carpet, full of holes, were laid out on the ground some ten books. Giacomo, without speaking to the man who, stretched out like his books, was sleeping at one side and snoring in the sun, fell on his knees and began to cast an uneasy and anxious eye over the backs of the books. Then he arose, pale and crestfallen, and wakened the *bouquiniste* with a shout and asked him:

"Ah, friend, you do not have here *The Mystery of Saint Michael?*"

"What?" said the merchant, opening his eyes. "You do not mean to speak about a book which I have? Look around for yourself!"

"The imbecile!" said Giacomo, kicking him with his foot. "Have you others than these?"

"Yes, let's see, here they are."

And he showed him a little packet of pamphlets tied with cords. Giacomo broke the cords and read the titles of them in a second.

"Hell," said he, "it is not that. Have you not sold it, perhaps? Oh, if you have got it, give it, give it! One hundred pistoles, two hundred, all that you wish!"

The *bouquiniste* looked at him, astonished. "Oh! perhaps you mean to speak of a little book which I gave yesterday for eight maravedis to the curé of the Cathedral of Oviedo?"

"Do you remember the title of this book?"

"No."

"Was it not *The Mystery of Saint Michael*?"

"Yes, that's it."

Giacomo turned away a few steps and fell in the dust like a man worn out by an apparition which possesses him.

When he came to himself, it was evening and the sun which reddened the horizon was in its decline. He raised himself and went home sick and despairing.

A week later, Giacomo had not forgotten the sad disappointment, and his wound was still throbbing and bleeding. He had not slept at all for three nights, for this day there was to be sold the first book which had been printed in Spain, a copy unique in the kingdom. It was a long time that he had wanted to have it. So he was happy the day that they told him that the owner was now dead.

But an uneasiness seized his spirit. Baptisto could buy it; Baptisto, who for some time had taken from him, not the customers—that concerned him very little—but all that which appeared rare and old; Baptisto, whose fame he hated with the hatred of an artist. This man became burdensome to him; it was always he who took away the manuscripts. At public sales he bid and he obtained. Oh! how many times the poor monk, in his dreams of ambition and of pride, how many times he saw come toward him Baptisto's long hand which passed across the crowd as on the days of a sale, come to rob him of a treasure of which he had dreamed so long, which he had coveted with so much love and egotism! How many times also had he been tempted to end with a crime that which neither money nor patience had been able to accomplish. But he drove back this idea in his heart, tried to divert his thoughts from the hatred which he bore to this man and went to sleep on his books.

Early in the morning he was in front of the house in which the sale was to take place. He was there before the auctioneer, before the public, and before the sun.

As soon as the doors opened he precipitated himself in the stairway, went into the room, and asked for this book. They showed it to him. That was already a happiness.

Oh! never had he seen anything so beautiful or that pleased him more. It was a Latin Bible, with Greek commentaries. He looked at it and admired it more than all the others. He clasped it between his fingers, smiling bitterly, like a man who is starving in sight of gold.

Never, moreover, had he desired anything so much. Oh! how he coveted it then, even at the price of all that which he had, his books, his manuscripts, his six hundred pistoles, at the price of his blood. Oh! how he would have liked to have this book! To sell all, all to have this book, to have only it, but to have it for himself, to be able to show it to all Spain, with a smile of insult and pity for the King, for the princes, for the savants, for Baptisto, and say: "Mine, this book is mine!" and to hold it in his two hands for his life, to fondle it as he touches it, to take in all its fragrance as he smells it!

At last the hour arrived. Baptisto was in the centre, with serene face, calm and peaceful air. They came to the book. Giacomo offered at first twenty pistoles. Baptisto kept quiet and did not look at the Bible. Already the monk advanced his hand to seize this book, which had cost him no little trouble and anguish, when Baptisto started to say:

"Forty!"

Giacomo saw with horror that his antagonist got excited in proportion as the price mounted higher.

"Fifty!" he cried with all his strength.

"Sixty!" replied Baptisto.

"One hundred!"

"Four hundred!"

"Five hundred!" added the monk regretfully. And while he stamped his feet with impatience and anger, Baptisto affected an ironical and wicked calmness. Already the sharp and cracked voice of the usher had repeated three times: "Five hundred." Already Giacomo was consumed with happiness. A sigh which escaped from the lips of a man came near causing him to faint, for the bookseller of the Palace Square, pressing forward in the crowd, said:

"Six hundred!" The voice of the usher repeated four times: "Six hundred"—and no other voice replied to him. Only there was seen, at one end of the table, a man with pale forehead, with trembling hands, a man who laughed bitterly with that laugh of the damned in Dante. He lowered his head, thrust his hand in his chest, and when he withdrew it, it was warm and moist, for he had flesh and blood at the end of his fingernails.

They passed the book from hand to hand, so as to bring it within reach of Baptisto. The book passed before Giacomo. He smelled its fragrance; he saw it pass an instant before his eyes, then stop before a man who took it, laughing. Then the monk lowered his head to hide his face, for he was weeping. On returning by the streets, his walk was slow and painful. His face was strange and stupid, his figure grotesque and ridiculous. He had the air of an intoxicated man, for he staggered. His eyes were half-closed; he had red and burning eyelids. The perspiration ran down his forehead, and he stammered between his teeth, like a man who has drunk too much and who has partaken too freely at a banquet. His thought was no longer under control; it wavered like his body, without having either end or intention; it was unsettled, irresolute, heavy, and bizarre. His head weighed like lead, his forehead burned like a brazier.

Yes, he was drunk with that which he had felt, he was fatigued with his days, and he was surfeited with existence. That day—it was a Sunday—the people promenaded in the streets, talking and singing. The poor monk listened to their chatting and their songs. He gathered in the road some scraps of phrases, some words, some cries, but it seemed to him that it was always the same sound, the same voice. It was a vague, confused hubbub, a music bizarre and noisy, which buzzed in his head and which crushed him.

"Say," said one man to his neighbour, "have you heard tell of the story of that poor curé of Oviedo who was found strangled in his bed?" Here, there was a group of women who took the evening air on their doorsteps. Here is what Giacomo heard in passing before them:

"Say then, Martha, do you know that there was at Salamanca a rich young man, Don Bernardo—you know, the one who, when he came here a few days ago, had a fine black mule, so pretty and so well equipped, and who made it paw the paving stones? Well, then, the poor young man, they told me at church this morning, that he was dead!"

"Dead?" said a young girl.

"Yes, little one," replied the woman. "He is dead, here, at the Hotel de Saint-Pierre. First he felt bad in his head; then he had a fever; and at the end of four days they buried him."

Giacomo heard still other things. All these souvenirs made him tremble, and a ferocious smile came to play around his mouth.

The monk went home, worn out and sick. He stretched out on the bench of his desk and slept. His chest was oppressed; a raucous and hollow sound came from his throat. He awoke with fever. A horrible nightmare had exhausted his strength.

It was then night, and it had just struck eleven at the neighbouring church. Giacomo heard cries of "Fire! Fire!" He opened his windows, went into the street, and actually saw flames which shot up above the roofs. He went back and was going to take up his lamp to go into his shop when he heard before his windows men running past and saying: "It is in the Palace Square. The fire is at Baptisto's!"

The monk gave a start; a loud peal of laughter rose from the depths of his heart, and he proceeded with the crowd toward the bookseller's house. The house was on fire; the flames rose up, high and terrible, and driven by the winds, they darted toward the fine blue sky of Spain, which looked down on agitated and tumultuous Barcelona like a veil covering up tears. They saw a man half-naked; he was desperate; he was tearing his hair; he rolled on the ground, blaspheming God and raising cries of rage and despair. It was Baptisto.

The monk contemplated his despair and his cries with calmness and happiness, with that wild laughter of the child laughing at the tortures of the butterfly whose wings he has plucked.

They saw in an upper story flames which were burning some bundles of paper. Giacomo took a ladder, leaned it against the blackened and tottering wall. The ladder trembled under his steps. He mounted on a run and arrived at that window. Curses! It was nothing but some old books from the bookshop, without value or merit. What to do? He had entered; it was necessary either to advance in the midst of this inflamed atmosphere or to descend again by the ladder of which the wood was beginning to get hot. No! He advanced.

He crossed several rooms; the floor trembled under his steps; the doors fell when he approached them; the beams hung down over his head; he ran into the midst of the fire, panting and furious.

He needed that book! He must have it or death!

He did not know where to direct his course, but he ran.

At last he arrived before a partition, which was intact. He broke it with a kick and saw an obscure and narrow apartment. He groped, he felt some books under his fingers. He touched one of them, took it, and carried it away out of this room. It was it! It, *The Mystery of*

Saint Michael! He retraced his steps, like a man lost and in delirium. He leaped over the holes; he flew into the flame, but he did not find again the ladder which he had placed against the wall. He came to a window and descended outside, clinging with hands and knees to the tough surfaces. His clothing began to get on fire, and when he arrived in the street he rolled himself in the gutter to put out the flames which were burning him.

Some months passed and one no longer heard talk about the bookseller Giacomo, except as one of those singular and strange men at whom the crowd laughs in the streets because it does not at all understand their passions and their manias.

Spain was occupied with more grave and more serious interests. An evil genius seemed to be hanging over it. Each day, new murders and new crimes, and all seemed to come from an invisible and hidden hand. It was a dagger suspended over every roof and over every family. There were people who disappeared suddenly without any trace of blood spilled from their wound. A man started out on a journey; he never came back. They did not know to what to attribute this horrible scourge, for it is necessary to attribute misfortune to someone who is a stranger, but happiness to oneself. In fact, there are days so ill omened in life, epochs so baneful to men, that not knowing whom to crush with his maledictions, one cries out to heaven. It is during these unfortunate epochs for the people that one believes in fatality.

A quick and industrious police had tried, it is true, to discover the author of all these crimes. The hired spy had slipped into all the houses, had listened to all the words, heard all the cries, seen all the looks—and had learned nothing. The prosecutor had opened all the letters, broken all the seals, searched in all the corners, and had found nothing.

One morning, however, Barcelona had left off its robe of mourning to crowd into the courts of justice, where they were going to condemn to death the man whom they supposed to be the author of all these horrible murders. The people hid their tears under a convulsive laugh, for when one suffers and when one weeps, it is a consolation, self-centred, it is true, to see the sufferings and tears of others.

Poor Giacomo, so calm and so peaceful, was accused of having burned the house of Baptisto, of having stolen his Bible. He was charged also with a thousand other accusations. He was there, seated on the bench for murderers and brigands. He, the honest biblio-phile, the poor Giacomo, who thought only of his books, was now compromised in the mysteries of murder and the scaffold.

The room was glutted with people. At last the prosecutor raised himself and read his report. He was long and diffuse; it was with dif-ficulty that one could distinguish the principal action from paren-theses and reflections. The prosecutor said that he had found in the house of Giacomo the Bible which belonged to Baptisto, since this Bible was the only one of its kind in Spain; now it was probable that it was Giacomo who had set fire to the house of Baptisto to possess himself of this rare and precious book. He stopped and seated him-self, out of breath.

As to the monk, he was calm and undisturbed and did not reply even by a look to the multitude which was insulting him.

His advocate rose, spoke long and well. Then, when he believed he had shaken his audience, he raised his robe and drew out from it a book. He opened it and showed it to the public. It was another copy of this same Bible.

Giacomo raised a cry and fell back on his bench, tearing his hair. The moment was critical. A word from the accused was awaited, but no sound came from his mouth. At last he seated himself, looked at his judges and at his attorney like a man who is just wakening.

They asked him if he was guilty of having set fire to the house of Baptisto.

"No, alas!" he replied.

"No?"

"But are you going to condemn me? Oh! Condemn me, I beg of you! Life is a burden to me. My attorney has lied to you. Do not be-lieve him. Oh! Condemn me; I have killed Don Bernardo, I have killed the curé, I have stolen the book, the unique book, for there are not two of them in Spain! My lords, kill me! I am a miserable wretch!"

His attorney came toward him and, showing him this Bible, said: "I can save you, look!"

Giacomo took the book and looked at it.

"Oh! I who believed that it was the only one in Spain! Oh, tell me, tell me that you have deceived me! May misfortune attend you!"

And he fell in a faint.

The judges returned and pronounced the sentence of death upon him.

Giacomo heard it without a shudder, and he seemed calmer and more tranquil.

They gave him hope that by asking pardon from the Pope, he would perhaps obtain it. He did not wish it at all and asked only that his library be given to the man who had the most books in Spain.

Then, when the people had dispersed, he asked his attorney to have the goodness to lend him this book. The man gave it to him. Giacomo took it lovingly, dropped some tears on the leaves, then tore it with anger and threw its fragments at the person of his defender, saying to him:

"You have lied about it, Mister Attorney! I told you truly that it was the only copy in Spain!"

Bibliomania

BY ROGER ROSENBLATT

The following is an excerpt from Bibliomania, *a one-man show written and first performed by noted essayist Roger Rosenblatt at New York's American Place Theater in 1994.*

The custom of borrowing books confutes nature. In every other such situation, the borrower becomes a slave to the lender, the social weight of the debt so altering the balance of a relationship that a temporary acquisition turns into a permanent loss. This is certainly true with money. Yet it is not at all true with books. For some reason a book borrower feels that a book, once taken, is his own. This removes both memory and guilt from the transaction. Making matters worse, the lender believes it, too. To keep up appearances, he may solemnly extract an oath that the book be brought back as soon as possible; the borrower answering with matching solemnity that the Lord might seize his eyes were he to do otherwise. But it is all play. Once gone, the book is gone forever. The lender, fearing rudeness, never asks for it again. The borrower never stoops to raise the subject. . . .

There's no spectacle that is as terrifying as the sight of a guest in your house whom you catch staring at your books. It is not the judgmental possibility that is frightening. The fact that one's sense of discrimination is exposed by his books. Indeed, most people would much prefer to see the guest first scan, then peer and turn away in boredom or disapproval. Alas, too often the eyes, dark with calculation, shift from title to title as from floozie to floozie in an overheated dance hall. Nor is that the worst. It is when those eyes stop moving that the heart, too, stops.

The guest's body twitches; his hand floats up to where his eyes have led it. There is nothing to be done. You freeze. He smiles. You hear the question even as it forms: "Would you mind if I borrowed this book?" Mind? Why should I mind? The fact that I came upon that book in a Paris bookstall in April 1969—the thirteenth, I believe it was, the afternoon, it was drizzling—that I found it after searching all Europe and North America for a copy; that it is dog-eared at passages that mean more to my life than my heartbeat; that the mere touch of its pages recalls to me in a Proustian shower my first love, my best dreams. Should I mind that you seek to take all that away? That I will undoubtedly never get it back? Then even if you actually return it to me one day, I will be wizened, you cavalier, and the book spoiled utterly by your mishandling? Mind?

"Not at all. Hope you enjoy it."

"Thanks. I'll bring it back next week."

"No rush. Take your time." [Liar.]

Never lend books—nobody ever returns them; the only books I have in my library are those which people have lent me.

—ANATOLE FRANCE

The Book Action

BY SOLLY GANOR

Solly Ganor's tale of survival told in his 1994 memoir, Light One Candle, *includes the following remarkable story about the rescue of books during the horror of war and persecution. As a boy, Ganor befriended Chiune Sugihara, the Japanese diplomat who provided thousands of exit visas for desperate Jews facing certain death in Dachau and other concentration camps.*

By the end of 1941 thousands of frozen German soldiers were being transported by rail back into Germany. Although the campaign had inflicted staggering casualties on the Soviets, it had also taken an enormous toll on the Wehrmacht, which lost some 800,000 men. The Russian offensive had been halted, however temporarily, by "General Mud" and "General Winter." German supply lines were stretched to the breaking point.

But somehow the Wehrmacht had to be supplied and supported. On January 20, 1942, Reinhard Heydrich, the "blond beast," chaired the Wannsee Conference on the Final Solution of the Jewish question. There he proposed to a group of top Nazi officials that the Jews of Europe be worked to death building roads into Russia.

In the occupied territories the Germans pressed local industries into service. Few Jews had any illusions about their fate after the

"Big Action," but remaining useful to the Germans seemed to be our only hope for survival. The Jewish Council organized ghetto workshops, which produced necessary goods for the Germans in exchange for food and erratic token payments.

Unlike the Jewish councils and capos in most ghettos and camps, the Kaunas Council and its Jewish police force managed to hold the community together, opening vocational training schools in carpentry and other basic skills for the youth. The classes provided effective cover for more traditional education and for the operations of Zionist youth organizations. Through these and other clandestine means, the Council and the ghetto inmates struggled to keep some remnants of civilization alive.

The deportations to Riga on February 6 were soon followed by more sad news. Late that month the Germans ordered all books in the ghetto to be turned over to the authorities. Anyone caught with books after the deadline would be executed. The people of the book, as we had been known throughout the ages, were to be separated from our ancient companions.

Earlier in the year the Germans ordered an area about a block from where we lived to be evacuated, and that part of the ghetto remained abandoned. There were strict orders not to enter it, but it wasn't long before Cooky and I were sneaking in to look for scraps of firewood or whatever else could be salvaged from the place. It was risky, but it was clear to me that unless I took a few risks my chances for survival were nil. I figured I didn't really have anything to lose.

After several such "raids" we discovered the best of all treasures— an attic with some old books in it. It could be reached only through an opening in the ceiling, and after some scavenging we managed to put together a rope ladder we could haul up behind us. It became another good hiding place, and it was perfect for what we came to call "operation library."

When Cooky joked that we could probably hide half the books in the ghetto in our new attic, he immediately regretted it. He knew exactly what I was thinking, and he didn't like it. Even though he had regained some of his old vitality since his visit to the Ninth Fort, he no longer had any nerve. I had to push him.

Nearly everyone complied with the order and began delivering their precious books to the assembly point.

It snowed the night before the deadline, and the ghetto was covered by a thick white blanket the next morning. My mother had tears in her eyes as she helped me load her beloved books into my homemade sled. The final load consisted of ten volumes of Russia's best authors, all bound in red leather with gold embossed lettering. Tolstoy, Lermontov, Dostoyevsky, Turgenev, Pushkin, Gogol—the thoughts, passions, ideals, and feelings of literary giants were in those books. The set was a wedding gift from Jochil.

I felt a deep compassion for my mother. She had never quite recovered from Herman's disappearance behind the walls of the Seventh Fort, and now her brother Jochil had been deported to Riga, perhaps never to be seen again. Mother rarely laughed or smiled these days. Like me, she escaped from her grief by reading. She would sit almost motionless for hours, only moving two fingers to flip the pages. Nothing else existed when she read. Not even food interested her. And now they were even taking her books away.

"Keep them, Mommy," I wanted to tell her. "We are all going to be killed anyway. You might as well enjoy your books while you can." But I kept my silence. Mother found it difficult enough keeping in touch with our terrible new reality.

"Make sure you take these books straight to the German storage center," she said to me sadly, and as if sensing my thoughts, she added in a stern voice, "Don't even think of hiding them, you hear me? It isn't worth getting shot on account of books."

I quickly averted my eyes. My mother could always sense my thoughts when she looked into my eyes.

Cooky waited for me on the corner of Gimbuto. He also had a sled loaded with books, and he looked jittery.

"Let's go," I said firmly. I knew he hated this idea, but I also knew he would follow me. We quickly crossed the road leading to the forbidden quarter, and within half an hour we had hauled all the books into the attic.

The same day we brought four more loads of books given to us by neighbors who had no sleds and were glad that someone would take them away.

But I wasn't satisfied, and I had an idea. Cooky put up a bigger protest this time, but in the end he went along. I got both of us work sorting the books brought to the assembly point. The man in charge, Mr. Grodnik, was sorting the books by language and subject matter, and he was glad to let us carry the sorted stacks from the first floor to the second. When I reported for work the next day, I announced that Cooky was at home sick. He was actually waiting behind the house, below a small window in the stairwell. All day I ran up the stairs with a load of books under each arm. As I rounded the first landing, I dropped the stack under my left arm out the window into the snow below, where Cooky waited, then continued up the stairs and deposited the remainder in stacks as instructed. After about an hour I could almost do this without breaking stride.

It was risky business, and despite the cold I was soon dripping with sweat. After two or three days of this Cooky was caught by a German guard. He gave the guard the story we had concocted, that he was delivering books and looking for the entrance to the building, and the German believed him, giving him only a kick for his stupidity. Cooky wet his pants in fright that day and refused to go on with the scheme. By then, however, we had accumulated quite a stash. A few ghetto inmates saw us trundling the books to our hiding place, but they paid us no mind. As it turned out, others in the ghetto were doing the same thing we were.

I sneaked books back to the house only one at a time and kept them hidden from the family. But it weighed on my conscience. Here we were with this rich collection of literature, and we only used it for our own selfish ends. Soon Cooky and I began giving out books, first to our closest friends and relatives, later to more and more people who became "customers." The word got around.

Cooky and I both began attending trade school, in carpentry. One day I was approached by Mr. Edelstein, our instructor, who taught mathematics before the war and tried to instruct us in math when we weren't pounding nails. He asked me point-blank if I could get hold of any textbooks, especially in mathematics. I first denied that I had any sources, but when he insisted I told him I would inquire. Cooky had in fact cursed me for saving some schoolbooks, especially those in mathematics. He hated math. "Is this what I risked my neck for?" he yelled when he saw them. There was one newer-looking geometry book among these that I smuggled into school for Mr. Edelstein. He was so delighted that he gave me a big hug. "Do you know what a treasure this is? Look! It's in Hebrew and was printed in Tel Aviv only a few years ago. Where on earth did you get it?"

We'd just put the textbooks in the corner and I never really looked at them. I told Cooky about a dream I'd had in which I'd let animals into the Ark, two by two, and Cooky thereafter called the schoolbooks our alligators, snakes, and hyenas.

Mr. Edelstein, a rather shy man with big brown eyes and thinnish hair, had taught at the high school in Kaunas. He came from a small town where Lithuanian partisans locked the Jewish population into the synagogue, then set the building on fire. His whole family had been burned alive. Despite what he'd experienced, he still believed in noble ideals, and was convinced that good would eventually triumph over evil.

He had no relatives in the ghetto, and like nearly all single men, he had "adopted" a family that no longer had a working male at its head. The Jewish Council made such assignments in order to protect single women, children, and elderly people. S. A. Lieutenant Gustav Hermann, the German head of the labor office, apparently understood that his workers' morale depended upon keeping their families intact insofar as possible, so the Jewish Council created many fictitious families where none existed. Mr. Edelstein lived with a family of five.

Mr. Edelstein had grown very fond of his adopted family, and like others often traded with the Lithuanian guards to get them extra food. When I brought him the book he put it in a bag full of clothing he was carrying. That afternoon when I left school I passed him at the gate, where he had stopped to trade with the guard. Evidently Mr. Edelstein asked for more food than the guard was willing to give him. Suddenly the Lithuanian began shouting, "What's this you got hidden there, Jew boy? A book? And in your heathen language, too. You know I could shoot you for possessing books. How would you like that for special payment?"

I was only about ten yards away and turned to see what was happening. A German military car approaching the gate from the other side came to a stop, and an SS officer stepped out, demanding to know what was going on. I felt the bottom drop out of my stomach.

Mr. Edelstein stood ashen-faced while the Lithuanian showed the book to the SS officer. The German turned the pages slowly, then demanded to know where Mr. Edelstein had gotten that book. I couldn't hear Mr. Edelstein's answer, but the German slapped him a few times and shouted, "Don't lie to me, you filthy Jew! This book was printed in Palestine and is in some kind of code! Who is your contact? Where did you get this book? Tell me or I will kill you!"

I stood frozen in horror as he and the guard began beating my teacher. Any minute I expected Mr. Edelstein to point a finger at me, but instead he made a barely perceptible gesture for me to go.

With that I found my feet and started running. I was turning into a side street when I heard a shot. I looked back to see Mr. Edelstein fall to his knees. The German put his pistol to his head and fired again, and Mr. Edelstein fell over and lay still.

That night I had a terrible nightmare about the Ninth Fort. Cooky and I were falling into that mass grave, and I could see Lena far above me, falling. Suddenly she was on top of me and the hole in her throat kept getting larger and larger, pumping out a thick mass of blood that covered my face, my mouth, my nose. I was drowning. I woke up screaming, although the screams were only in my mind. For five minutes I just lay there trying to catch my breath. The reality I woke up to wasn't a great improvement. My teacher had been murdered, and it was my fault.

I stayed home from school and cried the whole day. Finally Cooky came over and tried to cheer me up, but I was inconsolable. Me and my stupid books. For the first time I fully realized the danger I had exposed everyone to with my foolishness. My mother was right. It was senseless to get killed on account of books. I wouldn't listen to her, and now Mr. Edelstein was dead. To this day I remember his feeble gesture waving me away from there. All he had to do was point in my direction to save himself, but he would not.

"Don't be stupid. You don't really believe that the German would have let him live if he had betrayed you! He obviously would have shot both of you, and Mr. Edelstein realized it," Cooky tried to argue. "Besides, he should have been more careful." But no amount of logic was going to bring Mr. Edelstein back.

He was buried in the ghetto cemetery, only a short distance from where he was shot. Except for the family he lived with and a few of his pupils, including Cooky and myself, few attended his burial. He had no relatives, and violent death was such a common occurrence in the ghetto that nobody paid much attention.

There was no funeral, as all religious practices were forbidden by the Germans. Only the boys he shared a room with were crying as the burial party slipped him into the grave. I just stood there stunned, unable to utter a sound, until sprinkles of rain and a blackening sky sent everyone scurrying for shelter.

For the next ten days I didn't go to the trade school. I was too ashamed to face the other teachers and pupils, who all probably blamed me for Mr. Edelstein's death. Instead, I once again became an "Angel" replacing Isaac Trotsky at the airport. The "Angel" system had become common practice in the ghetto: boys my age replaced the ill and received food in exchange. I spent most of my time breaking the hard clay ground with a pickax. It was heavy, and you had to have real strength to wield one for any length of time. In their weakened conditions many adults could barely swing them. For this they were abused and given murderous beatings by the Ukrainian foremen.

I stuck it out both because Aunt Dora fed me and because she was the one person who could help when it came to my teeth. I spent many sleepless nights with terrible toothaches, which were sometimes so excruciating that I would run all the way to Dora crying like a baby. With her limited resources she could only help a little, but it was enough. It was partly out of gratitude that I agreed to replace Isaac at the airport, usually one day at a time. It took him ten days to recuperate from his most recent beating, however, and at the end I could barely stand on my feet. Somehow I staggered back to the ghetto that day, and more or less collapsed on Dora's step. I had not yet turned fourteen and was undernourished, and those ten days were too much.

Dora felt very guilty when she saw my state. She made me come every evening for a whole month afterward to give me extra rations. By ghetto standards Dora was a wealthy woman, as her services were in demand, and she continued to receive food smuggled in by her old cook.

Those ten days were purgatory, but somehow they helped expunge my guilt over Edelstein. I gained a little perspective on the whole event, and with the extra rations and several days' rest I was ready to return to school. Much to my surprise, neither the teachers nor the pupils connected Edelstein's death to the book I had given him. He was simply caught trading and died, as so many people did.

Another surprise was the fact that Cooky went to our "library" almost every day. I had sworn I'd never go near the place again. Perhaps he kept going because he didn't actually see the murder of Mr. Edelstein. Perhaps he somehow became courageous when I got scared.

From time to time he would bring me a book or two, and after about a month I finally returned with him. In this evil place people not only lost faith in God, they lost faith in society and in mankind itself. Only in the books did I find consolation. Then one day my mother came back early from work and caught me reading. She was so upset that I promised myself I would not bring books home anymore.

Cooky and I spent more and more time up in our attic hideout, reading or discussing what we'd read, and one day Cooky took out an old Bible we had among the Hebrew books. I'm not sure what prompted me to salvage it, as my upbringing was secular; perhaps I thought that a library without a Bible wouldn't be a Jewish library.

"I think we should say Kaddish for Mr. Edelstein," Cooky said after some hesitation. I looked at him in astonishment. Whenever we discussed religion, Cooky dismissed it. Both his parents were agnostic, and Cooky was brought up by them to despise religion.

"I know what you are thinking, but I think we owe it to him. After all, he did get killed because of our book. I think perhaps he would have wanted someone to say Kaddish for him," Cooky explained with some embarrassment. And so I wrote down the words of the Kaddish on a slip of paper, and the next day after school we stopped at the cemetery and read the words at his unmarked grave. Strangely enough I felt better for it, and I continued to visit and tend Edelstein's grave in the months to come. When the weather warmed I planted some peas there. To my surprise they grew into bushes and eventually bore fruit, which Cooky and I shared. I knew Mr. Edelstein wouldn't mind.

Where books are burned in the end
people will be burned, too.

—HEINRICH HEINE

From
Areopagitica

BY JOHN MILTON

Books are not absolutely dead things, but do contain a potency of life in them to be as active as that soul was whose progeny they are; nay, they do preserve as in a vial the purest efficacy and extraction of that living intellect that bred them. I know they are as lively, and as vigorously productive, as those fabulous dragon's teeth; and being sown up and down, may chance to spring up armed men. And yet, on the other hand, unless wariness be used, as good almost kill a man as kill a good book. Who kills a man kills a reasonable creature, God's image; but he who destroys a good book, kills reason itself, kills the image of God, as it were in the eye. Many a man lives a burden to the earth; but a good book is the precious life-blood of a master spirit, embalmed and treasured up on purpose to a life beyond life.

Books Unread

BY THOMAS WENTWORTH
HIGGINSON

This essay first appeared in The Atlantic Monthly *in 1904. The pity is it is simply too long to put on a tombstone.*

> *No longer delude thyself; for thou wilt never read thine own memoranda, nor the recorded deeds of old Romans and Greeks, and those passages in books which thou has been reserving for thine old age.*

—MARCUS ANTONINUS, III, 14

In the gradual growth of every student's library, he may—or may not—continue to admit literary friends and advisers; but he will be sure, sooner or later, to send for a man with a tool-chest. Sooner or later, every nook and corner will be filled with books, every window will be more or less darkened, and added shelves must be devised. He may find it hard to achieve just the arrangement he wants, but he will find it hardest of all to meet squarely that inevitable inquiry of the puzzled carpenter as he looks about him. "Have you really read all these books?" The expected answer is, "To be sure, how can you doubt it?" Yet if you asked him in turn, "Have you actually used every tool in your tool-chest?" you would very likely be told, "Not one half as yet, at least this season; I have the others by me, to use as I need them." Now if this reply can be fairly made in a simple, well-defined, distinctly limited occupation like that of a joiner, how much more inevitable it is in a pursuit which covers the whole range of thought and all the facts in the universe. The library is the author's tool-chest. He must at least learn, as he grows older, to take what he wants and to leave the rest.

This never was more tersely expressed than by Margaret Fuller when she says: "A man who means to think and write a great deal must, after six and twenty, learn to read with his fingers." A few men of leisure may satisfy themselves by reading over and over a single book and ignoring all others, like that English scholar who read Homer's *Iliad* and *Odyssey* every year in the original, devoting a week to each canto and reserving the minor poems for his summer vacation. Nay, there are books in the English language so vast that the ordinary reader recoils before their text and their footnotes. Such, for instance, is Gibbon's *Decline and Fall of the Roman Empire,* containing substantially the history of the whole world for thirteen centuries. When the author dismissed the last page of his book, on June 27, 1787, in that historic garden at Geneva, knowing that he was to address his public at once in four different languages, is it not possible that he may have felt some natural misgiving as to whether any one person would ever read the whole of it? We know him to have predicted that Fielding's *Tom Jones* would outlast the palace of the Escorial and the imperial eagle of Austria, but he recorded no similar claim for his own work. The statesman Fox, to be sure, pronounced the book to be "immortal" simply because, as he said, no man in the world could do without it; and Sheridan added, with undue levity, that if not luminous, it was at least voluminous. But modern readers, as a rule, consult it, they do not read it. It is, at best, a tool-chest.

Yet there lies before me what is perhaps the most remarkable manuscript catalog of books read that can be found in the English-speaking world, this being the work of a man of eighty-three, who began life by reading a verse of the Bible aloud to his mother when three years old, had gone through the whole of it by the time he was nine, and then went on to grapple with all the rest of literature, upon which he is still at work. His vast catalog of books read begins with 1837 and continues up to the present day, thus covering much more than half a century, a course of reading not yet finished and in which

Gibbon is but an incident. One finds, for instance, at intervals, such items as these: "Gibbon's *Decline and Fall of the Roman Empire,* read twice between 1856 and 1894"; "Gibbon's *Decline and Fall,* third reading, 1895"; "Gibbon's *Decline and Fall,* vols. 1 and 2, fourth reading"; followed soon after by "Gibbon's, vols. 3–6, fourth reading"; "Gibbon's, vols. 7–8, fourth reading." What are a thousand readings of *Tom Jones* compared with a series of feats like this? And there is a certain satisfaction to those who find themselves staggered by the contemplation of such labor, when they read elsewhere on the list the recorded confession that this man of wonderful toil occasionally stooped so far as cheerfully to include That Frenchman and Mr. Barnes of New York.

The list of books unread might properly begin with those painted shelves of mere book covers which present themselves in some large libraries, to veil the passageway. These are not books unread, since they are not books at all. Much the same is true of those which perhaps may still be seen, as formerly, in old Dutch houses round Albany: the effigies of books merely desired, but not yet possessed; and only proposed as purchases for some day when the owner's ship should come in. These were made only of blocks of wood, neatly painted and bound in leather with the proper labels, but surely destined never to be read, since they had in them nothing readable. Almost as remote from the real books are those dummies made up by booksellers to be exhibited by their traveling agents. Thus I have at hand a volume of my own translation of Epictetus, consisting of a single "signature" of eighteen pages, repeated over and over, so that one never gets any farther; each signature bearing on the last page, by one of Fate's simple and unconscious strokes, the printed question, "Where is progress, then?" (page 18). Where, indeed! Next to these, of course, the books which go most thoroughly unread are those which certainly are books, but of which we explore the backs only, as in fine old European libraries; books as sacredly preserved as was once that library at Blenheim—now long since dispersed—in which, when I idly asked the custodian whether she did not find it a great deal of trouble to keep them dusted, she answered with surprise, "No, sir, the doors have not been unlocked for ten years." It is so in some departments of even American libraries.

Matthew Arnold once replied to a critic who accused him of a lack of learning that the charge was true, but that he often wished he had still less of that possession, so hard did he find it to carry lightly what he knew. The only knowledge that involves no burden lies, it may be justly claimed, in the books that are left unread. I mean those which remain undisturbed, long and perhaps forever, on a student's bookshelves: books for which he possibly economized, and to obtain which he went without his dinner; books on whose back his eyes have rested a thousand times, tenderly and almost lovingly, until he has perhaps forgotten the very language in which they are written. He has never read them, yet during these years there had never been a day when he would have sold them; they are a part of his youth. In dreams he turns to them: in dreams he reads Hebrew again; he knows what a Differential Equation is; "how happy could he be with either." He awakens, and whole shelves of his library are, as it were, like fair maidens who smiled on him in their youth and then passed away. Under different circumstances, who knows but one of them might have been his? As it is, they have grown old apart from him: yet for him they retain their charms.

Books which we have first read in odd places always retain their charm, whether read or neglected. Thus Hazlitt always remembered that it was on the 10th of April, 1798, that he "sat down to a volume of the *New Eloise* at the inn at Llangollen over a bottle of sherry and a cold chicken." In the same way I remember how Professor Longfellow in college recommended to us, for forming a good French style, to read Balzac's *Peau de chagrin;* and yet it was a dozen years later before I found it in a country inn, on a lecture trip, and sat up half the night to read it. It may be, on the other hand, that such haphazard meetings with books sometimes present them under conditions hopelessly unfavorable, as when I encountered Whitman's *Leaves of Grass* for the first time on my first voyage in an Azorian barque; and it inspires to this day a slight sense of nausea, which it might, after all, have inspired equally on land.

Wordsworth says in his *Personal Talk,* "Dreams, books are each a world"; and the books unread mingle with the dreams and unite the charm of both. This applies especially, I think, to books of travel: we buy them, finding their attractions strong, but somehow we do not read them over and over, unless they prove to be such books as those of Urquhart—the *Pillar of Hercules* especially, where the wealth of learning and originality is so great that we seem in a different region of the globe on every page. One of the most poetic things about

Whittier's temperament lay in this fact, that he felt most eager to visit each foreign country before he had read any books about it. After reading, the dream was half fulfilled, and he turned to something else, so that he died without visiting any foreign country. But the very possession of such books, and their presence on the shelves, carries one to the Arctic regions or to the Indian Ocean.

"After all," as the melancholy Rufus Choate said, "a book is the only immortality," and sometimes when a book is attacked and even denounced, its destiny of fame is only confirmed. Thus the vivacious and cheery Pope, Pio Nono, when asked by a too daring author to help on his latest publication, suggested that he could only aid it by putting it in the Index Expurgatorius. Yet if a book is to be left unread at last, the fault must ultimately rest on the author, even as the brilliant Lady Eastlake complained, when she wrote of modern English novelists: "Things are written now to be read once, and no more; that is, they are read as often as they deserve. A book in old times took five years to write and was read five hundred times by five hundred people. Now it is written in three months, and read once by five hundred thousand people. That's the proper proportion."

Any man with a moderate income can afford to buy more books than he can read in a lifetime.

—HENRY HOLT

Ten Books That Shaped the American Character

BY JONATHAN YARDLEY

For their April/May 1985 issue, the editors of American Heritage *magazine invited Jonathan Yardley, book editor and columnist for* The Washington Post, *to write an article entitled "Ten Books That Shaped the American Character." Although his first instinct was to compile a list of books that changed the political life of America, on further reflection he decided to make a list of those that affected the cultural, social, and domestic life of the nation. Some of the books he discussed—like* Walden—*are books one would expect to see on such a list, but others will in all likelihood come as a surprise. Here, then, are the ten books he chose, as well as the runners-up. This list can be compared to the one compiled by Robert B. Downs for his* Books That Changed America, *which appears on page* 96.

THE LIST

1. *Walden* by Henry David Thoreau (1854)
2. *Leaves of Grass* by Walt Whitman (1855)
3. *Ragged Dick, or Street Life in New York* by Horatio Alger (1867)
4. *The Adventures of Huckleberry Finn* by Mark Twain (1884)
5. *The Boston Cooking School Cookbook* by Fannie Farmer (1896)

6. *The Theory of the Leisure Class* by Thorstein Veblen (1899)
7. *The Souls of Black Folk* by W. E. B. Du Bois (1903)
8. *In Our Time* by Ernest Hemingway (1925)
9. *How to Win Friends and Influence People* by Dale Carnegie (1936)
10. *The Common Sense Book of Baby and Child Care* by Benjamin Spock, M.D. (1946)

THE RUNNERS-UP

The Life and Memorable Actions of George Washington by Mason Locke Weems (1800)
The Clansman by Thomas Dixon (1905)
Main Street by Sinclair Lewis (1920)
Etiquette: The Blue Book of Social Usage by Emily Post (1922)
Babbitt by Sinclair Lewis (1922)
The Man Nobody Knows by Bruce Barton (1925)
The Grapes of Wrath by John Steinbeck (1939)
Hiroshima by John Hersey (1946)
The Lonely Crowd by David Riesman (1950)
The Catcher in the Rye by J. D. Salinger (1951)
Peyton Place by Grace Metalious (1956)
Catch-22 by Joseph Heller (1961)
The Death and Life of Great American Cities by Jane Jacobs (1961)
The New York Times Cook Book by Craig Claiborne (1961)
The Feminine Mystique by Betty Friedan (1963)
Roots by Alex Haley (1976)

Books That Changed America

BY ROBERT B. DOWNS

Fifteen years before the editors of American Heritage *asked Jonathan Yardley to compile his "Ten Books That Shaped the American Character" (see page 94), Robert B. Downs had written a book with a similar purpose. Published by Macmillan in 1970,* Books That Changed America *provided an analysis of twenty-five books whose impact on the American consciousness had, in his estimation, profoundly affected our way of life. It's clear from Downs's list that he had taken a somewhat broader view than Yardley, who concentrated specifically on books that affected the cultural, social, and domestic life of the nation and who accordingly included only popular books. Nevertheless, it's suggestive of the diversity of thought on this subject that not a single book appears on both Downs's and Yardley's lists.*

Twenty Years at Hull House by Jane Addams (1910)
An Economic Interpretation of the Constitution of the United States by
    Charles Austin Beard (1913)
*Experiments and Observations on the Gastric Juice and the Physiology
    of Digestion* by William Beaumont (1833)
Looking Backward by Edward Bellamy (1888)
The Nature of the Judicial Process by Benjamin Cardozo (1921)

Silent Spring by Rachel Carson (1962)

The Mind of the South by Wilbur Joseph Cash (1941)

Medical Education in the United States and Canada by Abraham Flexner (1910)

The Affluent Society by John Kenneth Galbraith (1958)

The Contagiousness of Puerperal Fever by Oliver Wendell Holmes (1843)

History of the Expedition Under the Command of Captains Lewis and Clark by Meriwether Lewis and William Clark (1814)

Middletown: A Study in Contemporary American Culture by Robert Staughton Lynd and Helen Lynd (1929)

The Influence of Sea Power Upon History 1660–1783 by Alfred Thayer Mahan (1890)

Reports by Horace Mann (1837–1849)

Prejudices by H. L. Mencken (1919–1927)

An American Dilemma; The Negro Problem and Modern Democracy by Gunnar Myrdal (1944)

Common Sense, Addressed to the Inhabitants of America by Thomas Paine (1776)

The Jungle by Upton Sinclair (1905)

The Book of Mormon by Joseph Smith (1830)

The Shame of the Cities by Lincoln Steffens (1904)

Uncle Tom's Cabin by Harriet Beecher Stowe (1852)

The Principles of Scientific Management by Frederick Winslow Taylor (1911)

Resistance to Civil Government by Henry David Thoreau (1849)

Democracy in America by Alexis de Tocqueville (1835–1840)

The Significance of the Frontier in American History by Frederick Jackson Turner (1893)

The Commerce of Reading

BY MICHEL DE MONTAIGNE

Michel de Montaigne is considered the originator of the essay form, the first two volumes of his Essays *having appeared in 1580 and the third in 1588. While in general the author deals with life from an urbanely skeptical point of view, that attitude is not evident in his essay on reading, in which he refers to the pastime as "the best viaticum I have yet found out for this human journey, and I very much pity those men of understanding who are unprovided with it." This translation, by Charles Cotton and revised by William Hazlitt, was first published by Templeman in London in 1842.*

The [commerce of books] goes side by side with me in my whole course, and everywhere is assisting to me; it comforts me in my age and solitude; it eases me of a troublesome weight of idleness, and it delivers me at all hours from company that I dislike; and it blunts the point of griefs if they are not extreme, and have got an entire possession of my soul. To divert myself from a troublesome fancy 'tis but to run to my books; they presently fix me to them, and drive the other out of my thoughts; and do not mutiny at seeing I have only recourse to them for want of other more real, natural, and lively conveniences; they always receive me with the same kindness. "He may well go a-foot," say they, "who leads his horse in his hand"; and our

James, King of Naples and Sicily, who, handsome, young, and healthy, caused himself to be carried up and down on a hand-barrow, reclining on a pitiful feather pillow, and clad in a robe of coarse gray cloth, with a cap of the same, but attended nevertheless by a royal train of litters, led horses of all sorts, gentlemen and offi-cers, therein showed but a weak and unsteady austerity; the sick man is not to be pitied who has his cure in his sleeve. In the experience and practice of this sentence, which is a very true one, all the bene-fit I reap from books consists; and yet I make as little use of it almost as those who know it not; I enjoy it as a miser does his money, in knowing that I may enjoy it when I please; my mind is satisfied with this right of possession. I never travel without books, either in peace or war; and yet I sometimes pass over several days, and sometimes months, without looking at them; I will read by and by, say I to my-self, of tomorrow, or when I please, and time meanwhile steals away without any inconvenience; for it is not to be imagined to what de-gree I please myself, and rest content in this consideration, that I have them by me, to divert myself with them when I am so disposed, and call to mind what an ease and assistance they are to my life. 'Tis the best viaticum I have yet found out for this human journey, and I very much pity those men of understanding who are unprovided with it. I rather accept of any sort of diversion, how light soever, in the feeling that this can never fail me.

When at home, I a little more frequent my library from whence I at once survey all the whole concerns of my family. As I enter it, I thence see under my garden, court, and base-court, and into all the parts of the building. There I turn over now one book, and then an-other, of various subjects, without method or design. One while I meditate; another I record, and dictate as I walk to and fro, such whimsies as these with which I here present you. 'Tis in the third story of a tower, of which the ground-room is my chapel, the second story an apartment with a withdrawing-room and closet, where I often lie to be more retired; above it is this great wardrobe, which formerly was the most useless part of the house. In that room I pass away most of the days of my life, and most of the hours of the day; in the night I am never there. There is within it a cabinet handsome and neat enough, with a very convenient fireplace for the winter, and windows that afford a great deal of light, and very pleasant prospects; and were I not afraid, less of the expense than of the trouble, that frights me from all business, I could very easily adjoin on either side, and on the same floor, a gallery of an hundred paces long, and twelve broad, having sound walls already raised for some other design, to the requisite height. Every place of retirement requires a walk; my thoughts sleep if I sit still; my fancy does not go by itself, my legs must move it; and all those that study without a book, are in the same condition. The figure of my study is round, and has no more bare wall than what is taken up by my table and chair; so that the remaining parts of the circle present me a view of all my books at once, set upon five rows of shelves round about me. It has three noble and wide prospects, and is sixteen paces in diameter. I am not so continually there in winter; for my house is built upon an eminence, and no part of it is so much exposed to the wind and weather as that, which pleases me the better for being of troublesome access and a little remote, as well upon the account of exercise, as being also there more retired from the crowd. 'Tis there that I am in my kingdom, and there I endeavor to make myself an absolute monarch, and to sequester this one corner from all society, whether conjugal, filial, or social; elsewhere I have but verbal authority only, and of a confused essence. That man, in my opinion, is very miserable, who has not a home where to be by himself, where to entertain himself alone, or to conceal himself from others. Ambition sufficiently plagues her votaries by keeping them always in show, like the statue in a market place: "A great fortune is a great slavery." They have not so much as a retreat for the necessities of nature. I have thought nothing so severe in the austerity of life that our religions affect, as what I have observed in some of their orders; namely, to have a perpetual society of place by rule, and numerous assistants among them, in every action whatever; and think it much more supportable to be always alone, than never to be so.

If any one shall tell me that it is to degrade the muses to make use of them only for sport, and to pass away the time, I shall tell him that he does not know the value of that sport and pastime so well as I do; I can hardly forebear to add further, that all other end is ridiculous. I live from hand to mouth, and, with reverence be it spoken, only live for myself; to that all my designs tend, and in that terminate. I studied when young for ostentation; since, to make myself wise; and now for my diversion, never for gain. A vain and prodigal humor that I had after this sort of furniture, not only for supplying my own need, but moreover for ornament and outward show, I have long ago quite abandoned.

Books have many charming qualities to such as know how to choose them; but every good has its ill; 'tis a pleasure that is not pure and unmixed any more than others; it has its inconveniences, and great ones too; the mind, indeed, is exercised by it, but the body, the care of which I have not forgotten, remains in the meantime without action, grows heavy and melancholy. I know no excess more prejudicial to me, nor more to be avoided in my declining age.

Book Collecting

BY ROBERTSON DAVIES

Robertson Davies was the author of numerous novels, plays, criticism, and essays. In this essay—which first appeared in Holiday *magazine in 1962 and later in the 1970 collection* The Enthusiasms of Robertson Davies—*the author discourses on the difference between the individual who collects rare books because they're valuable and the one who collects them because he loves books, ultimately making it clear which is, as he puts it, "the collector who really matters."*

Some months ago I was visiting friends in Ireland who took me to call on a neighbour, a titled lady who, they told me, was in financial straits. I was surprised to be shown into a library which I knew at once would bring several thousand pounds if she chose to sell it. I therefore assumed that she must prize her books highly and tried to lead the conversation toward literature and collecting, but with no success. She would talk only about farming, gardening, and the difficulties of maintaining a large house with no staff.

At last I asked her point-blank about the library. Her eyes misted. For an instant I felt I had intruded upon a secret sorrow or shown some sort of North American grossness. But her reply reassured me.

"I suppose it is quite nice," said she. "My husband's father knew quite a lot about it, but we've never troubled ourselves. There's a

Shakespeare Fourth Folio somewhere, but I haven't seen it for a long time, and a first edition of *Pride and Prejudice,* though I think it's been lost. Oh, and we have the first printed edition of the Venerable Bede's book"—she waved toward a copy of the *Historia Ecclesiastica Gentis Anglorum,* which I had already spotted, and the cover of which was hanging loose—"and some other things."

Indeed there were some other things. I had made a quick tour of the shelves while the others chatted. The library was suffering painfully from neglect but was still a splendid accumulation, and there was nothing wrong with it that a good book repairer and a lot of love and saddle soap could not put right. As my hostess talked on about how short of money she was, I asked her why she did not sell her library, since she did not appear to attach much importance to it.

"I'd have no idea what to ask," said she. "Several years ago I met a little man at dinner who wanted to know if we had any books. An American—a medical man, I think. I said yes, and asked him to come to see them sometime. Do you know, he turned up the very next day! just at teatime, and we had some people in, so my husband went to the door and said it wouldn't be convenient, and I think they can't have got on, because the little man never came again."

"I don't suppose the American's name could have been Rosenbach, could it?" I asked.

"Yes, that was it," said she. "I thought he was rather pushing."

This encounter must have been one of Doctor Rosenbach's few defeats during his famous tour of Ireland, when he scooped up so many fine things for his clients. Edwin Wolf and John F. Fleming's recent biography of him makes no mention of the incident, which was not important to Rosenbach, but it might have proved a profitable experience for the lady who had mislaid her Shakespeare Folio to have received the most astute and highest-paying book dealer of our time.

I have found this story useful as a means of discovering what interest people have in books. Those who think of them principally as objects of value exclaim at the lost opportunity to do business with Rosenbach. Those who love books for themselves grieve at the neglect of a fine, perhaps a brilliant, library. And of course there are a few who glory in the aristocratic spirit which sets a tea party ahead of a sorely needed business deal.

This last point of view is of immense psychological interest but has no place in a discussion of book collecting. Members of the first group, who think of books as valuable objects to be bought and sold, are interesting only when they achieve something approaching the proportions of a Rosenbach. If they buy and sell on a lesser scale, they might as well be dealing in rare stamps; like so many collectors of all sorts, they are mere hagglers and swappers, occasionally goaded by an obsession to complete an assemblage of objects to which they have themselves set arbitrary limits. If a man determines, for instance, that he will get together examples of all the books Horace Walpole produced on his private printing press at Strawberry Hill, he has set himself a difficult and expensive task, for this realm is confused by clever forgeries. Such a man may be—or become—a real Walpole enthusiast, but the chances are that it is the difficulty the collection presents and the particular sort of status attached to its assemblage that enchant him.

Is there anything wrong with such an attitude? No; it ranks with collecting pictures by a famous painter, or school of painters, not because you like them but because they are valuable. It is a way of gaining face, and I suppose it is sometimes an evidence of the creative spirit; if you cannot make a work of art yourself, you can at least make a distinguished collection of such works. The galleries and museums, and through them the public, owe an incalculable debt to this spirit. But my real admiration is reserved for people who collect books because they love them.

If you love books, why is any good edition not as dear to you as a first edition, or one which presents some special features? Edmund Wilson attacked Rosenbach and his imitators in 1926, saying, "All this trade is as deeply boring to people who are interested in literature as it seems to be fascinating to those others who, incapable of literary culture, try to buy the distinction of letters by paying unusual prices for bibliographical rarities." That is partly true, but if we visit those great libraries in ancient universities where the collections of book lovers of the past are preserved as unities, we soon know better. In those splendid rooms we feel the presence of something noble, which has played a great part in shaping a man's mind to a noble form. We sense books as things with more character than the commercial productions of a trade. It is splendidly austere to say that Shakespeare is just as much Shakespeare in a paperback edition as he is in the beautiful Nonesuch Press edition of 1929 or the First Folio of 1623, but not all of us are such literary Calvinists. We value beauty and we value associations, and I do not think we should be sneered at because we like our heroes to be appropriately dressed.

It is the snobbery of book collecting that disgusts. Suppose our friend the collector shows us his first edition of Max Beerbohm's *Zuleika Dobson;* we handle the chunky, red-brown book with pleasure, reflecting that it was in this form, and in this pleasant type, that Max first saw his child presented to the world; for a moment we are close to the London of 1911. We think of the author with affection and seem almost to see him across the void of fifty years. But then our friend the collector begins to boast a little: his copy, he points out, is a Gallatin 8 (b); and furthermore, it has the ornamental frame on the spine stamped in green, instead of in gold. He urges us not to mistake it for a mere Gallatin 8b, which is a much inferior article, printed in 1912 and (from the dizzy eminence attained by the owner of a Gallatin 8 (b)) hardly worth having. Perhaps we begin to sicken of our friend the collector and tell him that we have only a Modern Library edition, which we read every year, with growing appreciation. This may well be a lie, but we have to put the ass in his place somehow. We are driven into bibliographical Puritanism by his antiliterary nonsense.

This is what can happen, but worse may befall. We may begin to yearn for his treasure. We do not covet his house, nor his wife (who gives dismal evidence of his lack of taste), his ox nor his ass, but with a searing flame we lust intolerably for his book. We know what it cost him, because he has not been able to refrain from telling us; he ordered it from a bookseller in England (whom he calls "my bookseller," as though he owned the fellow bodily) and so he got it for less than twenty dollars, which is considerably less than he would have had to pay for the same copy in New York.

We have twenty dollars in our pocket this minute. But it is not money that matters, nor our ability, at last, to get a Gallatin 8 (b) of *Zuleika* for our own. It is his book we want, and we want it now.

In this fevered state men have stolen. Book collectors are often tempted to steal, and if they are not of iron character, they do so. Rosenbach, in his *Books and Bidders,* admits to the temptation: when in doubt as to whether he could buy the very copy of Johnson's *Prologue* used by Garrick at the opening of Drury Lane in 1747, he wished that he might be weak enough to steal it. If he ever stole, he will answer for his deed in distinguished company. Sir Thomas Bodley, founder of the great Bodleian Library at Oxford, had to be watched by his friends; Pope Innocent X, before he gained the triple tiara, was involved in a scandal over a rare book he stole from the famous collection of Montier; Don Vicente, a monk of the Convent of Pobla in Aragon, murdered several collectors in order to get their best books; and of course men in great political positions, like Cardinal Mazarin and Cardinal Richelieu, stole whole libraries under the guise of dispersing the property of enemies of the state. Frederick Locker-Lampson, the poet, confessed that he very nearly married Lady Tadcaster to get his hands on her Shakespeare Folios and Quartos. This is a lust which cannot be described and is so terrible that I could not wish anyone to feel it.

Between stealing and what may be called Borrowing with Mental Reservation I do not see any great difference. Conscious of this viciousness in my own bosom (oh, what struggles with the monster, in the dead of night and in the dusky recesses of libraries!), I used for many years a book-plate which bore Doctor Johnson's admonition "To forget, or pretend to do so, to return a borrowed object is the meanest sort of petty theft." I wonder if the scoundrels who stole from me have troubled to steam that label out of my books.

Setting aside all the unworthy creatures who value rare books for the wrong reasons, let us look at the true collectors, splendid fellows like you and me. Why do we collect books? There is no single, honest answer. It is not solely the love of beauty, which may be the mainspring of the man who collects pictures, or furniture, or china. The book lover will have some beautiful books on his shelves, but there will be some ugly little articles as well. One of my special favourites is a hideous, ill-printed jest-book of 1686; it is stained and thumbed, managing somehow to suggest that it was carried in the pockets of several generations of veterinarians as they went about their business; but it is a rarity. Yet I can honestly say that it is not its rarity that comes first with me; when I read it, I am transported back nearly three centuries to the reign of James II, and its jokes (fearful jokes they are, blunt and dirty) are more congenial than if I had the same book in a neat modern reprint. To the book collector the historical sense is at least as potent as the love of beauty.

Unique qualities are prized, of course, but only a rich man can hope to possess many books which have no mates anywhere in the world. I have a modest example of this kind, a copy of George Cruikshank's *Punch and Judy* which contains all the proofs which were pulled for the publisher, Prowett, taken from his scrapbook. Great collections, like that of Pierpont Morgan, contain hundreds of unique volumes. The ultimate in this line is, of course, the manuscript of a book. Morgan acquired the exquisite, touching original script of Thackeray's *The Rose and the Ring* with the author's own water-colour illustrations; a facsimile has been made, which is in itself enough of a rarity to be a pleasant possession. These things run high; Rosenbach paid £15,400 for the manuscript of *Alice in Wonderland,* at a time when the pound was worth close to five dollars.

An interesting type of unique book is that which dealers describe as "extra-illustrated." In the early nineteenth century people used to make such books for their own pleasure. A man who acquired a biography of his particular hero might also own a considerable number of portraits, significant landscapes, and even letters written by the hero; he sent these away to the binder with his book, and in time it came back to him, handsomely recased, with all the pictures and letters neatly mounted on extra sheets and bound into the text. Such books can be of great interest and value, or they can be junk; it depends on the taste of the original owner. I have one or two books of this kind relating to the theatre, and the additional matter they contain makes them valuable to me; I am not so foolish as to suppose that they would interest anyone who was not bewitched by the theatre of the early nineteenth century.

Collectors, if they are realists, must make up their minds early in life whether they are getting together a group of books which they hope will grow in value or simply a collection which gives them pleasure. The man who expects to gain a day's posthumous fame when his library disappears into the maw of a university must never lose sight of his primary aim. The professional bibliophiles will paw over his books and be quick to despise him if he has bought any fakes or anything unworthy—and how quick legatees are to spot anything which is not up to their demanding standards. But the man who collects only for his own pleasure may buy anything he pleases, not caring that when he dies he will be called a magpie and that books he has loved will be bought for ten cents apiece by the dealers. He will have some fine things, of course, but as individual items they are not likely to fetch the prices they would bring if he had controlled his desires and bought only the ingredients of a coherent collection. The fellow who can leave his alma mater every book and every scrap of manuscript relating to or owned by Button Gwinnett is a greater man, in this realm, than the fellow who troubles the university librarian with attractive odds and ends.

The former will put the Gwinnettologists forever in his debt, and tiny pinches of incense, in the form of footnotes, will be cast into his funerary flame. "The late Enoch Pobjoy, to whom Gwinnett scholars are obliged for the new light his collection has thrown on Gwinnett's sanitary arrangements"—that is what he will be. But the collector who has lived only for pleasure, what of him?

Well, so far as I am concerned, he is the only collector who really matters. He is a man who loves books and reads them. He loves books not only for what they have to say to him—though that is his principal reason—but for their look, their feel, yes, and even their smell. He is a man who may give books away, but who never thinks of buying a musty immortality with his library. His affair with books is a cheerful, life-enhancing passion.

Considering what a nuisance books are, it is astonishing what a number of collectors of this stamp one meets. For books are a des-

There are 10,000 books in my library, and it will keep growing until I die. This has exasperated my daughters, amused my friends, and baffled my accountant. If I had not picked up this habit in the library long ago, I would have more money in the bank today; I would not be richer.

—PETE HAMILL, "D'ARTAGNAN ON NINTH STREET:
A BROOKLYN BOY AT THE LIBRARY"

perate nuisance; a library of even a few thousand volumes anchors a man to one house, because it is such a task to shift them.

I face the ordeal of a move myself, and regardless of how much I try to concentrate on the realities of the matter, I catch my mind wandering toward fearful calculations as to the amount of shelf room I can possibly hope for in the new house.

Will it be necessary to sink to the horror of a stack room, a book hell, in the basement? Or (for cheerfulness will keep breaking in) will it be possible to devise some splendid new arrangement so that in a twinkling of an eye, any book may be found?

The one thing that never occurs to me is to get rid of some books or to forswear buying any more. And that, I suppose, is what being a collector really means.

HOLIDAY, MAY 1962

"Holy cow! What kind of crazy people used to live here anyway?"

Bibliomaniacs

BY JOHN MICHELL

John Michell's classic 1984 book, Eccentric Lives and Peculiar Notions, *from which this essay is excerpted, might well have included a biography of Michell himself. His interests ranged from Atlantis to flying saucers, and he wrote several best-selling books on ancient wisdom. Tales of bibliomania taken to extremes have appeared elsewhere, but never with the bizarre touch Michell provides.*

Bibliomania, the passionate desire to handle, possess, and accumulate books, has been the subject of warnings by many writers, mostly those who have been touched by it themselves. Others, however, have defended it on the grounds that, since as one grows older one's level of insanity inevitably increases, it is best to adopt one of the more liberal forms of madness such as obsession with books.

Some truly horrid examples are recorded of fanatical book collecting, and of those who have been ruined by it, alienated wives and families, and even been driven from their own homes by their libraries. Thomas Rawlinson, a collector of the early eighteenth century, stuffed his rooms at Gray's Inn so full of books that he had to sleep in the passage. He then moved into a large mansion which he shared with his brother and did the same thing there. By the time Thomas died, aged forty-four, there was scarcely a place where the brothers could sit among the books, papers, and dust of their collection.

A bibliomaniac of Paris, M. Boulard, bought books indiscriminately until he owned more than 600,000 of them. Shelf space in his house had long given out, so he filled trunks and cupboards with books, and then the attics, cellars, storerooms, and the floors of every other room. The weight was so onerous that the house began to collapse, so Boulard bought more houses, six in all, which he filled entirely with books, gradually driving out the tenants before the rising flood of his collection.

Bibliomania is the title of a book published in 1809 by the Rev. Thomas Frognall Dibdin, whose principal subject was the outstanding bibliomaniac of his time, Richard Heber. Dibdin came from a show-business family; his uncle was the writer of such long-popular songs as "Tom Bowling" and "'Twas in the good ship *Rover*," later to be parodied by rugger players. With Heber and other bibliomaniacs of the time Dibdin founded the Roxburghe Club, where the first toast was to "the cause of Bibliomania all over the world," followed by more toasts to famous printers and book collectors of ages past. It was a time when book prices were low, and Dibdin and his fellows could pick up for a few shillings manuscripts now worth many thousands of pounds. He had a sharp nose for a bargain and, though a clergyman, did not spare even his reverend colleagues when it came to book business. On a visit to Lincoln Cathedral he noticed in the library some rare old volumes, the worth of which was quite unrecognized by the unworldly clerics. Dibdin offered to help improve the library by providing it with up-to-date books by the best authors in exchange for the old ones. The Lincoln clergy accepted and were delighted with the £300 worth of modern books which the Rev. Dibdin chose for them. Their mood changed, however, when they heard that their benefactor had sold just one of the old books from their library for £1,800. When Dibdin called again, eager to make a further exchange, they shut the door of the library in his face.

Richard Heber was a prodigy of bibliomania. Born in 1774, the son of a rich clergyman at Hodnet in Cheshire, he compiled at the age of eight a catalogue of the library he had already built up, with detailed instructions on how the books were to be bound. Throughout his school days he bought far beyond the limit of his means, becoming a familiar figure at book auctions. His father saw his rectory being overrun by books, followed by accounts from dealers and book-binders, and did his best to curb Richard's frenzy. It was in vain. Richard's magpie career went on unchecked and he became a discriminating buyer of old rarities. He was also that rare type among bibliomaniacs, a scholar, actually reading some portion of the writings he accumulated. When he went up to Oxford he further annoyed his father by editing for publication a classical work which the good clergyman found improper.

When old Mr. Heber died, leaving a fine estate and fortune, Richard was freed of his only previous restraint, lack of money. His book-buying exploits became fantastic. It seemed as if he wanted to own every book that ever was, and not just one copy of each. He used to say that every gentleman needed at least three copies of a book, one for his country house library, one for reading, and one to lend to friends. But three copies was by no means his limit. Several of his collections of different copies or editions of the same work would have formed a considerable library on their own. He would buy the entire contents of a bookseller's catalogue or collections of many thousands of books in one lot, and he would also make difficult journeys of hundreds of miles in pursuit of a single coveted volume. Only once was he diverted from his career, and only for a short time, when he contemplated marriage. Not that it really was a deviation, for the wife he almost chose was Miss Richardson Currer of Yorkshire, the most renowned of English women book collectors. The proposal, in fact, was for a marriage of libraries, but either the couple or their books did not suit each other, for nothing came of the match.

Heber's appetite for books, said Dibdin, displayed "a rapaciousness of hunger and thirst, such as the world never saw before, and is unlikely to see again." Holbrook Jackson summed him up as "a bibliomaniac if ever there was one . . . a bibliomaniac in the most unpleasant sense of the word; no confirmed drunkard, no incurable opium-eater, had less self-control; to see a book was to desire it, to desire it was to possess it, the great and strong passion of his life was to amass such a library as no individual before him had ever amassed . . . His collection was omnigenous, and he never ceased to accumulate books of all kinds, buying them by all methods, in all places, at all times."

Toward the end of his life Heber became a recluse, gloating over his treasures behind the shutters of his London house in Pimlico. In one of its rooms he had been born, and in 1833 he died in it, despairing and alone, shortly after he had sent a substantial order to a bookseller. It was his inner citadel, fabulous among bibliophiles because no one else had ever been allowed to enter it. The inquisitive Dibdin hurried at once to Pimlico to be the first to break in. "I looked around me in amazement," he wrote. "I had never seen rooms, cupboards, passages, and corridors, so choked, so suffocated, with books. Treble rows were here, double rows were there. Hundreds of slim quartos—several upon each other—were longitudinally placed over thin and stunted duodecimos, reaching from one extremity of a shelf to another. Up to the very ceiling the piles of volumes extended; while the floor was strewn with them, in loose and numerous heaps. When I looked on all this, and thought what might be at Hodnet, and upon the Continent, it were difficult to describe my emotions."

From the piles of paper Dibdin was at last able to unearth Richard Heber's will. Like Shakspere's, it made no mention of any books. Indeed, it was some time before the executors could locate the manifold branches of his gigantic library. Two houses in London were found to be stuffed with books, and so was the large mansion he had inherited in Cheshire. Other houses, similarly filled, were located in Paris, Brussels, Antwerp, and Ghent, and another in Germany. No one has ever been certain whether these eight repositories housed the entire library of Richard Heber or whether he had other store-places about Europe where unknown literary treasures may still be lurking.

A Monstrous Paper Collector

At the sale of Richard Heber's manuscripts in 1836 the largest buyer was a Worcestershire landowner, Sir Thomas Phillipps, who went on to become the largest collector ever known of old papers and documents. Born in 1792, he inherited at the age of twenty-six his father's estate at Middle Hill near Broadway, married the daughter of an Irish general, and used the influence of his father-in-law to have himself made a baronet. Sir Thomas had a considerable income, all of which, together with all the money he could raise through mortgaging his property, he spent on buying manuscripts.

No individual's life has ever been better documented than that of Sir Thomas Phillipps, partly because he never threw away a scrap of paper, hoarding household bills and drafts and copies of all his correspondence, and partly because of A. N. L. Munby's five published volumes of Phillipps's *Studies* (later boiled down to one volume entitled *Portrait of an Obsession*). Described in this work is the amazing series of transactions by which Phillipps built up a collection of ancient and medieval manuscripts, far more extensive than that of the British Museum or any university library. It is the most detailed history of the most extreme of bibliomaniacs. "Tim" Munby was himself afflicted by bibliomania, but he controlled the disease through its only known antidote by becoming a bibliophile. He collected not only books but curious anecdotes about book dealers and their customers, many of which he published in later years when he was librarian at King's College, Cambridge. Some of the best were about himself. As a young man, while working for the famous dealer Bernard Quaritch, he had acquired two medieval manuscripts which he then sold to finance a half share in a 1925 type 40 Bugatti. It was a fine vehicle, but it was always breaking down, one of its gaskets giving repeated trouble. Munby repaired it with a piece of thick vellum cut from an old book. When people asked him the age of the Bugatti he was thus able to reply, "Parts of it date back to the fifteenth century."

There is no record of any such tomfoolery in the life of Sir Thomas Phillipps. He was serious, dry, cross, and utterly obsessed. Apart from a few minor hobbies, such as abusing the Pope and issuing violently anti-Catholic tracts, his whole time was spent acquiring books and manuscripts. He would buy whole valuable libraries, booksellers' entire stocks, old records thrown out by government departments, and cartloads of waste paper on the way to be pulped. Among the rubbish were many items of worth and rarity, which were thus saved from destruction. Phillipps offered higher prices for collections of old documents than the waste-paper dealers could pay and thus broke their monopoly of the market. Other collectors followed his example, and preservation of thousands of unique records and historical documents is credited to Sir Thomas's obsession with paper.

It was impossible for any one man to catalogue this continually waxing library, but Phillipps did his best. He pressed his wife, three daughters, and their governess into the task of listing manuscripts and copying out those which he thought worth publishing. A succession of resident printers issued catalogues and small editions of texts for the benefit of scholars. These activities were constantly interrupted by the intrusion of creditors. On many occasions Phillipps was so deeply in debt that he seemed on the verge of ruin. Yet he always pulled through, never selling from his library, ever adding to it. His estate buildings collapsed because he refused to spend money repairing them, and his family were forced to live, like him, as misers. He was ruthless with booksellers, demanding lengthy credit and books on approval and then refusing payment or the return of goods until compelled by law. His treatment drove several into bankruptcy, but he could always find others to accept his huge orders.

At the age of thirty he had to flee abroad to avoid creditors. The move only made matters worse because at that time, in the turmoil after the Napoleonic Wars, many great European libraries were being dispersed. Ignoring his debts, Phillipps bought manuscripts wherever he could, enriching his collection with items which would now be almost priceless. Meanwhile he had hired a printer, Adolphus Brightley, who arrived at Middle Hill to find that he was expected to lodge and work in Broadway Tower, a monument on a lonely hilltop. This was impossible since the Tower was dilapidated, its windows had no glass in them, and the only water available was that which poured through the roof and down the walls. In any case its rooms were all occupied by some local indigents. Phillipps's agent, who had become adept at running the estate without spending money, took charge of the young printer, found him temporary lodgings, and joined him in a plea for help to their absent employer. But not even a small sum could be spared for the printer's expenses. Like all Phillipps's dependants, he had to learn to fend for himself. He and the agent somehow evicted the people from the Tower and patched it up sufficiently for the printing press to be installed. There Brightley worked for over three years, unable to leave because all his capital was invested in the materials of his trade. In that time he gave loyal service, learning Latin and Anglo-Saxon to assist his work of printing transcriptions of old manuscripts. Finally his employer's meanness and bad temper became too much for even his tolerance, his wages fell hopelessly into arrears, and he gave notice. The string of printers who succeeded him suffered as badly, or worse, and left more promptly. Each in turn was set to work on Phillipps's catalogue of his manuscripts, and each used a different size, colour, and type of paper for the work. The finished catalogue, which Phillipps distributed to certain libraries and the few scholars he respected, has a unique reputation as the book which was produced by the greatest number of printers.

Lady Phillipps's father, General Molyneux, saved the day by taking over management of the Middle Hill estate and arranging a settlement of its proprietor's debts. Phillipps was thus able to return home. Immediately he began a spate of book-buying which belittled even his earlier efforts. As crates and cartloads of paper poured into it, the interior of the mansion at Middle Hill rapidly shrank. Most of the rooms were unusable for normal purposes, being filled with books, as were all the corridors in which there was barely enough room for two people to pass. When the dining room became clogged with manuscripts Phillipps locked it up, and the family had to make do with one sitting room on the ground floor and three bedrooms upstairs, poorly furnished, with peeling wallpaper and broken panes. In order that the books might easily be removed in case of fire, they were stored in long, coffin-like boxes, piled one on top of another, the fronts of which opened downward on horizontal hinges. The walls of the Phillippses' bedroom were so thickly lined with these boxes that only a few square feet of floor remained for Lady Phillipps's dressing-table.

The strain of keeping house under these circumstances, constantly persecuted by bailiffs and writ-servers and with no sympathy from her bibliomaniac husband, became too much for Lady Phillipps. She lost her spirits, took to drugs, and died at the age of thirty-seven. Immediately after the funeral Phillipps began a search for her replacement. What he needed in a wife was money, nothing else. All his affections were given to books. "I am for sale at £50,000," he wrote to a friend. But it was not easy to find a docile bride with that size of dowry. It was ten years before Phillipps married again, and in that period he was continually active in negotiations with fathers of unmarried ladies. Munby reckons that he made seventeen serious bids before he finally closed a deal. His approaches were crude and pecuniary. One prospective father-in-law accused him, justly, of behaving like a Smithfield cattle dealer. Finally, after much haggling, he struck a bargain for a clergyman's daughter with £3,000 a year. She was stout and amiable, and the marriage went happily until in his last years Phillipps's eccentricities became intolerable.

He also offered his daughters on the marriage market, beginning when the eldest was twelve by proposing her to his old friend, Charles Madden, who had charge of manuscripts at the British Museum. But Henrietta Phillipps had ideas of her own. One of her father's agreeable habits was of hospitality to scholars. He enjoyed the company of the many visitors to Middle Hill who came to consult his manuscripts, although he was often unable to locate a particular document among the boxes and unopened crates of his collection. The fateful visitor was James Orchard Halliwell, a brilliant young scholar from Cambridge and one of the most enigmatic figures of nineteenth-century literature. He was a dandified youth of obscure birth whose manuscript studies had procured him the highest academic honours and election as Fellow of the Royal Society before his nineteenth birthday. Later he became the leading collector of Shakespearean documents and rarities and author of the acknowledged best *Life of Shakespeare*. He had the greatest influence in forming the modern Shakespeare cult at Stratford-on-Avon. He was also one of the few people ever to get the better of Sir Thomas Phillipps.

Phillipps had corresponded with Halliwell about manuscripts before inviting him to Middle Hill. The young man was ingratiating and presented himself as Phillipps's eager disciple. Once in the house he began courting Henrietta—and promptly asked for her hand in marriage. Her father in his usual way turned the subject to money. Halliwell had little to show in the way of income or prospects, which were what Phillipps most required of a son-in-law. And there was another objection: some nasty rumours were going around about Halliwell's character and reputation. It was even said that he was that most dreaded enemy of the bibliomaniac—a sly book thief. Phillipps withheld his consent to the marriage and, when the couple married without it, was relentless throughout the rest of his life in persecuting them.

His first opportunity for revenge on his son-in-law came soon after the wedding. Halliwell was accused of stealing manuscripts from Trinity College, Cambridge, and then selling them. The evidence was black against him, but he defended himself vigorously, speaking at public meetings and issuing an explanatory pamphlet. Somehow the matter never came to court. Phillipps, who had been urging on the prosecution, was dismayed, and he became even more so when he realized that his estates, which were entailed upon his heir, would eventually pass to the Halliwells. Lawyers advised him that there was no way of preventing James Halliwell, through his wife, from inheriting Middle Hill. That being the case, Phillipps decided on a scorched-earth policy. Halliwell would succeed to a wilderness. Ignoring all protests from his heirs and trustees, he cut down the fine avenues and copses on the estate, ruining its appearance and value. With the money raised by the timber he bought an enormous mansion in Cheltenham, Thirlestaine House, and in 1863 began moving his library there from Middle Hill. This vast operation took more than eight months to complete. A fleet of over a hundred wagons, drawn by 230 carthorses, groaned and sometimes collapsed under the weight of the Phillipps Library on its journey over the Cotswolds. Thirlestaine House, with its central block and two wings, was so large that Phillipps moved about it on horseback while supervising the disposal there of his books and pictures. Middle Hill was left empty and derelict and allowed, even encouraged by Phillipps, to fall into ruin. Cattle roamed its gardens and ground-floor rooms, and nothing was done to prevent the local vandals from smashing its windows and remaining fittings—most of which Phillipps had himself removed so as to make the house useless to his heirs.

The last years at Thirlestaine House saw the culmination of Sir Thomas Phillipps's mania. Without ceasing to acquire more manuscripts he began a new collection of printed books. Thousands of volumes, both cheap and rare, were poured into his library. He bought indiscriminately, gripped by a terrible new ambition. "I wish to have one copy of every book in the world!!!!!" he wrote to a friend. What with ordering books, unpacking, arranging, and cataloguing them, and corresponding with or receiving visits from scholars, he had no time for ordinary domestic life. He ate and slept among his books. His only diversions were printing learned texts and conducting his propaganda war against Roman Catholics. Catholic scholars were barred from his library.

The second Lady Phillipps detested Thirlestaine House. The parts not stuffed with books, she complained, were infested with rats, and the kitchen was in a separate wing on the other side of a road from the house, so dinners always arrived cold. She had a breakdown and was sent off to a cheap boarding-house in Torquay, where her husband kept her in embarrassing debt and sent angry letters in response to her pleas for money.

Phillipps's campaign of spite against his heirs was ultimately unsuccessful. When the old bibliomaniac died, aged eighty, Halliwell was energetic in repairing the roof of Middle Hill, finding a buyer for it, and breaking the entail on the estate. For the rest of his life he was a rich man. His wife, Henrietta, died a few years after her father, and Mr. J. O. Halliwell-Phillipps (as he now called himself) went on to make his name as the first authority on the life and times of Shakespeare. Despite their quarrel he had always admired his father-in-law, and he imitated him in printing small editions of manuscript texts of literary, topographical, or folklore interest. His particular form of bibliomania was love of rarities, so he would often buy back his own productions in order to destroy them, leaving just one or two copies in existence and thus defeating the main purpose of publishing in the first place. All his life he had collected and dealt in literary and other relics of Shakespeare, beginning with those he stole (including a *Hamlet* quarto of 1603 which he abstracted from Phillipps's library and mutilated to conceal its provenance). Early disgraces were in time forgotten, and he became a revered figure of scholarship. His remarkable Shakespeare collection was housed in a strange bungalow complex, to which he kept adding new buildings, at Hollingbury Copse near Brighton. He referred to it as "that quaint wigwam on the Sussex Downs which had the honour of sheltering more record and artistic evidences connected with the personal history of the great dramatist than are to be found in any other of the world's libraries."

The most generous obituary on the death of Sir Thomas Phillipps was written by Halliwell, who praised him for his great learning. Madden of the British Museum crossly disagreed. He was an old rival of Phillipps, who had consistently topped his bids on behalf of the national collection at sales of precious manuscripts. He referred to him as the Monopolizing Bugbear. In reply to Halliwell he declared that Sir Thomas had no degree of learning or scholarship and that his publications were worthless because they contained so many errors. Phillipps had at some time picked a quarrel with almost every one of his friends, but many of them wrote kindly about him, remembering the more benevolent aspects of his bibliomania, his kindness to young scholars, and his willingness to open his library to those capable of appreciating it. The monstrous form of his madness was so apparent that people made allowances for it, and he somehow retained the affections even of those he had most wronged or persecuted, such as his own family.

Disposing of the Phillipps Library was far beyond the powers of his heirs for several generations. Sales of its now incredibly valuable contents have been going on from the nineteenth century to the present. In sifting through the manuscripts, writes Munby, great treasures have come to light, items of unique worth which for a hundred years had lain buried within the Phillipps hoard. "We may hope," he adds, "that Bibliotheca Phillippica has not yielded up all its secrets yet."

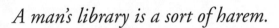

A man's library is a sort of harem.

—RALPH WALDO EMERSON, *THE CONDUCT OF LIFE*
(*1860*), "IN PRAISE OF BOOKS"

They Don't Call It a Mania for Nothing

BY HAROLD RABINOWITZ

"A Communist!"

"What?!"

"Absolute. A Communist."

I was dumbfounded. It took me a few moments to think of what to say. Arguing was out of the question. Chaim looked at me with an air of certainty, almost challenging me to deny it, practically looking at me with an accusatory squint as if he believed *I* was a Communist—or as if defending the accused would cast some doubts on me. I laughed and looked away, but Chaim was firm. His expression didn't change. The man was a Communist.

We had just spent a bleak winter's afternoon in Chaim's living room, watching a movie on afternoon television—*Planet of the Apes*—and several times I thought a movie of us watching the movie would be far more entertaining.

Chaim and his wife lived in a cozy two-bedroom apartment up in the Bronx just off Van Cortlandt Park, a neighborhood, I had discovered, that had two claims to fame: the first Son of Sam shooting took place down the street, and the neighborhood boasted a large immigrant Russian Jewish community. Chaim was a famous person in the community: a famous Yiddish writer whose work had appeared regularly in the *Jewish Daily Forward* when that paper thrived in the fifties. When Chaim took his daily constitutional in the neighborhood, he invariably encountered people (almost always men) who would argue with him about some point in the plot of an installment—that had appeared in the paper thirty years before! Chaim didn't dismiss them, though. I always thought he invited them just so he could argue. (One of the saddest things Chaim could say about an old friend was that "he had no one to argue with anymore.") And since I walked with him, and we seemed to get along, I guess I also felt something of an honored son of the community (though no one ever stopped me).

That particular afternoon was the end of a long period of time in the confluence of our lives, a period that had begun some two years earlier when a chance meeting in a lobby of a motel in Brookline, Massachusetts, led to my translating a work of Chaim's from the Yiddish and its being published by Alfred Knopf. There was always a sense of urgency as we worked on the translation. I would drop off a few chapters and go over the last few that had been reviewed by Chaim and his wife. It was a particularly chaotic time in my life, and I was glad to find refuge in their home. Chaim and I were bound by a few things that sometimes blurred the borders between us, the way married people begin to look like one another, or people look like their pets: we were both lapsed yeshiva students, fallen far from the faith but still respectful of the tradition because it was a tradition (and what else is there to be respectful of?); we were both uprooted—he from a war-ravaged home in Vilna, me from the more benign persecutions of a New England divorce; we were both devotees of the written word—we argued for hours on how to render a sentence or a phrase just right, and only after a few months of this was Chaim convinced that it was not my simple rebelliousness or the hurt of a miserable existence talking (and it took me no less time to think that about him); we were both admirers of intelligent women; we both mourned the fact that Chaim had had the Nobel Prize snatched from under his nose by "Bashevis'n," though Chaim begrudgingly admired the cunning with which his adversary had solicited the support of *The New York Times* and how he had campaigned for the prize with the help of the New York intelligentsia (and how—this Chaim really admired, possibly because it was the move he would have made—how he had, in his acceptance speech, made it virtually impossible for any other Yiddish writer to ever win a Nobel Prize); we both were mystified by poetry, though he had more of a right to be, having written seven or eight volumes of it, all of it great, some of it immortal; we both hated his wife's cooking, especially her coffee—even greater than the mystery of poetry was the mystery of what a person could do to a cup of coffee to make it taste that bad. And we both loved books.

No, we were both *crazy* about books. Chaim's apartment in the Bronx was what my apartment back in Brookline was going to become in twenty or thirty years. The front door could not be completely opened because there was a floor-to-ceiling bookcase behind it (and all bookcases were floor to ceiling; anything less was wantonly wasteful). All the hallways of the apartment were lined on both sides with books; Chaim was a portly person, but even a thin person had to walk sideways through the connecting hallways of the apartment. And don't forget the area above the doorways—every one of them had shelving loaded, creaking menacingly under the two and three layers of books in each shelf of the bookcase, with books placed sideways on top of the rows. Chaim and I had discussed the merits of putting books in front of books on shelves the way artisans might compare notes on some craft like leather tanning. (And Chaim was envious that most of my books were in single rows on the shelves, just as I knew that inevitably I'd have to resort to doubling up, a milestone in any book collector's life.)

The breakfront in the living room had certainly once held their china in the display case and silverware in the drawers; all of that was packed solid with books. (You may think you get the idea, but wait, I'm not finished.) There were, of course, bookshelves covering every square inch of wall space in the living room, but there were also stacks of books under the sofa, and there were books neatly but compactly stacked under the end tables on either side of the sofa—from the floor to the shelf midway up the length of the tables, and then from that shelf to the top, and then some books on top of the tables on which the lamps that illuminated the room stood. (The legs of those tables curved and the edge of the books followed the curves in and out up the length of the table.) The same was true of the coffee table in front of the sofa—and the same was true of the sofa itself: books filled the space between the top of the back of the sofa and the shelves over the sofa (in front of which a large painting hung—covering the books behind it—of a woman I later discovered was

Chaim's mother-in-law). There were several small card tables in the living room, and each of them had books stacked under them—but with enough room for someone to sit at the table, perhaps a bit sideways if one was not as short-legged as Chaim. And there were shelves in the recessed windows, and those shelves were packed with books, allowing only a tiny spot of light to peek through from the outside. I had asked Chaim early on why he didn't simply have the bookcase that covered all of that wall and snaked over, around, and under the window built straight across the hall (some carpenter or handyman had certainly put a child through college on Chaim), and he said he didn't want to block the windows entirely—but I knew the real reason: he'll get around to that soon enough; meanwhile why waste such good space?

The space under the tables; the corners of every room (who goes there?), including the kitchen next to the sink and the bathroom behind the toilet; the bottom half of the laundry hamper (yes, I looked); and the rear of the kitchen cabinets—the front half was room enough for the few dishes and foods a couple used—all were packed with neatly stacked books. One night, while Chaim and I were eating some of his wife's broiled flounder (just a guess), he asked me if I knew what the effect of extreme cold was on books, and I could feel the woman in the kitchen tense up until I assured him that it would ruin the binding and warp the paper. The refrigerator was safe (for the time being).

This was all just a warm-up for Chaim's study. Chaim had actually divided the study lengthwise with a bookcase that had obviously been added to over the years to the point that it now went nearly the entire length of the room. The bookcases were packed with books, two or three deep, and on both sides—only the most narrow passage behind this construction with books on both sides. At the end of the room was barely enough room for a chair and a small typing table on which was a Yiddish Olivetti portable typewriter on which Chaim created his novels, his poetry, his essays. To get behind those room-dividing bookcases, the typing table had to be moved in, and anyway the space back there was too narrow for Chaim to get into; he had to send me crawling in there, to look for a book on the bottom shelf, and able to see anything only because he had run an extension cord there and rigged a construction lamp with a hook on the end. (I was only sent there twice: once to find a book that would settle an argument about Gogol; another time to get a volume of the old *Jewish Encyclopedia.* Both times I came out like someone rescued after being lost for a week in underground caverns.) Every closet in the apartment—and they were spacious closets—was packed solid with books, and that meant when one opened the closet door, one was confronted with a wall of books, floor to ceiling, with every available space filled and with the top book in each stack wedged forcibly in place.

Not the floor of the apartment; not the building—the Bronx listed under the weight of Chaim's books.

In the two years I had been coming there, maybe two or three hundred days spent in that apartment from morning till night, I never saw anyone else there—no visitor, no delivery person, no handyman—no one. I asked Chaim about this on one of our walks (I later understood that great Yiddish writers simply do not have or permit visitors; then again, maybe it was the threat of coffee that kept everyone away), and he said something about not wanting people to think him strange for having so many books. I thought he was talking about the annoying line all book collectors endure: Have you read all of these books? I told him about Dr. Johnson's stock response: Yes, and some of them twice! Chaim stopped walking and looked at me disdainfully. "If anyone asks you if you've read all those books," he said, "it means you don't have enough books."

So this is where we were: in Chaim's living room, whiling away a winter's afternoon, watching *Planet of the Apes.* Ordinarily I would have thought it impossible to convince Chaim to spend a few hours watching such a movie. If he could ask about a side dish, "Is this a vegetable for a writer like me?" then what would he say about *Planet of the Apes?* But this was an afternoon to be waiting for a phone call. The book we had translated was published and received good reviews, but a few weeks ago we were told it was on the short list for the Pulitzer Prize. There followed the frenzied phone calls to people who are supposed to know about such things, and we kept hearing the same thing from many quarters: after disbelief that Chaim's book was even being considered, it would be between his book and Anne Tyler's *Dinner at the Homesick Restaurant.* There followed the weeks of endless conversations about what chance Chaim had, what chance any Yiddish writer had in America—of winning a Pulitzer, of selling well, of being recognized. Who but the people we met on our walks cared about the family life of a rabbi's wife, of the politics of a European shtetl, of courtyard intrigues in the Jewish section of Vilna? I understood my role very well in these discussions. I was supposed to play the part of the consoler, the assurer, the advocate. Of course they would, Chaim, or at least the more cultivated readers would appreciate you. I honestly didn't believe it then any more than I believe it now, but I'm a good soldier and I did my duty.

On this day, we were told, the decision was going to be made. Someone was going to call us—from the publisher or from the committee, we didn't know which. Continuing to work on the next translation was out of the question; even the usual pointless hand-wringing was too nerve-racking. When I saw in the paper that *Planet of the Apes* was playing on television that afternoon, I thought it would be the perfect release. This is what America liked, I said, and if he would watch it patiently, he would see that its plot lines were not so different from Chaim's stories and that the setting was every bit as far removed from Main Street America as the alleyways behind the synagogues of Europe.

But it was rough going. Explaining the twists of the plot of *Planet of the Apes* to Chaim—in Yiddish, and in terms he could relate to . . .

"You see, the woman died because there was a leak in the capsule where she was in suspended animation . . . but they had to, because the space voyage was going to take so long . . . the gorilla (*die malpe*) thinks he's as dumb as the humans on the planet because he can't speak . . . that *malpe* is a scientist; that's right, a scientist . . . They turned the other astronaut into a human as dumb as the ones on the planet; that's what the scar on his head shows . . . No, that's the *malpe*'s boyfriend . . . She knows he's intelligent and can talk, but she's afraid of . . . yes, that one, the doctor . . . No, that girl didn't come with them on the spaceship; she's one of the humans on the planet; Charlton Heston just likes her, that's all . . . When the doll talks, that shows that people on this planet once talked; why else would they make dolls that talk? . . . No, that's the real Statue of Liberty; they returned back to earth. Yes, they were going someplace else, but they wound up back on earth a few hundred years later . . . No, that's the real Statue of Liberty . . . Right, the real one; so the war where everything was destroyed took place on earth, and that's why Charlton Heston's banging the water and yelling, 'You did it, you really did it . . .' "

That's when Chaim accused the screenwriter of being a Communist.

"A Communist!?" I said. "What makes you say he's a Communist?"

"Because he wants to show that that will be the end of the United States. Absolute, a Communist. And this is what Americans want?"

"It's very popular. I think they made two sequels. At least."

"Hear that?" he called out to the kitchen. "This is what they like."

That's when the phone rang. It rang several times, and it seemed to me that neither Chaim nor his wife would answer it, and then it occurred to me that they thought I would answer it, that I should answer, as if somehow it was me who had gotten into this impossible situation. I ran into the study and answered the phone. When I returned to the living room, they were waiting and looked at me expectantly.

"Well, the good news is we beat out Anne Tyler. The bad news is we were first runner-up. We didn't win."

Chaim looked at his wife and smiled resignedly. Who can figure out these people? he seemed to shrug.

"Who *did* win?" she asked.

"That was also a surprise," I said. "Someone I never heard of—and a book I never heard of. Something called *The Color Purple* by an Alice Walker."

There was a silence for a moment, and then all three of us seemed to be moved by the same idea at the same moment; Chaim said it aloud: "Get the car," he instructed his wife, "and we'll go down to Barnes and Noble and see this book."

Chaim and I were dropped off on the corner of Fifth Avenue and 18th Street while his wife parked in a lot down the street; we waited for her on the corner. There across the street was the main store, but I knew we weren't going there; I don't believe Chaim had ever set foot in that store—and perhaps never in any store that sold books at retail prices. We were denizens of the used-book stores, the "*shenk*," he called them—Yiddish for tavern—because we were like drunkards whenever we went book hunting. And, my God, Chaim and I had spent many hours combing through used-book shops in Manhattan, in Boston, and even near Chaim's summer home in the Adirondacks. We went every chance we could and spent many hours looking and searching. Chaim looked for sets—two volumes of Poe or seven of Balzac. I looked for books and authors I knew about, books I hadn't gotten when I was taking a course, or perhaps a work by an author whose books I already had, only not everything that author had written—a work in philosophy or the volume of Stephen Jay Gould I was missing. Chaim would look at the books I collected (we would pick a place in the shop where we would place the books we had collected, to be culled from later, and I was in charge of making sure no one walked off with any of them, even though we wound up actually buying only a few of the books we squirreled away) with disgust. "How could you compare this fine three-volume set of the stories of de Maupassant with that garbage by Barbara Tuchman?" he would say. But you've got everything Barbara Tuchman ever wrote, I'd answer—in fact, some of her books you have several copies of! Yes, well, I forget that I have them, he'd say sadly, so I buy extra copies. I had learned long ago not to bother pointing out that he had changed the subject.

That's one of the things that all bookaholics share, like a common symptom of a genetic disease. You come across a fine volume and you can't remember if you have it, or maybe you have it with a different jacket, or maybe in paperback and here is this fine hardcover copy—or is your copy back at home also hardcover? It's gotten so I can tell when I see that furrowed faraway gaze in the eyes of a customer in a used-book store, having come to a dead stop, that he is trying to conjure up his bookcases in his mind's eye and remember whether or not he has the book he has found. This is part of the sweet agony that Chaim went through every time he set foot into a used-book shop—and it wasn't getting any less agonizing. A few times when he had come across a book he wanted, but couldn't recall if he had it, I remembered seeing a copy on his shelf and said so. Chaim was strangely unappreciative; he seemed to sneer at me. I couldn't tell whether it was because I was depriving him of this agony I call sweet or he was simply angry at any indication that I was in some way inventorying (and how could I not be coveting?) his books. After that, I just kept my mouth shut.

Chaim's wife came down the street and we were ready to enter what we called "the shul"—the synagogue. The Barnes & Noble

Sales Annex was, Chaim pointed out, something like an old-world synagogue at that. It had a men's section and a women's section—the men looking at the books about sports and airplanes (and sneaking surreptitious glances at the lingerie photography), and the women looking at fiction (and sneaking a peek at the firemen's calendars). And there were the old characters who were always there because they didn't seem to have anywhere else to go—perhaps sitting and reading an old book or a pointless obsolete textbook they had no reason to be looking at, except for the fact that it was so large and so cheap. And it had a *shames*—a sexton-like young man, a bit disheveled and distracted, who it turned out was the manager of the store. His name was Walter, and we were the bane of his existence, because Chaim could not buy a book without bargaining with the shopkeeper, and in this case, that unenviable role was Walter's.

Chaim would bargain with anyone about a book, even if he found it in a 50-cent bin in front of the Strand (though he never did that with anything else; in fact, I thought he was a generous tipper and particularly broad-handed when it came to money). At first I was always embarrassed by this, but he had gotten me involved in the process and I had to admit that it was part of the game. He'd argue for a discount, then not get it, and then he'd motion me to go to work: I'd tell the dealer that Chaim was a famous Yiddish writer who had fallen on hard times, that he was a scholar who needed the book for research, no matter what it was—while Chaim would stand stoic and hurt in the corner. It usually worked, but not with Walter, and there had been a few difficult moments over the past year when Walter was just a second or two away from calling the store guards from across the street to have us removed.

We went into the store and saw Walter standing near the cash register. He winced when he saw us and averted his eyes, but I walked up to him, said hello, and asked him where I might find a particular book.

"What book?" he asked.

"We're looking for a book by a writer named Alice Walker. *The Color Purple*."

"I think that's a new book. You'll have to get that across the street."

I stood there a moment and wondered how to proceed.

"Across the street. You'll have to get it—"

"I know, I know. But the thing is that we can't . . ."

"What? I know, he's a poor Yiddish writer . . ."

"Look," I said quietly, "Walter. We want to see this book because . . . my friend just found out he lost the Pulitzer Prize to this book, and we just wanted to take a look at—"

"This book beat him out of the Pulitzer Prize?"

I nodded.

"Wait here." With that Walter closed down the cash register, walked out of the store, and went directly across the street. I motioned to Chaim, who was standing at the far end of the store, that everything was under control. A few minutes later, Walter came back with three copies of *The Color Purple* and gave them to me.

"How much is that?" I asked.

I was ready to start haggling when he abruptly said, "No charge." I shrugged and brought them to Chaim and his wife, who I had assumed was being forced to make this trip by Chaim, but it now seemed that she was every bit as eager as we were to see this book. We each retreated to a corner of the store and read.

It took about two hours, and I'm not certain I've ever read a book with such inner turmoil before.

When I had finished I turned to find Chaim and found them together in a corner of the store, with Chaim being told what was going on in the book. It was apparent that they had not gotten very far into it, but I could see Chaim was stilled by what he was hearing. He turned to me and asked, "What do you think?"

"I hate to say it," I said, "but I don't think we have anything to be ashamed of."

"Pay for the books and let's go."

"Already paid for."

The three of us left—I nodded to Walter, who seemed to be smiling at me as I walked by—and made our way to the parking lot and into the car.

The trip back to the Bronx started in silence. I sat in the backseat, but I could feel the thoughts running through Chaim's mind: Beaten again. Cheated again—or maybe not cheated, but certainly, at least, beaten. It was afternoon and the day was getting dark and cold as we crawled up the FDR Drive. Somewhere around 125th Street, Chaim turned toward me and asked, "So how much did that *paskudnyak* Walter charge you for those books?"

I paused and then said, "Nothing."

"Nothing?"

"Well, I told him why we wanted them . . ."

"To read them there."

"Right, and that you had just been beaten out for the Pulitzer Prize by that book."

I don't think I could have outraged Chaim if I had told him I was Stalin's long-lost bastard child. He was livid and started cursing me in Polish. I tried to calm him down. "No, no, I didn't say it in those words," but the damage had been done.

"Turn this car around! We're going back and throwing these into his face!" And there were several moments in all the screaming that Chaim made a move to grab his wife's arm or the wheel and the car swerved a bit, which caused more screaming.

I guess I understood what I had done wrong—and maybe this was a subtle way of getting back at Chaim for all the times he had forced me into the uncomfortable position of bargaining for him. But he was livid and it looked as if it were going to be a long ride home and an even longer night when we got to the Bronx. Chaim was calling me every curse word in the book and breathlessly swearing I had ruined his life and made everything he had worked for like dirt (things I had heard many times from my mother when my forgetting to buy a container of milk on my way home had had similarly calamitous consequences). We were on the Major Deegan Expressway when, for some reason, I blurted out, "He was blacklisted!"

Chaim turned toward me and said, "Who?"

"The writer of *Planet of the Apes.* He had to write it under a pseudonym because he was blacklisted."

Chaim exploded in laughter; it was as if all the energy of his explosion of anger was now erupting in a volcano of mirth. He was bouncing around on the front seat so violently that his wife was having even more difficulty driving than when he was physically attacking her a few minutes earlier. "What did I tell you? Of course he's a Communist! And he tells me he isn't a Communist . . ."

"I didn't say he wasn't a Communist. I just said . . ."

But Chaim was laughing that exaggerated laugh in which each "ha!" comes out as a projectile that offers a glancing blow against the head.

We returned to Chaim's apartment. I sat in the living room; Chaim's wife puttered in the kitchen, sullen and disappointed; and Chaim was in his study on the phone. He spent the rest of the night there, taking one call after another. I don't know if people were calling him (to console him, perhaps, or to rub it in) or if he was calling them, but I could hear him talking into the phone at the top of his lungs, cursing me for telling Walter about why we wanted copies of *The Color Purple,* and for taking them from him at no charge, and poking fun at me for trying to fool him into thinking the writer of *Planet of the Apes* was not a Communist. A few times I sauntered to the door of the study and looked in, and if he was talking about *Planet of the Apes,* he'd smile at me knowingly, triumphantly. And if he wasn't, I would just go back to the living room and not look in.

It was hard for me not to hear just about everything Chaim was saying, and I don't remember him saying anything to any of those callers the entire night about not winning the Pulitzer Prize.

Bibliolexicon

Bibliobibule	One who reads too much
Biblioclast	One who tears pages from or otherwise destroys books
Bibliodemon	A book fiend or demon
Bibliognoste	One who is knowledgeable about editions, colophons, printers, and all the minutiae of books
Bibliographe	One who describes books
Biblioklept	One who steals books
Bibliolater	One who worships books
Bibliolestes	A book robber or plunderer
Bibliomancer	One who practices divination by books
Bibliomane	One who accumulates books indiscriminately
Bibliomaniac	A book lover gone mad
Bibliophage	One who eats or devours books
Bibliophile	One who loves books
Bibliophobe	One who fears books
Bibliopole	One who sells books
Biblioriptos	One who throws books around
Bibliosopher	One who gains wisdom from books
Bibliotaphe	One who buries or hides books

What Is the Matter with the Bookshop?

BY A. EDWARD NEWTON

It is virtually impossible to walk into any used-book shop in the Mid-Atlantic states and not encounter one of A. Edward Newton's collections of essays about books—and even some books from Newton's own vast library. One could almost throw darts at the title pages of Newton's books and be assured of hitting a memorable piece. Here are two of the editors' favorites—from A Magnificent Farce *(1921) and* The Greatest Book in the World *(1925), respectively—with a cartoon and a list sandwiched in between.*

Some time ago my friend Mr. William Harris Arnold told me that he had written a paper on the welfare of the bookstore. When it appeared in the *Atlantic Monthly*, I read it attentively, and I disagree with his conclusions. As it seems to me that the subject is one in which all who read should be interested, I should like to present my views for what they may be worth.

Mr. Arnold's remedy for the situation, admittedly difficult, in which the retail booksellers find themselves is to have publishers grant to booksellers "the option of taking books by outright purchase or on memorandum"—that is to say, on sale, and subject to return. I remember once, years ago, hearing the late Andrew Carnegie say to a body of businessmen that, if he were in a business in which it was impossible for him to tell, at least approximately, how much money he had made or lost in a given month, he would get out of that business. He said that the next best thing to making money was to know that you were not making it—and apply the remedy. Now, if a publisher should establish in any large way the custom of disposing of his publications "on sale," as the phrase is, I should like to know when, if ever, he could go before his creditors, represented by authors, printers, paper-makers, and binders, and declare himself solvent and worthy of their further confidence.

It seems to me that publishers assume sufficient risk, as it is. Many books, I fancy, just about pay their way, showing very little of either profit or loss; there may be a small profit resulting from the average book, and the exceptional book shows either a handsome profit—or a large loss. *The Four Horsemen of the Apocalypse* is the most recent of great successes: edition followed edition in such quick succession that the publishing facilities of New York City were heavily drawn upon to keep up with the demand. On the other hand, many years ago, the publication of *Endymion,* by Disraeli, then earl of Beaconsfield, occasioned an enormous loss. His publishers brought out this novel in the then customary three-volume form for, I think, two guineas. No one read into the middle of the second volume. It was a complete failure. A few months after publication every second-hand bookshop in London was trying to dispose of uncut, and unopened, "library" copies at about the cost of binding. It must be admitted that these are extreme instances: the profit in the one case must have amounted to a small fortune; the losses in the other might have driven the publisher into bankruptcy.

The publishing business has always been regarded as extra-hazardous—more respectable than the theatrical business and less exciting, but resembling it in that one never knows whether one is embarked upon a success or a failure until it is too late to withdraw. And it has always been so. Sir Walter Scott, whose career as a publisher is not always remembered, said that the booksellers, as publishers were called in his day, were "the only tradesmen in the world who professedly and by choice dealt in what is called 'a pig in a poke,' publishing twenty books in hopes of hitting upon one good speculation, as a person buys shares in a lottery in hopes of gaining a prize"; and Sir Walter had reason to know, as had also Mark Twain.

I remember that, some years ago, a little book, *A Publisher's Confessions,* was issued anonymously by Doubleday, Page & Co. It recited the difficulties, financial and other, of a firm of publishers and is now generally understood to have been written by Walter Hines Page, our late ambassador to the Court of St. James's. The writer's conclusion was that men of such distinction as those who control the organizations known as Scribner's, Macmillan, and others of like standing, could earn very much more by devoting their abilities to banking, railroads, or other lines of business; for, he said, "publishing as publishing is the least profitable of all professions, except preaching and teaching, to each of which it is a sort of cousin." And it is to this harassed person, perplexed, by reason of the nature of his calling, beyond most businessmen, that Mr. Arnold would add the financing of the countless bookstores, in many cases in incompetent hands, all over the country, from Maine to California. His suggestion is interesting, but I doubt if publishers in any large numbers will take kindly to it. They will probably feel that Mr. Arnold, whom I last saw in his own library surrounded by his own priceless books, apparently free from problems of any kind, has suggested a remedy worse than the disease from which they are suffering.

It is, however, to the bookseller rather than to the publisher that my heart goes out. The publishers of the present day, at least those I know, ride around in limousine cars while the booksellers walk—the floor. When Hogg threatened to knock the brains out of a bookseller, Sir Walter Scott cried, "Knock the brains into him, my dear Hogg, but for God's sake don't knock any out." The difficulties from which he is chiefly suffering are two: first, the unfair competition of certain department stores; and second, that we, the readers, have deserted him. A rich, intelligent, and extravagant people, we know nothing, and seemingly wish to know nothing, of the pleasure of buying and owning books. As I see it, the decay of the bookshop set in years ago with the downfall of the lyceum, the debating society, and the lecture platform. We have none of these things now, and if we had not largely given up reading as one of the consequences, I should not be sorry; but the mental stimulation that comes from personal contact has been lost, and seemingly there is nothing that will take its place. Of course, when I say that we have none of these things, I mean in proportion to our population and wealth.

When it comes to book-buying, we seem so loath to take a chance. We pay four or six or ten dollars for a pair of tickets for a "show"—how I hate the word!—sit through it for an entire evening, and when asked what we thought of it, answer briefly, "Rotten," and dismiss the matter from our minds. Now book-buying is, or ought to be, a pleasure. If one comes in contact with a fairly well-informed salesman or saleswoman, it may be a delight. And there are such. To speak of those I know, if you care for illustrated or extra-illustrated books, where can you find a more interesting character than George Rigby in Philadelphia? And there is Mabel Zahn, at Sessler's—"Dere Mable," as I sometimes call her: many a time she has shamed me with her knowledge. And there is Leary's, one of the largest and best second-hand bookshops in the country; you are not importuned to buy, you may browse there by the hour. We in Philadelphia hold its proprietor in such esteem that we made him mayor of our city, and finally governor of our state. He has known me ever since I was a little boy, and it was a proud day for me when I thought I could safely refer to him as my friend Ned Stuart.

Leary's is one of the few bookshops in which bargains may still be found. My friend Tinker—dear old Tink—never comes to Philadelphia without spending a few hours at Leary's; and only yesterday James Shields, that astute bookman, dropping in upon me to ask a question, which, naturally, I was unable to answer, showed me a ten-dollar bill he had just extracted from Lawler, Rosenbach's manager, for a book he had just "picked up" at Leary's for fifty cents. These things can still be done, but it takes more exact knowledge than I have been able to acquire. One thing yet remains to be told: the price at which Lawler sold the book. Who knows?

In an effort to escape the blame that should be ours, we sometimes say that Mr. Andrew Carnegie, who scattered public libraries all over the land in an effort, relatively successful, to die poor, is responsible for the plight in which the booksellers find themselves; but I am willing to acquit the libraries of all blame. They do an immense amount of good. I never go to a strange city without visiting its library, and I count many librarians among my friends; but I am, nevertheless, always overwhelmed in the presence of countless thousands of books, as I might be in the presence of crowned heads; indeed, I think that, idle curiosity once gratified, crowned heads would not impress me at all.

And so it is that, not being a scholar, or altogether indigent, I do not much use any library except my own. I early formed the habit of buying books, and, thank God, I have never lost it. Authors living and dead—dead, for the most part—afford me my greatest enjoyment, and it is my pleasure to buy more books than I can read. Who was it who said, "I hold the buying of more books than one can peradventure read, as nothing less than the soul's reaching towards infinity; which is the only thing that raises us above the beasts that perish"? Whoever it was, I agree with him; and the same idea has been less sententiously expressed by Ralph Bergengren in that charming little poem in *Jane, Joseph and John*, the loveliest book for children and grown-ups since R.L.S. gave us his *Child's Garden of Verses*.

My Pop is always buying books:
So that Mom says his study looks
Just like an old bookstore. The bookshelves are so full and tall,
They hide the paper on the wall,
*   And there are books just everywhere,*
*   On table, window-seat, and chair,*
And books right on the floor.

And every little while he buys
More books, and brings them home and tries
To find a place where they will fit,
And has an awful time of it.

Once, when I asked him why he got
So many books, he said, "Why not?"
I've puzzled over that a lot.

Too many of us, who are liberal, not to say lavish, in our household expenses seem to regard the purchase of books as an almost not-to-be-permitted extravagance. We buy piano-players and talking machines, and we mortgage our houses to get an automobile, but when it comes to a book, we exhaust every resource before parting with our money. If we cannot borrow a book from a friend, we borrow it from a library; if there is anything I like less than lending a book, it is borrowing one, and I know no greater bore than the man who insists on lending you a book which you do not intend to read. Of course, you can cure him, ultimately, by losing the volume; but the process takes time.

My philosophy of life is very simple; one doesn't have to study the accursed German philosophers or any other to discover that the way to happiness is to get a day's pleasure every day—I am not writing as a preacher—and I know no greater pleasure than taking home a bundle of books which you have deprived yourself of something to buy.

"I never buy new books," a man once said to me, looking at a pile on my library table; "I've got to economize somewhere, and they are so expensive."

"And yet," I retorted, "you enjoy reading; don't you feel under any obligation to the authors from whom you derive so much pleasure? Someone has to support them. I confess to the obligation."

When I think how much pleasure I get from reading, I feel it my duty to buy as many current books as I can. I "collect" Meredith and Stevenson, the purchase of whose books no longer benefits them. Why should I not also collect George Moore or Locke or Conrad or Hergesheimer? which, by the way, I do. And while you may not be able to get such an inscription in your copy of the first edition of Drinkwater's *Abraham Lincoln* as I have in mine, you should get a copy of the book before it is too late. All these men are engaged in carrying on the glorious tradition of English literature. It is my duty to give them what encouragement I can; to pay tribute to them. I wish I were not singular in this.

But to return to the bookshop. In addition to having to compete with the many forms of amusement unknown fifty years ago—it would be superfluous for me to do more than mention the latest of them, the "movie"—the bookshop elects to sell a "nationally advertised" article in competition with the department store. The publishers allow what would be a fairly liberal margin of profit, if the bookshops were permitted to keep it; but the department stores cut that margin to the quick. For reasons that are well known, it is profitable for them to do so: with their immense "turnover" and their relatively small "overhead," they can afford to sell certain popular books at cut prices, for the reason that at the next counter they are selling chocolates, marked "WEEKEND Special, 70¢ Regular Price $1.00," which do not cost over forty cents, perhaps less; and often they do get a dollar for these boxes. And what is true of chocolates is true of practically everything they sell, except books and a few other specialties, which they use as "leaders."

Books are the only "nationally advertised" specialties that anyone pretends to sell in shops almost exclusively devoted to them. Time was, and it was a sad time, when the monthly magazines, *Atlantic, Harper's, Scribner's,* and the rest, which cost $28 per hundred, wholesale, were retailed in a large store in Philadelphia for twenty-five cents each. The highest court to which the question can be carried has ruled that the seller can sell at any price he pleases, provided that he does not misstate the facts, as, for example, that his immense purchasing power enables him to undersell his competitors. In some few cases the publishers provide "specials," too: they give extra discounts for quantities; and there are always, alas, "remainders," sold at a loss by the publishers and at quite a tidy little profit by the retailer; but in general the facts are as I have stated.

It must be admitted that the department store helps the publisher by selling hundreds of thousands of copies of books like *Dere Mable* and the *Four Horsemen. The Young Visitors,* too, whether it be by Barrie or another, sold enormously; but just so large as is the sale of books like these, just so small is the sale of books of enduring merit. Perhaps I am wrong, but I fancy that men prefer to buy what I may call good books, while women buy novels and the lighter forms of literature.

Now, fancy a man going into a certain department store that I have in mind and asking for a copy of *Tom Jones.* He is met by a young lady in a low-cut dress, standing in high-heeled slippers, with her hair gathered up in large puffs which entirely conceal her ears; her nose has been recently powdered, and she looks as if she might be going to a party. "*Tom Jones!*

" she says, "is it a boy's book? Juveniles, second to the right." "No, it's a novel," you say; and she replies, "Fiction, second to the left."

You move on, avoiding a table on which is a sign, "The Newest Books Are on This Table," and you meet another young lady, also ready for a party, and repeat your question. "Is it a new book?" she says. "No," you explain; and she conducts you to a case containing hundreds of volumes of the Everyman's Series—and an excellent series it is. But the books have been skillfully shuffled, and what you seek is hard to find. While you and she are looking, someone "cuts in" and inquires for a copy of *Java Head,* to which she promptly replies, "One sixty-nine," and conducts her customer to a large pile, behind which she disappears and is seen, by you, no more.

You keep on looking until someone comes to your rescue and asks if she can do anything for you. You say, "*Tom Jones,*" and she, being an intelligent person, says, "Fielding," and conducts you to the fine-book department, where you are finally shown a set of Fielding flashily bound in what appears to be morocco, marked $40. You demur at the price and explain that you want *Tom Jones* to read, not a set to put upon your shelves; finally, thanking the "saleslady" for her trouble, you go out empty-handed, having wasted half an hour.

If this paper should be read by the proprietor of a retail store, or by his intelligent clerk, I can hear him cry, "You are quite right, but we know all this. Have you any remedy?" Certainly I have nothing to suggest which will prove a royal road to fortune; but I do suggest the selling of good second-hand books along with current publications, and I would stress the second-hand, and call it the rare-book department, for the profits of that department will be found to be surprisingly large. I would say to the proprietor of the bookshop, "Bring some imagination to bear on your business." Imagination is as necessary to a successful tradesman as to the poet. He is, indeed, only a day laborer without it. I am reminded of one of the clever bits in Pinero's play *Iris.* A tan, distinguished-looking man enters; his appearance instantly challenges attention, and the ingenue inquires who he is and is told, "That is Mr. Maldonado, the great financier." Then comes the question, "What is a financier?" and the telling reply, "A financier, my dear, is a pawnbroker—with imagination."

The point is well made. What quality was it in Charles M. Schwab which, while most of the great businessmen in America were wringing their hands over what appeared to be their impending ruin, when the war broke out, sent him off to England, to return quickly with hundreds of millions of dollars' worth of orders in his pocket? Imagination! It was this same quality, working in conjunction with the imagination of the late J. P. Morgan, which led to the formation of the great Steel Corporation.

There may be little room for the display of this supreme qualification in the retail book business, but there is room for some. Be enterprising. Get good people about you. Make your shop windows and your shops attractive. The fact that so many young men and women enter the teaching profession shows that there are still some people willing to scrape along on comparatively little money for the pleasure of following an occupation in which they delight. It is as true to-day as it was in Chaucer's time that there is a class of men who "gladly learn and gladly teach," and our college trustees and overseers and rich alumni take advantage of this and expect them to live on wages which an expert chauffeur would regard as insufficient. Any bookshop worthy of survival can offer inducements at least as great as the average school or college. Under pleasant conditions you will meet pleasant people, for the most part, whom you can teach and from whom you may learn something. We used to hear much of the elevation of the stage; apparently that has been given over; let us elevate the bookshop. It can be done. My friend, Christopher Morley—

> . . . Phoebus! what a name
> To fill the speaking-trump of future fame!

in his delightful *Parnassus on Wheels,* shows that there may be plenty of "uplift" and a world of romance in a traveling man well stocked with books. Indeed, a pleasant holiday could be planned along the lines of Roger Mifflin's novel venture in bookselling. I prophesy for this book, some day, such fame as is now enjoyed by Stevenson's *Travels with a Donkey.* It is, in fact, just such a book, although admittedly the plump white horse, Pegasus, lacks somewhat the temperamental charm of R.L.S.'s best-drawn female character, Modestine.

I was in a college town recently, and passing a shop, I noticed some books in the window and at once entered, as is my habit, to look around. But I stayed only a moment, for in the rear of the shop I saw a large sign reading, "Laundry Received before 9 A.M. Returned the Same Day"—enterprise, without a doubt, but misdirected. If the bookshop is to survive, it must be made more attractive. The buying of books must be made a pleasure, just as the reading of them is; so that an intellectual man or woman with a leisure hour may spend it pleasantly and profitably increasing his or her store.

Every college town should support a bookshop. It need not necessarily be so splendid an undertaking as the Brick Row Print and

Book Shop at New Haven, over which Byrne Hackett presides with such distinction, or even the Dunster House Book-Shop of Mr. Firuski of Cambridge. And to make these ventures the successes they deserve to be, faculty and students and the public alike should be loyal customers; but it should be remembered that these shops need not, and do not, depend entirely upon local trade. Inexpensive little catalogues can be issued and sent to customers half-way round the world.

Speaking of catalogues, I have just received one from a shop I visited when I was last in London, called "The Serendipity Shop." It is located in a little slum known as Shepherd's Market, right in the heart of Mayfair. It may be that my readers will be curious to know how it gets its name. "Serendipity" was coined by Horace Walpole from an old name for Ceylon-Serendip. He made it, as he writes his friend Mann, out of an old fairy tale wherein the heroes "were always making discoveries, by accidents and sagacity, of things they were not in quest of." Its name, therefore, suggests that, although you may not find in the Serendipity Shop what you came for, you will find something that you want, although you did not know it when you came in. Its proprietor, Mr. Everard Meynell, is the son of Alice Meynell, who, with her husband, did so much to relieve the sufferings of that fine poet Francis Thompson, and who is herself a poet and essayist of distinction. Is not every bookshop in fact, if not in name, a Serendipity Shop?

I have no patience with people who affect to be fond of reading, and who seem to glory in their ignorance of editions. "All I am interested in," they say, "is the type: so long as the type is readable, I care for nothing else." This is a rather common form of cant. Everything about a book should be as sound and honest and good; but it need not be expensive.

I have always resented William Morris's attitude toward books. Constantly preaching on art and beauty for the people, he set about producing books which are as expensive as they are beautiful, which only rich men can buy, and which not one man in a hundred owning them reads. Whereas my friend Mr. Mosher of Portland, Maine—I call him friend because we have tastes in common; I have, in point of fact, never met him or done more than exchange a check for a book with him—has produced, not a few, but hundreds of books which are as nearly faultless as books can be, at prices which are positively cheap. As is well known, Mr. Mosher relies very little upon the bookshops for the marketing of his product, but sells practically his entire output to individual buyers, by means of catalogues which are works of art in themselves. We may not fully realize it, but when Mr. Mosher passes away, booklovers of another generation will marvel at the certitude of his taste, editorial and other; for he comes as near to being the ideal manufacturer as any man who ever lived.

I would not for a moment contend that a man in the retail book business will in a short time make a fortune. We are not a nation of readers, but a young and uncultured people. It is not to be forgotten, however, that we graduate every year an immense number of men and women from our colleges. Potentially, these are, or ought to be, readers; they will be readers, if publishers and booksellers do their duty.

If a library is the best university, as we have been told it is, the bookseller has his cue. Let him make his shop attractive—a centre from which culture may be radiated. Customers have to be educated. When a new line of goods, of whatever kind, is being introduced, "missionary work," as we manufacturers call it, has to be done.

New York City has several fine bookshops: for example, Brentano's, one of the great bookshops of the world; but Brentano's has its fine-book department, as have Scribner's and Dutton's and Putnam's; and these so-called fine-book departments are doing expensively, as befits New York, what I would have every bookshop do according to its locale, as McClurg is doing in Chicago.

The advantages that would accrue are several. More readers would be made. The book business of the department stores would not be interfered with in the least—they would remain, as now, the best customers for certain classes of publishers, who might expect to have some day, in addition, a more thriving class of booksellers than now. And better books would be published—better, that is, in print, paper, and binding.

In the fine-book department, which I'm urging every bookseller to start without delay, I would keep out trash; I would admit only good books—good, I mean, in every sense of the word except moral. The department should be in charge of the most intelligent man in the shop, if there be an intelligent man; and I would get one if I had not one, and in these days of profit-sharing, I would give him an interest in the profit of that department. I would buy, too, good books from the second-hand English booksellers, who sell very cheaply; and above all things I would not forget the wisdom stored up in the distorted proverb,

Early to bed and early to rise,
Work like h——, and advertise.

Ten Memorable Books
That Never Existed
(and Where They Were
Mentioned)

Books titles are sometimes used to add to the plausibility of fiction or legend. Below are ten books that are alleged to have been written by fictional characters, or to have existed, but for the existence of which there is no evidence.

1. *The Curious Experience of the Patterson Family on the Island of Uffa* by John H. Watson (alluded to in several Sherlock Holmes stories as a work Dr. Watson wrote before meeting Holmes)
2. *Mad Tryst* by Launcelot Canning (mentioned by Edgar Allan Poe in *The Fall of the House of Usher*)
3. *The Memoirs of the Hon. Galahad Threepwood* (a nonexistent autobiography found in several stories by P. G. Wodehouse)
4. *Modern Warfare* by Gen. Tom Thumb (a fake book in the library of Charles Dickens)
5. *Necronomicon* by Abdul Alhazred (a manual on corpse-eating that appears in the horror tales of H. P. Lovecraft)
6. *Hansard's Guide to Refreshing Sleep* (another of the phony sets that Charles Dickens used to fill the shelves of his library and poke fun at his rivals)
7. *On Polishing Off the Canonical Hours* by Master Greedyguts (a satirical manual for the clergy referred to by François Rabelais)

8. *The Seven Minutes* by J. J. Jadway (the scandalous book in Irving Wallace's novel of the same title; surprisingly never written by some enterprising writer)
9. *Practical Handbook of Bee Culture* by Sherlock Holmes (a fictional contribution by the great detective)
10. *The Book of Adam* (a book mentioned in the Talmud and in rabbinic literature that, it seems, never actually existed)

The Last of His Race

BY A. EDWARD NEWTON

Not long ago there died a gentleman, scholar, and book-collector, whose place in the game we are playing it will be difficult and perhaps impossible to fill. Need I say that I refer to Beverly Chew? There have been and there now are greater collectors than he, but I feel quite sure that no other amateur has ever exerted in this country the widespread influence that he did, or had an equal amount of bibliographical learning.

Mr. Chew was born in the beautiful little college town of Geneva, New York, on March 5, 1850, in a fine old mansion situated on a bluff overlooking the lake, and he died in another old-fashioned house not far from the spot where he was born. He was a graduate of Hobart College, a small college in Geneva, and throughout his life he remained closely identified with the institution in which he was educated. After his graduation he went to New York, and in due course he became a successful banker. For many years he was vice president of the Metropolitan Trust Company, until, a few years ago, he retired from active business. At the time of his death he was Geneva's most distinguished citizen, but he was so modest and unassuming that perhaps not all of his neighbors knew this fact. The great passion of his life was books, and his knowledge of them inexhaustible and impeccable.

I am able to place with some certainty the time when I first met Mr. Chew: it was almost thirty-five years ago, just before I was married, at a reception at the Grolier Club in New York, of which he was one of the earliest members, serving the Club with honor and filling every office from librarian to president. My ignorance in those days was abysmal compared with his knowledge, and somehow in the course of conversation he asked me what I collected, and, replying, I said, with some confidence, "The older poets," meaning thereby not Longfellow or Tennyson or Browning, but rather Keats and Shelley. I shall never forget his look of reproach as he said: "You don't call Keats and Shelley 'the older poets,' I hope"; and subsequently, when I came to know him better, I learned that his definition of "older poets" would be those who had died before 1640—men of whose very names I, at that time, had never heard. But with the passing of years we became warm friends, and those who knew him well will agree with me that no man was more kindly, generous, and courteous than he.

Mr. Chew came of an excellent family, remotely connected with the distinguished Chew family of Germantown, Philadelphia. His grandfather was Collector of the Port of New Orleans and officially entertained La Fayette upon his last visit to this country. It so happened that his father, then an infant, was to be christened at the time of the visit, and the great man held the boy, who was named Alexander La Fayette, the name being handed down in the family.

Shortly after his graduation he married Clarissa Pierson, with whom he lived in the most perfect happiness until her death in May 1889. He had been heard to express the wish that he too might die in May, and this melancholy wish was granted him: after a long period of unconsciousness, he passed away, peacefully on May 21, 1924. He was a high churchman and in New York was a regular and devout attendant of the Church of St. Mary the Virgin. To visit the fatherless and widows in their affliction was a part of his creed; the number and extent of his kindly charities will never be known, for he almost never spoke of these things even to his most intimate friends. His funeral service was held in Trinity Church, Geneva, which he had loved as the church of his boyhood, and his body was carried up the aisle by college boys, members of his fraternity, the Sigma Phi, to which his father and his three brothers belonged. It was a gray day, but the light streamed in through the windows of yellow glass—of which he was so proud; glass made in Geneva a century ago, the manufacture of which is a lost art—and made a golden haze, a proper atmosphere for the beautiful and impressive service of the Church of England Prayer Book. Prior to the service at the church he lay at rest in his library, surrounded by his books, his closest friends, that he knew and loved so ardently.

Next to books Mr. Chew loved prints; portraits, which are a form of biography; especially old examples of famous engravers like Marshall, who engraved the portrait of Shakespeare for the *Poems* (1640), the beautiful Sucklin [*sic*] for *Fragmenta Aurea* (1640), and the Herrick for the *Hesperides* (1648); or Faithorn, who engraved the superb portrait of Killigrew in the 1664 edition of *Comedies and Tragedies,* which Mr. Chew once told me he thought was the finest portrait in any book. And I do not forget the lovely little plates in another favorite book of his, Lovelace's *Lucasta.* Lovelace! what a name for a poet! And Faithorne! "whose charm can save from dull oblivion or a gaping grave," as his friend Mr. Thomas Flatman has it. Mr. Chew's collection of portraits of Milton was, I suppose, the finest ever gotten together. But why call the roll? Whoever did fine work with pen or pencil or brush or type had in Beverly Chew his keenest appreciator.

I have not yet mentioned Mr. Chew's most remarkable characteristic—his marvelous memory. Certain great men are curiously endowed: I have been told that the late Pierpont Morgan could, merely by thinking of figures, make them dance about in his brain and finally add, multiply, and divide themselves while his confreres were looking for a lead pencil; Mr. Chew's memory was of this same disconcerting order. He never seemed to forget anything relating to a book. And there is so much to be remembered! Think how many books there are; think, too, that every great book has some special characteristic which must be present or lacking, as the case may be, if that book is to pass the scrutiny of a collector such as Mr. Chew was and find a place upon his shelves. And these points, so important in what they indicate, are seemingly so trifling and insignificant in themselves: a date, a misplaced word or letter even. Many years ago, I bought at auction a first edition of Hawthorne's *Scarlet Letter.* When I got it home and examined it I found therein a long letter written by Mr. Chew to its former owner, in which he says, "When I returned home and examined page by page the first and second editions of the 'Scarlet Letter,' I find that I was correct in my statement, namely—" then followed a minute description, ending with: "and the book should have the word 'reduplicate' on page 21 instead of the word 'repudiate.' " Of my personal friends, the only man that I would mention as in the class with Beverly Chew is Mr. Thomas James Wise of London, but Mr. Wise's opportunities have been much greater than Mr. Chew's, for he has sat at the gate, whereas, curiously enough, Mr. Chew never went abroad. No, I can hardly bring myself to think that the present generation of book-collectors is as distinguished as that to which Mr. Chew belonged. I suppose we fall naturally into the way of investing those who have gone with qualities which we may lack, perhaps; and yet, as I think of men like Robert Hoe and Samuel P. Avery, Charles B. Foote and Frederick R. Halsey, Edward Hale Bierstadt, and William Loring Andrews, it does seem as though there were a falling off in the present generation.

I have referred to Mr. Chew's taking me up so promptly when I spoke of the "older poets"; his own favorites, I came to know, were those of the seventeenth century; I suppose his knowledge of this period was unequaled. Wherever one goes among bookmen, either in this country or in England, the bibliographies published by the Grolier Club are constantly referred to; with the publication of these Mr. Chew had much to do. The librarian of the Club, Miss Granniss—who succeeded Mr. H. W. Kent, to whom book-collectors are under so many obligations—has told me of her work on the Club's volumes of English bibliography from Wither to Prior. Most of the collations had been made by Mr. Bierstadt, and after his death the work was carried on by a committee. Mr. Chew, it appears, had been appointed to oversee the proofreading, a most tedious and difficult task, one of his countless services to the Club. Questions, of course, arose by the hundred; these Miss Granniss was in the habit of listing during the week for submission to Mr. Chew, and on Saturday afternoons he would punctually appear and, after settling himself in his chair and lighting his cigar, would exclaim, "Fire away!" Whereupon she would begin; and says she, in the letter from which I am quoting:

> I can hardly recall a question which he was not able to answer at once "out of his head," though I remember occasional admonitions to verify this blank leaf, or that

variation in spelling by such and such copies or reference books, but I am sure that I never found him mistaken. The information which he had spent a lifetime in acquiring was cheerfully and instantly put at the service of anyone really interested.

Shortly after the war I went to London, and spending, as my custom is, some time in the British Museum, I chanced one day upon that distinguished gentleman, Mr. Alfred W. Pollard, then Keeper of the Printed Books, and in conversation with him I happened to refer to the *Census of Shakespeare's Plays in Quarto* which had recently been published by the Yale University Press, under the joint direction of Miss Henrietta C. Bartlett of New York and Mr. Pollard. The book is a splendid example of scholarly bibliography upon an extremely difficult subject, and Mr. Pollard, referring to the exasperating annoyances and delays incident to sending proof backward and forward across the ocean during the war, said, "I thought the job would never get done, and at last I wrote Henrietta and told her that if she could prevail on Mr. Chew to read the proof I would be satisfied. I was quite willing to put my name to anything that had received his approval." What a tribute from a great scholar to the busy man of affairs! "If you want a thing done, go to a busy man," is an old adage.

Of the many societies and clubs and institutions of which Mr. Chew was a member I shall not speak; they all, I feel, as we of the Grolier Club do, mourn his loss. An old friend has been taken from us. One may make friends but not old friends—it takes time to make an old friend, as it does to make an old book.

Was Mr. Chew a poet? I do not know, but he wrote at least one poem which has found its way into the anthologies, "Old Books Are Best."

It is a little more than a year ago that, after several days spent in Buffalo with my dear friend and fellow collector, Mr. R. B. Adam, I decided not to go on to New York without visiting Mr. Chew in Geneva. I am glad that I did. He met me at the station and conducted me—rather ceremoniously, for he was a gentleman of the old school—to his home, pointing out with something like pride the house in which he was born, on the main street of the pretty collegiate town. In the evening after dinner we sat in his library and smoked and talked, and put our hobby horses through their paces until late into the night; and as we retired he told me that my visit to him was a compliment, and I replied that my invitation was an honor. "And so to bed." The next morning, being an early riser, seeing the door of his bedroom closed, I passed very quietly and silently tiptoed downstairs into the library; the old gentleman was there before me. In an easy chair by the window he sat with several newspapers, unopened, by his side. In his hand was a book, which by the help of a magnifying glass he was reading as I entered; he put it by to greet me affectionately and was I thought a trifle embarrassed at being seen with this artificial aid to failing eyesight. To change the subject, I spoke of the book he had in his hand; it was a first edition of Herrick's *Hesperides* (1648), and I told him that my copy was a better one. This put him on his mettle at once, and he spoke of the fine copy—bound by Roger Payne, as I remember—that had been in the collection he had sold to Mr. Henry E. Huntington.

It is well known that some ten or twelve years ago Mr. Chew disposed of his library—the greater part of it, that is—to Mr. Huntington. The transaction was a difficult one; Mr. Huntington wanted the books, and Mr. Chew—getting on in years, and never a very rich man—thought that he could not afford to decline a liberal offer. After some delay, due to Mr. Chew's reluctance to part with his books, the proposition was accepted; but when the hour of separation came, it was too much of a wrench. Mr. Chew, with tears in his eyes, went to Mr. Huntington and told him he could not bring himself to part with the volumes, but he said, "If ever I can bring myself to sell, I shall sell only to you." Mr. Huntington was disappointed but understood Mr. Chew's feeling and, fine gentleman that he is, instantly released Mr. Chew from his bargain. Several years passed; the books were becoming increasingly valuable; another offer was made—and accepted— and as Mr. Huntington handed Mr. Chew a very large check, he said, "And, Mr. Chew, I would gladly hand you a check for double the amount for your knowledge." Such a compliment is twice blest: "It blesseth him that gives and him that takes." And taking a thought from Omar's *Rubaiyat,* I often wonder what a man does with his money when he has exchanged his library for it. I know what Mr. Chew did: he at once began collecting again, and at the time of his death he had a small but very choice collection—he would have been the last to call it a library—for he could not live without books.

A pretty story is told of Mr. Chew's love for a rare book. Hearing that Mr. Huntington had secured two copies of the first edition of Shakespeare's *Sonnets* with the two different imprints, he called upon him and asked for the privilege of holding the two books— they are perhaps two of the most valuable books in the language— in his hands at the same time, one in each hand. I would like to have had a photograph taken of him at this moment, but I have an excellent picture of him, looking at a copy of Herrick, one of his favorite books, the one I saw him examining when I was last with him in Geneva.

Another story. During the last years of Mr. Chew's life in New York it was his habit not to go downtown on Saturdays, but to spend the morning quietly among his books in his apartment in the Royalton; knowing this, it became my custom, when in New York on a Saturday, to call upon him. One morning we had spent several hours together when I suddenly remembered that Drake, the bookseller in Fortieth Street, had asked me to call to look at some books just in from London. So cutting my visit short, more especially as Mr. Chew too pleaded an engagement, with professions of mutual regard and regret we parted and I went at once to Drake's. I had not been there more than ten minutes when in walked Mr. Chew; his engagement was the same as mine. We laughed heartily at each other and turned to the books. "Here is something you should buy, if you haven't it," said Mr. Chew, taking up a copy of *Piers Plowman* in old binding, calling attention to the corrected date, 1550. "But it is out of my line," I replied. "It shouldn't be," said he. Then my eye chanced to light upon a copy of Blake's *Poetical Sketches,* George Cumberland's copy with his so-called bookplate, one of Blake's last engravings, therein. "And you should have this," I said, knowing that his copy had gone into the Huntington Library. Mr. Drake looked on with amusement. "Go to it, gentlemen; I cannot afford salesmen such as you"; and when a little later we left the shop to lunch together, I was the owner of *Piers Plowman* and Mr. Chew had a copy of Blake's *Poetical Sketches* in his pocket.

Looking back, one recollects that the year 1918 was a particularly pleasant one for book-buyers, and booksellers too. It saw the end of the war, money was plentiful, and several fine libraries were dispersed at Mitchell Kennerley's Anderson Galleries. I have in mind especially the Hagen collection, sold in May, and the Herschel V.

Jones library in December. There was a feeling of good-fellowship abroad, and after these sales a group of us were wont to forgather at the Plaza around a well-spread table, there to fight our battles o'er again. Mr. Chew, who would always be invited to join these parties, was an old friend of Mr. Hagen, and had written an introduction to his sale catalogue, and was especially interested in the sale of his library. In the introduction he had written: "If I were asked what is the scarcest item in the sale, I should unhesitatingly say that charming little volume containing four of the poems of John Skelton, Poet Laureate to King Henry VII. Two of these little booklets were in the Hoe library, but this lot of four from the Locker library is probably unique." It was not often that Mr. Chew would give a "tip" on a book, but this was a sure thing, and the item realized just a trifle short of ten thousand dollars. The high prices pleased but did not surprise him. "They will go higher still," he said. At both of these sales I bought—for me—largely, being guided, as far as my means would allow, by Mr. Chew's judgment. Once again I record that my extravagances were investments, and my economies proved to be a willful waste of money.

Our friend is gone, if any man can die,
Who lived so pure a life, whose purpose was so high.

When his will was opened, it was found that Mr. Chew had followed in the steps of the great French collector Edmond de Goncourt, who left instructions that his drawings, his prints, his curiosities, his books—in a word, all those things which had been the joy of his life—should not be consigned to the cold tomb of a museum, to be subjected to the stupid glance of the careless passer-by; but required that they should be dispersed under the hammer of the auctioneer, so that the pleasure which the acquiring of them had given him should in turn be given someone of his own taste.

Thus to his friend Mitchell Kennerley, the president of the Anderson Galleries, passed—for sale—Mr. Chew's entire collection, with the exception of four paintings: his portraits of Ben Jonson by Gerard Honthorst, Pope and Dryden by Sir Godfrey Kneller, and a pastel of Dryden by Edward Lutterel; and his fine collection of German, Dutch, and Flemish silver bindings, of which he had some fifty or more specimens; these he bequeathed to the Grolier Club.

No doubt he felt, and correctly, that there they would receive the same loving care that they had in his own library and would serve to link his name with those of other benefactors of the Club, which is the most important, successful, and authoritative book-club in the world. Long may it continue to flourish!

When the announcement was made that Mr. Chew's library would be sold, the book-collecting world was agog. What books had he, and what would they fetch? I knew pretty well what I wanted and had made up my mind to pay the price. Someday I shall write a paper on the psychology of the auction room: such curious things happen there. Important items are frequently almost given away; occasionally they bring more than they are worth. Who can tell why? At last the expected evening came; the sale was well attended.

First let me say that an important book sale in New York is very different from a similar event in London. In London it is hardly apt to be a thrilling affair, no matter how important the items. At Sotheby's the auctioneer stands or sits in a large pulpit, while in front of him is a long, narrow table, one end of which abuts upon the pulpit, while ranged on each side of the table are the important members of "the trade," as the booksellers are always called. The book, if it be an important one, is handed by the auctioneer's assistant to the first man on the right-hand side, who glances at it and passes it to his next neighbor, who also looks at it and passes it on. At the end of the table it crosses over to the man on the left and gradually makes its way back to the auctioneer, who then knocks it down to the highest bidder with as much enthusiasm as though he were selling a cabbage. Enthusiasm is never good form in England. But let us assume that the knock-out is in operation, as it may well be, and that an outsider, a collector, seeing an item bringing half what it is worth, ventures to bid. His bid will be accepted, of course, but instantly there is competition: someone in the trade will bid quietly but persistently against the outsider until either he drops out or the book is his at three times what it is worth. He has made his experience; if he has secured the treasure, he is likely to hate himself and it; if he has lost it, the booksellers are likely to hate him; in any event he is unlikely to bid again. "The trade" is a ring, and a ring is something which has neither beginning nor end.

A book auction in New York is a very different affair: it may well be a social event, a game in which you may join, if you think you have the skill; but remember that here, too, you are playing against professionals. An amateur swordsman with a broomstick may be able to disconcert a professional with a rapier, but the chances are against it. My own plan, after years of experience, is to give my bids to the particular bookseller most likely to buy, for stock or for a client, the item that I especially covet. For example, if an item like *Robinson Crusoe* is coming up, to free myself from Dr. Rosenbach's competition I will give my bid to him with the highest limit I am willing to pay. He in turn will have to outbid Lathrop Harper and Walter Hill and Gabriel Wells. If, on the other hand, I want a *Songs of Childhood* by Walter Ramal, De la Mare's first book of poems and now much sought—or *A Shropshire Lad*—a slender volume which brought over two hundred dollars at Anderson's not long since, whereas I paid only one hundred and thirty for mine less than a year ago—I would give my bid to James F. Drake and take my chance with Rosy. If then, having secured the good will of the trade, some little odds and ends come up of no special importance, I do not hesitate to bid myself. But an important item I would never attempt to buy myself; and I have seen thousands of dollars spent uselessly by persons giving important commissions to the wrong agent.

But this is a digression. On the first evening of the Chew sale the room was crowded; all the leading booksellers and many distinguished librarians and collectors were there. I noticed many ladies, particularly Miss Greene and Miss Thurston representing the Pierpont Morgan library, Miss Granniss of the Grolier Club, and Miss Henrietta Bartlett. A few hours before the sale began Mitchell Kennerley received a telegram from the erstwhile collector Mr. Jones of Minneapolis, reading: "I shall attend the Chew sale not to buy but to pay my respects to a great collector"; the same spirit, I fancy, prompted other collectors to attend. Frank B. Bemis of Boston was there, but I did not see him bidding, and it was not until the sale was over that we exchanged confidences and I learned that several important items would find a resting-place in his lovely home on the North Shore.

Who shall say what a book is worth? I suppose there cannot be a better criterion than the price paid. A *Paradise Lost* in original binding attracted much attention. The volume had a famous pedigree and had a pencil note dated September 6, 1857, written on the fly leaf by a former owner, Sir M. Digby Wyatt, which read: "This edition is the first and has the first title-page; it is worth nearly £10 and is rapidly rising in value." It certainly is: it brought the record price, fifty-six hundred dollars. Mr. Chew had bought the volume from Quaritch not many years ago for fifteen hundred. I was glad to see a first *Robinson Crusoe,* three volumes, original binding, a fine copy but in no way better than my own, bring fifty-three hundred and fifty dollars, while a Blake *Songs of Innocence and Experience,* for which Mr. Chew paid seventeen hundred and fifty dollars, brought also the record price for that item, fifty-five hundred dollars. The Cumberland copy of Blake's *Poetical Sketches,* which I sold him that day at Drake's for four hundred and fifty dollars, brought nine hundred; while a copy of *Piers Plowman,* quite as good as the copy he sold me on the same occasion, brought two-thirds less than the price I paid, thus confirming a belief that I have long had: that the tendency in the New York auction rooms is for star items to bring more and less important items frequently to bring less than they are worth. By a fluke I lost a superb first edition of Hudibras in three volumes, in original calf, which I had intended to buy, and I discovered later that this desired item went to Jerome Kern; I congratulate him upon its acquisition.

Nevertheless, my "bag" was satisfactory, if not splendid; I especially wanted and secured Hooke's *Amanda.* It is an excessively scarce little volume of poems published "by a gentleman of Trinity College in Cambridge" in 1653 and perhaps owes its vogue among collectors to the lines in Andrew Lang's "Ballade of the Bookman's Paradise":

> *There treasures bound for Longpierre*
> *Keep brilliant their morocco blue,*
> *There Hooke's* Amanda *is not rare,*
> *Nor early tracts upon Peru!*

I had seen this identical copy sold years ago at the Hoe sale, and since that time only one other copy has come upon this market. I also bought, through "Rosy," a fine Chapman's Homer dedicated "To the Imortal Memorie of the Incomparable Heroe, Henrye Prince of Wales"—my "royal book-collector," the edition which suggested to Keats his famous sonnet; a large paper Killigrew with the fine portrait, which Mr. Chew and I have so often admired; and a little Coryat, *Greeting to His Friends in England,* which I have long searched for. These, with a few pick-ups of no great importance, constituted my lot. It seems rather curious to see them in my own library; although I paid for them promptly, I have observed that it usually takes some time for an old book to become accustomed to new surroundings.

When a book-collector dies and his books are disposed of, that ends the matter—except in memory. I have referred to Mr. Chew as "the last of his race"; this is not strictly so. There yet remains one, the last leaf, so to speak, on the noble tree which in its prime was so splendid. I refer to my friend Mr. W. A. White of Brooklyn: he yet remains to us. He is a more distinguished collector than Mr. Chew, and perhaps a better scholar, but his influence has not been so great. He is known the world over for his Blakes, but—with a few other outstanding volumes—chiefly for his Elizabethans. When in 1916, the three hundredth anniversary of the death of Shakespeare, the Public Library of New York determined to keep the event by an exhibition of books by Shakespeare and his contemporaries, a superb exhibition was made. Miss Bartlett, an undoubted authority on the subject, had the matter in charge, and not everyone then knew that the exhibit was, in effect, a case or two of books from the library of Mr. White. He is so modest, so retiring, so seemingly the scholar, that no one would suspect he is a man of large business interests, yet ever and always ready to place himself, his knowledge, and his library at the disposal of those truly interested in his subject. With his passing, the second and greatest era in American book-collecting will come to an end—an era in which, no doubt, the honored name of Pierpont Morgan ranks highest, as the recent gift by his son of the great library formed by the father so abundantly proves.

Mr. Huntington yet remains to us, but he is not an individual; already he is an institution, and a noble one. Since he began collecting a few years ago, he has bought twenty million dollars' worth of books and given them away—to the State of California—"therefore of him no speech." If nowhere else in the world do we find such fortunes as in America, certain it is that nowhere else are these fortunes so immediately and freely shared with the public.

A new generation of book-collectors is in the making: the names of William Andrew Clark, Jr., R. B. Adam, Frank B. Bemis, Jerome Kern, Carl Pforzheimer, J. A. Spoor, J. L. Clawson, and others, occur to me. I hope, I earnestly hope, that they and others like them will keep alight the torch of learning—bibliographical and other—which, if not originally lit, was for so many years kept aglow by Beverly Chew and kindred spirits of the Grolier Club.

Books are becoming everything to me. If I had at this moment any choice of life, I would bury myself in one of those immense libraries . . . and never pass a waking hour without a book before me.

—THOMAS B. MACAULAY

The Perfect Book

BY WILLIAM KEDDIE

The Foulis's editions of classical works were much praised by scholars and collectors in the nineteenth century. The celebrated Glasgow
publishers once attempted to issue a book which should be a perfect
specimen of typographical accuracy. Every precaution was taken to
secure the desired result. Six experienced proof-readers were employed, who devoted hours to the reading of each page; and after it
was thought to be perfect, it was posted up in the hall of the university, with a notification that a reward of fifty pounds would be paid
to any person who could discover an error. Each page was suffered to
remain two weeks in the place where it had been posted, before the
work was printed, and the printers thought that they had attained
the object for which they had been striving. When the work was issued, it was discovered that several errors had been committed, one
of which was in the first line of the first page.

Books Are the Windows of the Soul

BY HENRY WARD BEECHER

Books are the windows through which the soul looks out. A home without books is like a room without windows. No man has the right to bring up his children without surrounding them with books, if he has the means to buy them. It is a wrong to his family. He cheats them! Children learn to read by being in the presence of books. The love of knowledge comes with reading and grows upon it. And the love of knowledge, in a young mind, is almost a warrant against the inferior excitement of passions and vices. Let us pity these poor rich men who live barrenly in great bookless houses! Let us congratulate the poor that, in our day, books are so cheap that a man may every year add a hundred volumes to his library for the price which his tobacco and his beer would cost him. Among the earliest ambitions to be excited in clerks, workmen, journeymen, and, indeed, among all that are struggling up in life from nothing to something, is that of forming and continually adding to a library of good books. A little library, growing larger every year, is an honourable part of a man's history. It is a man's duty to have books. A library is not a luxury, but one of the necessities of life.

How Reading Changed My Life

BY ANNA QUINDLEN

*Anna Quindlen is a Pulitzer Prize–winning columnist and the author of three best-selling novels—*Object Lessons, One True Thing, *and* Black and Blue, *among other books. In this selection from her 1998 contribution to the Library of Contemporary Thought series,* How Reading Changed My Life, *she shares her optimistic view of the role of reading and the future of books in the computer age.*

"Books are over," the editor of a journal to be found only on the Internet told me one day at a conference on the future of the newspaper business. Just my luck. After all these years of reading books I'd finally written one; when I took time to alphabetize my shelves, it came between Proust and Ayn Rand, which seemed representative of how I'd read all my life, between the great and the merely engagingly popular. I could still remember the time I had held my first hardcover book. The Federal Express truck raised a cloud of gravel and dust on a country road as I ripped into the envelope, removed the book, and lifted it up and down in my outstretched hands, just to feel the heft of it, as though it was to be valued by weight. I held it the way I'd seen babies held at religious ceremonies, a *bris,* perhaps, or a baptism. Hardcovers: every writer's ultimate ambition, whether she admits it or not.

It was a fearsome frisson that ripped through the business, the business of writing, the business of publishing, the business of news-papering, when I was well into all three. The computer had become like the most miraculous sort of technological Swiss Army knife: each time you thought you knew what it could do, it turned out that it could do more, faster, better, more accurately. I wrote my first novel on a big clunker of a machine that wheezed slightly when it stored information and had a mere 256 kilobits of memory. It just managed to hold the book, the word-processing program, and a few other odds and ends. My third novel was composed on a machine that fits into my handbag and weighs slightly more than a premature baby. The program corrects my punctuation and capitalization as I type; when I try to type a stand-alone lowercase *i,* it inflates it into a capital letter, correcting me peremptorily, certain I've made a mis-take. I could keep a dozen copies of my book on its hard disk and it wouldn't even breathe hard.

And there was less than a decade between the publication of those two books.

So it became easy, as the age of the computer washed in a wave of modems and cybersurfers over the United States at the end of the twentieth century, to believe those who said that books need never leave the soul of this new machine at all, that the wave of the future was this: *The Age of Innocence* on-line, to be called up and read with the push of a view button; *The Fountainhead* via the Internet, per-haps with all the tiresome objectivist polemical speeches set in a dif-ferent font for easy skipping-over (or even the outright deletions that Ayn Rand's editor should have taken care of). No paper, no shelf space, and the ultimate democratization of reading: a library in a box much smaller than a single volume of the old leatherbound *Ency-clopaedia Britannica.* To all the old fears of lack of literacy, of inter-est, of quality—was added the fear of microchips.

A small skirmish in these technowars broke out in the summer of 1997 in the pages of *The Horn Book,* the journal of children's litera-ture, and it was representative of both the worst-case scenarios and the realities of the future of publishing in an era of tearaway tech-nology. A writer and librarian named Sarah Ellis tried an experi-ment: she read on a laptop computer a book for children called *The End of the Rainbow.* But this was not just any book: it exemplified the greatest fears of those who love children's literature and know how difficult it can be to publish in a cost-conscious age. *The End of the Rainbow* was part of a series of Danish books about a boy named Buster published by Dutton; the sales trajectory of its predecessors had convinced the publisher to offer it free on the Internet rather than go to the expense of publishing it in book form.

Ms. Ellis gave Buster on the computer a fair shake, but she found the experience ultimately unsatisfactory. She concluded that the process of scrolling down, reading in a linear fashion, on a machine she associates with haste, were all antithetical to reading for pleasure. "The screen," she says, "turned me into a reluctant reader." When she went to the library and took out an earlier bound Buster book, her reluctance disappeared. "I experienced that feeling of surrender, of putting myself in someone's hands, which is one of the great pleasures of fiction," she wrote. And she reclaimed the experience of a book, pure and simple: "the soft scrape of my fingers against the pages, the glissando sound of flipping back to a previous chapter." The scrolling of the screen had not been equivalent of turning the pages. A laptop is portable, but not companionable.

Ms. Ellis believed her experiment raised many questions about the future of reading in the face of the ascendancy of computers, questions that will be raised over and over again in the years to come. But, reading her words, I found more questions answered than asked, and one essential one settled to my satisfaction. At the time that technocrats had predicted the imminent death of the book as we knew it, all of us in the world of print were in a kind of frenzy about how new technology would change our old businesses. In the five years between my first job as a copy girl and my hiring at *The New York Times* as a reporter, big papers had begun to retire their typewriters and bring in computer systems on which reporters would produce the day's copy and editors edit it. It was a modest revolution, given the advances still to come, but a revolution not without pain; one of the *Times's* most venerable reporters insisted he was too old to learn new tricks, and his copy had to be transcribed into the computer from the copy paper he continued to use in his old manual typewriter.

But the real revolution was said to be coming in the product itself. Panel after panel was held at journalism conventions about whether newspapers would be replaced by the downloading of the day's news onto a computer screen. It seemed only sensible to those whose cor-

respondence had become characters sent by modem from one computer to another instead of a file of business letters, inevitable that
the collection of folded newsprint that landed on the doormat with
a thwap before daybreak each morning could simply be replaced by
a virtual newspaper in a computer in the kitchen, coffee cup beside
the keyboard.

Perhaps that may someday come to pass, in one form or another;
perhaps someday it will seem quaint that anyone ever doubted that
the printed book between hard or soft covers was in its twilight at
the end of the twentieth century. But the decade after the initial
panic over the demise of printing upon paper seemed to foreshadow
a very different end. News indeed appeared on computers; so did
magazines, some created expressly for on-line users. There were even
books like the Buster book that Dutton put on the Internet rather
than risk commercial failure. But none of them convincingly supplanted the more conventional product. Both those in the business
of books and those in the business of computer technology realized
something that we readers apprehended most deeply in our hearts:
that people are attached, not only to what is inside books, but to the
object itself, the old familiar form that first took shape four centuries
ago. A laptop computer is a wondrous thing; it is inconceivable to
me now that I ever did without one, particularly in writing and revision. (There are still, of course, those novelists who like to speak
fervently of writing by hand in special lined journals, or using the
old Royal typewriter they were given when they went away to
Choate forty years before. Not me.) But a computer is no substitute
for a book. No one wants to take a computer to bed at the end of a
long day to read a chapter or two before dropping off to sleep. No
one wants to take one out of a purse on the New York City subway
to pass the time between Ninety-sixth Street and the World Trade
Center. No one wants to pass *Heidi* on disk down to their daughter
on the occasion of her eighth birthday, or annotate William Carlos
Williams on-screen. At least, no one wants to do it yet, even those
who are much farther along the cybercurve than I am. The dis-ease
Ms. Ellis felt reading a book on the computer, which she described
so eloquently in her *Horn Book* article, is what so many of the rest of
us feel, and why the book continues to prosper. Ms. Ellis wonders if
this is generational, if she finds reading a screen less satisfactory than
do children born to its blandishments. But I have three of those chil-

dren, and while they play games, trade mail, and do plenty of research on their computers, they do most of their reading in plain old ordinary books, some that belonged to me years ago. They seem to like it that way. My youngest grew up with a copy of *Arthur's Teacher's Trouble* on CD-ROM, an interactive version of the picture book that allowed her to use her mouse to make desks open and birds fly. But she never gave up reading the version on paper. "I like the real book," she said.

And a real book, not a virtual version, is more often than not what's wanted. After all, the publisher of Dutton Children's Books did not decide to publish *The End of the Rainbow* on-line because children were clamoring to read it on the computer. His reasons were financial, not philosophical; he simply did not believe he could afford the loss that the book would incur in conventional publication. The prophets of doom and gloom and the virtual library may use this to generalize about a future in which hundreds, perhaps thousands, of wonderful books are never published at all. But the fact is that publishing in all its incarnations—small presses, large presses, vanity presses, university presses—produces many more new titles today than it did fifty or a hundred years ago. More than 350,000 new books were added to the Library of Congress in 1995 alone; that institution, founded with funding of $5,000 two centuries ago, now has two hundred times the number of items once found in the legendary library in Alexandria.

And if some new books only manage to make their way onto the Internet, isn't that better than losing them entirely? New technology offered the publisher of Dutton Children's Books, Christopher Franceschelli, some useful middle ground between taking a substantial financial loss and not offering the book to readers at all. He wrote eloquently in a letter to the *Horn Book,* "We live in an era of transition perhaps not all that dissimilar to that of five hundred years ago. Then an entire culture had to wrestle with the meaning of the Western reinvention of movable type. Even then there were those who bemoaned the loss of texture, when the individually crafted, individually illuminated manuscript, with rubricated initials and tooled leather bindings, gave way to the radically simple black-and-white pages mechanically produced by Gutenberg and his descendants. Indeed there are those who would argue that the entire Protestant movement was only possible once the Book had lost its totemic value as literal manifestation of the divine Word to reappear as the book—cheap, portable, with a mutable text accessible to (and interpretable by) one and all."

And in his history of reading, Albert Manguel concludes, "It is interesting to note how often a technological development—such as Gutenberg's—promotes rather than eliminates that which it is supposed to supersede." Consider, for instance, the thousands of books sold every day on-line. In at least one way, those computer services that were said to spell *finis* to book buying in America have instead succeeded in making it easier for the technologically adept.

Katherine Paterson, in her library speech, took the long view, too, describing her despair at trying to find information on an on-line service and turning to an old encyclopedia and finding it there instead, but noting, too, "I think it well behooves us to realize that we are not the first generation to fear the changes that seem to engulf us. Plato, lest we forget, argued in the *Dialogues* that if people learned to read and write, poetry would disappear, for it was only in the oral tradition that poetry could be preserved properly."

Well, Plato was wrong. And so, I believe, are those people predicting the demise of the book, particularly its death by microchip. The discussions surrounding the issue always remind me of the discussions from my childhood about the gastronomic leap forward occasioned by the development of astronaut food. Soon, we heard, we would be able to eat an entire Sunday dinner in the form of a pill. Soon a Creamsicle could be carried around in your pocket, run under the hose, and reconstituted on a warm day, almost as good as new.

It's thirty years since man first walked on the moon, and when people sit down to a big old-fashioned supper it is still a plate of roast beef and mashed potatoes, not a capsule and a glass of water. When they buy a Creamsicle, it's three-dimensional, wet and cold and wonderful. That's because people like the thing itself. They don't eat mashed potatoes with gravy because they just need to be nourished, but because mashed potatoes and gravy are wonderful in so many ways: the heat, the texture, the silky slide of the gravy over your tongue. And that is the way it is with books. It is not simply that we need information, but that we want to savor it, carry it with us, feel the heft of it under our arm. We like the thing itself.

It is not possible that the book is over. Too many people love it so. It is possible that it has fallen upon hard times, but finding the evidence to prove this is more challenging than many people may think. It is true that there are almost no serializations of books in magazines anymore, a form of book that once made novels accessible for millions of readers who could not afford hardcovers. It is true that department stores no longer sell books, and that many of what pass for bookstores seem closer to gift shops, with far too many date-books and trinkets. It's a little terrifying, the fact that in many of the mall stores there is an entire long wall classified as Fiction and a small narrow section to one side of it called Literature. That second, smaller, section is reserved largely for dead people, dead people who represent much of the best the world of words has had to offer over its long span.

But the ultimate truth is that they aren't dead, those people. The writers of books do not truly die; their characters, even the ones who throw themselves in front of trains or are killed in battle, come back to life over and over again. Books are the means to immortality: Plato lives forever, as do Dickens, and Dr. Seuss, Soames Forsyte, Jo March, Scrooge, Anna Karenina, and Vronsky. Over and over again Heathcliff wanders the moor searching for his Cathy. Over and over again Ahab fights the whale. Through them all we experience other times, other places, other lives. We manage to become much more than our own selves. The only dead are those who grow sere and shriveled within, unable to step outside their own lives and into those of others. Ignorance is death. A closed mind is a catafalque.

I still remember sitting in the fading afternoon one day in a rambling old house in the country, speaking to the elderly matriarch of one of America's great publishing families, a woman known for her interest in all things political, social, intellectual. Near the end of our conversation she squared her shoulders, looked sharply into some middle distance behind me, and said, as though to herself, "I can't read any longer." The words were sad and sonorous as a church bell, and I felt that she had pronounced a sort of epitaph upon herself, and I felt that she felt it too: I can't read any longer.

Yet in her sorrow there was joy, the remembered joy of someone who had been a reader all her life, whose world had been immeasurably enlarged by the words of others. Perhaps it is true that at base we readers are dissatisfied people, yearning to be elsewhere, to live vicariously through words in a way we cannot live directly through life. Perhaps we are the world's great nomads, if only in our minds. I travel today in the way I once dreamed of traveling as a child. And the irony is that I don't care for it very much. I am the sort of person who prefers to stay at home, surrounded by family, friends, familiarity, books. This is what I like about traveling: the time on airplanes spent reading, solitary, happy. It turns out that when my younger self thought of taking wing, she wanted only to let her spirit soar. Books are the plane, and the train, and the road. They are the destination, and the journey. They are home.

After all manner of professors have done their best for us, the place we are to get knowledge is in books. The true University of these days is a collection of books.

—THOMAS CARLYLE, *OF HEROES, HERO-WORSHIP, AND THE HEROIC* (1841)

Three by Quindlen

Three Interesting Lists of Books

BY ANNA QUINDLEN

TEN BIG THICK WONDERFUL BOOKS THAT
COULD TAKE YOU A WHOLE SUMMER TO
READ (BUT AREN'T BEACH BOOKS)

Gone With the Wind by Margaret Mitchell
Vanity Fair by William Makepeace Thackeray
East of Eden by John Steinbeck
The Forsyte Saga by John Galsworthy
Buddenbrooks by Thomas Mann
Can You Forgive Her? by Anthony Trollope
Sophie's Choice by William Styron
Henry and Clara by Thomas Mallon
Underworld by Don DeLillo
Lonesome Dove by Larry McMurtry

THE TEN BOOKS ONE WOULD SAVE IN A
FIRE (IF ONE COULD SAVE ONLY TEN)

Pride and Prejudice by Jane Austen
Bleak House by Charles Dickens
Anna Karenina by Leo Tolstoy

The Sound and the Fury by William Faulkner
The Golden Notebook by Doris Lessing
Middlemarch by George Eliot
Sons and Lovers by D. H. Lawrence
The Collected Poems of W. B. Yeats
The Collected Plays of William Shakespeare
The House of Mirth by Edith Wharton

TEN NONFICTION BOOKS THAT HELP US UNDERSTAND THE WORLD

The Decline and Fall of the Roman Empire by Edward Gibbon
The Best and the Brightest by David Halberstam
Lenin's Tomb by David Remnick
Lincoln by David Herbert Donald
Silent Spring by Rachel Carson
In Cold Blood by Truman Capote
How We Die by Sherwin Nuland
The Unredeemed Captive by John Demos
The Second Sex by Simone de Beauvoir
The Power Broker by Robert A. Caro

Talking of Old Books

BY A. S. W. ROSENBACH

Few book collectors have been as successful at it as A. S. W. Rosenbach. Starting his collection when he was a college freshman with a $3.60 purchase of a pamphlet by Dr. Johnson (later valued at over $10,000), he amassed one of America's finest libraries, which became the foundation of the Rosenbach Museum in Philadelphia, one of the great museums dedicated to the book. Rosenbach wrote several books that show him to have had an engaging writing style. This piece is from his 1927 book Books and Bidders.

"GENIUS?" The tall old man with the fan-shaped beard looked eagerly at his companion, then settled back more heavily against the rows and rows of old books lining the walls to the ceiling on all sides of the room. "Of course Edgar was a genius, but in spite of being a gambler and a drunkard—in spite of it, I tell you!"

The other, a thin man of lesser years, his long, inquiring face meditative in the twilight, nodded.

"You are right," he agreed. "But what difference did it make? The only question is, would 'The Raven' have been any greater without his gambling and drinking? I doubt it."

The argument was on, and my uncle, Moses Polock, would lean forward now and again, waving his coatless arms—he handled books easier in shirt sleeves—in an effort to gain a point. His peculiarly young and penetrating blue eyes glistened. Opposite, George P. Philes, a noted editor and book collector, twirled a gray moustache and goatee while balancing in a tilted chair, listening calmly, and patiently relighting a half-smoked cigar which went out often as the verbal heat increased.

I would watch these two, dazed with their heated words concerning authors and their works; hear them make bookish prophecies, most of which came true. A favorite subject was their neurotic friend, Edgar Allan Poe. Both had befriended this singularly unfortunate and great writer, and each had certain contentions to make which led through the fire of argument to the cooler and more even discussion of reminiscences. But they did agree that it would take less than fifty years after Poe's death to make first editions of his works the most valuable of all American authors.

It was in 1885, when I was nine years old, that I first felt the haunting atmosphere of Uncle Moses' bookshop on the second floor of the bulging, red-brick building on Commerce Street in old Philadelphia. At that age I could hardly realize, spellbound as I was, the full quality of mystery and intangible beauty which becomes a part of the atmosphere wherever fine books are brought together; for here was something which called to me each afternoon, just as the wharves, the water, and the ships drew other boys who were delighted to get away from books the moment school was out. Whatever it was—some glibly speak of it as bibliomania—it entered my bones then and has grown out of all proportion ever since. The long walk from the bookshop to my home in the twilight, the moon, just coming up, throwing long shadows across the white slab of Franklin's grave which I had to pass, was sometimes difficult; but as I grew older I learned to shut my eyes against imaginary fears and, in a valiant effort to be brave, hurried past darkened corners and abysmal alleyways, inventing a game by which I tried to visualize the only touches of color in Uncle Moses' musty, dusty shop—occasional brilliantly bound volumes. Running along, I also cross-examined myself on quotations and dates from books and manuscripts through which I had prowled earlier in the day, unwittingly developing a memory which was often to stand me in good stead.

My uncle's appreciation of books showed itself long before he took over the publishing and bookselling business established in

Philadelphia in 1780, just before the close of the Revolution. Throughout his youth books had been dear to him, and his father, noting this, encouraged him to keep together the volumes he prized most. Yet he gained local attention, not as a book collector but as a publisher, when with a certain amount of initiative he brought out the works of the first American novelist, Charles Brockden Brown. But I early had my suspicions of him as a publisher. It seemed to me that he used the publishing business as a literary cat's-paw by which he might conceal his real interest and love—searching for, finding, and treasuring rare books.

After all, if one is in a trade, certain expectations are held by the public; and the older Uncle Moses grew the less willing he became to meet these expectations. To publish books and sell them was one phase; but to collect, and then to sell, he considered a different and entirely personal affair. A poor young man, Uncle Moses had acquired the business in an almost magical manner. Jacob Johnson, the original founder, began by publishing children's books only. But in 1800 he decided to branch out and took a partner, Benjamin Warner. Fifteen years later the firm was sold out to McCarty and Davis. After several successful years McCarty retired, and it was then that Moses Polock was employed as a clerk. They had spread out and were now publishing all sorts of books. Davis became very fond of his clerk and, when he died, in 1851, left him sufficient money in his will to purchase the business for himself. Luck was evidently with my uncle, for he made a great deal of money in publishing Lindley Murray's *Grammar* and other school-books of the time.

First as a publishing house and bookstore combined, Uncle Moses' shop became a meeting place for publishers and writers. Here it was that the ill-fed Poe came in 1835 to talk modestly of his writings and hopes.

Such men as James Fenimore Cooper, William Cullen Bryant, Noah Webster, and Herman Melville might be seen going up or coming down the narrow staircase leading to the second floor. George Bancroft, the historian, came, too, and Eaton, who wrote the *Life of Jackson;* George H. Boker, a distinguished Philadelphia poet, Charles Godfrey Leland, of *Hans Breitmann Ballads* note, and Donald G. Mitchell, who wrote as Ik. Marvel, and many others— they found their way along the uneven brick sidewalks of Commerce Street. Gradually, however, it developed into a rendezvous for the more leisured group of collectors.

Men—and occasionally a woman—who owned many an interesting and valuable volume came to browse and talk. Silent or voluble, enthusiastic or suspiciously conservative, each had in mind some book of Uncle Moses' he hoped one day to possess. For it took something more than money and coercion to make this old man give up his treasures. Even when he occasionally fell to this temptation and sold the precious volume, in place of the original he would make a pen-and-ink copy of the book, word for word, so that it was typographically perfect. This would take weeks to do, and only when he needed money badly did he consent to part with the original. I have some of these copies and treasure them as curiosities. Not only months but very often years of tireless perseverance were necessary to make him sell a favorite volume. Equally interesting was that other group which came daily—a group composed of impecunious and peculiarly erratic book lovers, found in book haunts the world over: a poverty-stricken intellectual class, who in filling their minds often forget to provide for their stomachs as well.

All the memories of my childhood center around the secluded and dusty corners of this shop, where I eavesdropped and prowled to my heart's content. My uncle, at first annoyed at having a little boy about the place prying into musty papers and books, eventually took delight in showing me rare editions purchased by him at auctions and private sales. As he grew older he became somewhat eccentric and, despite my extreme youth, insisted upon treating me as a book lover and connoisseur, his own equal. Although he lived to be a very old man, he retained the most marvelous memory I have ever known. He could tell without a moment's hesitation the date of a book, who the printer was, where it had been found, any physical earmarks it might have, its various vicissitudes, and how it had reached its final destination.

Among the noted collectors who came to match their wits and learning with my uncle was a younger man, Clarence S. Bement, who developed into one of the greatest American book experts. Even at that time he had a wonderful collection, and I well remember his subtle efforts to add to it constantly. He would talk in a firm, low, rather musical voice, obviously toned with persuasion, hoping to make his friend part with some cherished volume he coveted. As I watched Uncle Moses refuse, I saw a curiously adamant and at the same time satisfied expression spread over his features; I noticed, too, the dignity of movement as he gravely took the volume from Bement's fingers to look at it, with that expressive pride in ownership that verges on madness with many people to whom possession can mean but one thing: books.

Samuel W. Pennypacker, who in later years became governor of Pennsylvania, was another avid book collector and constant habitué of the old Commerce Street bookshop. His hobby was anything he could lay his hands upon from the Franklin press. He also collected all data relating to the early Swedish settlers of Pennsylvania and his German and Dutch ancestors, as well as any material concerning the development of the state. A large man he was, with serious eyes set in a rather square-shaped head. But his voice fascinated me most of all as it boomed about the shelves when he grew excited and took on an unforgettable Pennsylvania Dutch twang.

Pennypacker was a fervent admirer of George Washington, and he had once heard of a letter which General Washington wrote from one of the scenes of his childhood, Pennypacker's Mills. He couldn't seem to forget this letter, for he was always talking about it, hoping to trace it to its owner and eventually make it his own.

I shall never forget the day Uncle Moses told him he had found and bought this letter. He handed it to Pennypacker with a light of triumphant amusement in his eyes. After reading it, Pennypacker put it down on the table before him and, without raising his eyes, said in a peculiarly exhausted way, "Polock, I must have this letter. You can make any bargain you choose, but I must have it!" Hardly waiting for the other to reply, he rushed down the stairs, to return a few moments later with two books under his arm. My uncle's blue eyes were but mocking questions as he pushed them aside after glancing at their title pages. They were two valuable books, but not unusually so. Pennypacker had by this time unbuttoned his coat, and I saw him take from an inner pocket a thin, yellow envelope.

"These"—Pennypacker pointed to his two books—"and this." He opened the envelope and gave my uncle its contents. It, too, was a letter from George Washington, yet no sign of emotion swept the old man's features as he read. But the exchange was made rather quickly, I thought, and it would have been difficult to decide which bargainer was the more satisfied. I have read both letters many times since. The

Pennypacker's Mills letter was dated September 29, 1777, and addressed: "On public service, to the Honorable John Hancock, President of Congress, Lancaster." George Washington wrote in part:

> I shall move the Army four or five miles lower down today
> from where we may reconnoitre and fix upon a proper sit-
> uation at such distance from the enemy as will enable us
> to make an attack should we see a proper opening, or
> stand upon the defensive till we obtain further reinforce-
> ments. This was the opinion of a Council of General Of-
> ficers which I called yesterday. I congratulate you upon
> the success of our Arms to the Northward and if some ac-
> cident does not put them out of their present train, I
> think we may count upon the total ruin of Burgoyne.

The letter which my uncle received was written four years later from Philadelphia, in 1781, to Abraham Skinner, Commissary General of Prisoners, and was easily the more important, historically, of the two, as General Washington discussed throughout the surrender of Cornwallis and the exchange of prisoners at Yorktown. He instructed General Skinner not to consent to the exchange of Lord Cornwallis under any conditions.

Even I, with but a short experience as a mere onlooker in the collecting game, realized its greater value. After my uncle's death this Washington letter sold for $925, and it rests today as one of the treasures in the Pierpont Morgan collection.

A few years ago I bought back the Pennypacker's Mills letter for $130 from Governor Pennypacker's estate. Because of the incident it recalls I would never part with it.

When I was eleven years old I began book collecting on my own. My first purchase was at an auction in the old Henkels's auction rooms on Chestnut Street. It was an illustrated edition of *Reynard the Fox* and was knocked down to me for twenty-four dollars. My enthusiasm rather than my financial security swept me into this extravagance, and after the sale I had to go to the auctioneer, Mr. Stan V. Henkels, and confess that I was not exactly solvent. At the same time I explained I was Moses Polock's nephew, instinctively feeling, I suppose, that such a relationship might account for any untoward action concerning books. I had hardly got the words out of my frightened mouth when Mr. Henkels burst into a fit of laughing which—although I was too young, too scared and self-conscious to realize it at the time—was the beginning of a lifelong friendship between us.

When he ceased laughing, he looked down at me, a sombre little boy with a book under his shaking arm, and said, "I've seen it start at an early age, and run in families, but in all my experience this is the very first baby bibliomaniac to come my way!" With this admission he kindly consented to extend credit, and trusted me for further payments, which I was to make weekly from my school allowance. Giving him all the money I possessed, ten dollars, I marched from the auction room, feeling for the first time in my life that swooning yet triumphant, that enervating and at the same time heroic, combination of emotions the born bibliomaniac enjoys so intensely with the purchase of each rare book.

Stan V. Henkels—no one dared to leave out the middle initial—was a remarkable man. Even in his young days he resembled an old Southern colonel, the accepted picture we all have, a man of drooping moustache, rather patrician nose, and longish hair which he decorated with a large-brimmed, rusty black hat of the Civil War period. He insisted he was an unreconstructed rebel and was always willing to take on anyone in a verbal battle about the Civil War.

By profession an auctioneer of books, Mr. Henkels was the first person to make the dreary, uninteresting work of auction catalogues into living, fascinating literature, almost as exciting reading as fiction. Previous to this, anyone wanting to find out what was in a collection had little luck when searching through a catalogue, beyond discovering names and dates.

Observing this, and that certain items whose contents were of exceptional interest did not sell well, Henkels decided to find out for himself what was between the covers of the books he sold, and to learn what was often told so confidentially in the literary manuscripts and letters, and then to print the most interesting data he could find about each item. This was a great work in itself, and how he found the leisure to give to it was a mystery. Thus he brought in color and life, a human-interest setting, which added thousands of dollars yearly to his business, and which awakened feelings of gratitude in many collectors.

Seven years after buying *Reynard the Fox* on the installment plan, I made my first valuable literary discovery. I was studying then at the

University of Pennsylvania, and books enthralled me to a disastrous extent. I attended book sales at all hours of the day and night; I neglected my studies; I bought books whether I could afford them or not; I forgot to eat and did not consider sleep necessary at all. The early stages of the book-collecting germ are not the most virulent, but nevertheless they make themselves felt!

This night I went to the Henkels's auction room several hours before the sale. I looked at many of the books with great delight, sighed when I estimated the prices they would bring, and was beginning to feel rather despondent, when I happened to see a bound collection of pamphlets in one corner of the room.

Now for some unknown reason pamphlets, even from my boyhood, have been a passion with me. I cannot resist reading a pamphlet, whether it has value or not. The potentialities between slim covers play the devil with my imagination. It is true that books are my real love, but pamphlets flaunt a certain piquancy which I have never been able to resist. One might call them the flirtations of book collecting. I crossed to the corner, disturbed that I had not seen the volume earlier in the evening, that I had so little time to devote to it. But hurried as I felt—it was almost time for the sale to begin—I came upon a copy of Gray's *Odes.* It was not only a first edition, but the first book from Horace Walpole's famous Strawberry Hill Press, printed especially for him. Walpole had a weakness for gathering fame to his own name by printing the works of certain famous contemporaries. Delighted at finding this, I observed the title page of a pamphlet, which was bound with it. I could hardly believe my eyes! For in my hands I held, quite by accident, the long-lost first edition of Dr. Samuel Johnson's famous *Prologue,* which David Garrick recited the opening night of the Drury Lane Theatre in London in 1747. Although advertisements in the *General Advertiser* and *Gentleman's Magazine* of Doctor Johnson's day announced the sale of this work for the modest sum of sixpence, no one had ever heard of a copy of this original edition being in existence before or since. Boswell made an allusion to it in his *Life of Johnson,* but that was all that was known of this first issue of the little masterpiece of "dramatick criticism."

I closed my eyes in an effort to steady myself, leaning heavily against the wall. I wanted to buy this pamphlet more than I had ever wanted anything in the world. A wealthy and noted collector entered the room. I gave up hope. Again I looked at the pamphlet, and as I read Doctor Johnson's famous line on Shakespeare, "And panting Time toil'd after him in vain," I wished that I might be weak enough to take something which did not belong to me.

Suddenly my plans were made. I would have the *Prologue*! I would do anything honorable to obtain it. Having nothing but my future to mortgage, I desperately decided to offer that, whoever the purchaser might be.

Mr. Henkels announced the usual terms of the sale and I gazed cautiously about the room; every member of the audience was just waiting for that volume of pamphlets, I knew. Finally it was put up, and the very silence seemed to bid against me; when, after two or three feeble counter-bids, it became really mine for the sum of $3.60, I sat as one in a trance. The news soon spread among the experts of the exceptional find I had made, and I had many offers for it. Several years later, during my postgraduate course at college, when I needed money very badly, a noted collector dandled a check for $5,000 before my eyes. It was a difficult moment for me, but I refused the offer. In my private library I retain this treasured volume.

One day previous to this I was in the auction rooms when a white-haired Negro said Mr. Henkels had something interesting to show me if I would go to the top floor. I found him standing by an open window fronting Chestnut Street, exhibiting to several curious customers a small gold locket which had belonged to George Washington. It had been authenticated by his heirs, and also the gray lock of hair enclosed within it. As I joined the others, Mr. Henkels opened the locket and held it out for inspection. At that moment an unexpected gust of wind blew into the room and, sweeping about, took the curl very neatly from its resting place. So quickly did it happen it was a moment or so before we realized that the prized lock had been wafted out of the window. Then suddenly we all ran to the stairs and raced four flights into the street below. Up and down, searching the block, the gutters, and the crevices of stone and brick, we sought the lost lock of the Father of our Country. After an hour, or so it seemed, we gave it up as useless. As we returned to the entrance of the rooms the old Negro employee came out.

"Wait a minute!" Henkels exclaimed as an idea came to him.

He grabbed the ancient and surprised servant by the hair. Selecting a choice curly ringlet, he clipped it off with his pocketknife, then placed it carefully in George Washington's locket, closing it tightly.

Several days later I saw the locket put up for sale. The bidding was brisk, and the buyer later expressed himself as being exceptionally lucky. But Henkels, who was the soul of honor, could not listen quietly for long. He told of his, as well as Nature's, prank with the original lock of hair and offered to refund the money. The purchaser refused, saying he had given no thought to the contents anyway, that his interest lay only in the locket.

It is almost incredible, the number of stories that circulate about the civilized world containing misstatements and garbled information about the values and prices of old books. I am sometimes amused, at other times annoyed, to read in the daily papers statements of prices I and other collectors are supposed to have bought and sold books for. Reporters who descend upon us hurriedly to verify the story of some unusual sale can be divided into two classes, overenthusiastic and bored. The former often exaggerate the amount paid for a book and its value; the latter are likely to be careless about details and set them down incorrectly.

When I bought a Gutenberg Bible for $106,000 last spring, I was careful to read and correct the original announcement made of the purchase. Such an event was too important in the history of book collecting to be misstated. Even then, many papers carried a story which gave the impression that this was the only Gutenberg Bible in existence, when there are about forty-two known copies—differing in condition, of course. But collectors themselves have often been at fault for the broadcasting of misinformation, for they seldom take time to go out of their way to correct wrong impressions.

It is only in the past few generations that collectors have taken great care of their treasures—a lucky change, too, for had they all pawed books about, wearing them to shreds in the scholastic manner, few rare volumes would have been saved for us today. Acquisitiveness, that noble urge to possess something the other fellow hasn't or can't get, is often the direct cause of assembling vast, extraordinary libraries.

Book lovers who were contemporaries of Moses Polock treated him as though he would live forever. It has been noted that those who collect things outlive people who do not. No one notices this so much, perhaps, as the collector himself who has his eye on the collection of another, or the book collector who cannot sleep well at night for the thought of a valuable first edition he would like to own. Book collectors, I make no exceptions, are buzzards who stretch their wings in anticipation as they wait patiently for a colleague's demise; then they swoop down and ghoulishly grab some long-coveted treasure from the dear departed's trove.

Two years before my uncle's death I gave up my fellowship in English at the University of Pennsylvania to enter professionally the sport of book collecting and the business of selling. Uncle Moses was extremely pleased to have me as a competitor. He often said he believed I had all the necessary requisites for collecting, an excellent memory, perseverance, taste, and a fair knowledge of literature. Alas, all requisites but one—money! He thought if I were fortunate enough to acquire that, I would also have the other virtue—courage: the courage to pay a high price for a good book and to refuse a poor one at any price. And I was fortunate. Two gentlemen whose interest in books was as intense as mine made it possible for me to establish myself as a bookseller. The first, Clarence S. Bement, possessed a glorious collection over which he had spent years of constant study and search. All collectors were eager to secure his volumes, each being fine and rare. As a silent partner he was invaluable to me in many ways, and with the second, Joseph M. Fox, spurred me on to collecting the choicest books and manuscripts as they came on the market, pointing out the fact that at all times there is a demand for the finest things. Mr. Fox, one of the most lovable of men, lived in a very old Colonial house called Wakefield, in the suburbs of Philadelphia, in which he had discovered wonderful Revolutionary letters and documents.

It is difficult to know at what moment one becomes a miser of books. For many years preceding his death, Uncle Moses kept a fireproof vault in the rear of his office, where he secreted rarities no one ever saw. His books were as real to him as friends. He feared showing the most precious lest he part with one in a moment of weakness. One of the amusing incidents of his life was that he had sold a copy of the Bradford *Laws of New York,* published in 1694, to Doctor Brinley for sixteen dollars, and many years later he had seen it sell at the Brinley sale for $1,600. The money consideration did not cause his regret so much as the fact that he had felt an affection for this volume, which had rested upon his shelves for more than thirty years. By an amusing turn of the wheel of chance, which my uncle might have foreseen, the same volume would be worth today $20,000!

At the death of my uncle, in 1903, I came into possession of some of his wonderful books; others were purchased by private buyers and are today parts of various famous libraries. I was greatly thrilled when, as administrator of his estate, I entered his secret vault for the first time in my life. In the half light I stumbled against something very hard on the floor. Lighting a match, I looked down, to discover a curious bulky package. Examining it more closely, I found it was a bag of old gold coins. A reserve supply cautiously hoarded, no doubt, to buy further rarities.

My uncle's estate included several books from the library of George Washington, the finest of which was a remarkable copy of the *Virginia Journal,* published in Williamsburg, which I still have. Washington was one of the three presidents who collected books in an intelligent manner. There have been presidents who loved books—the late Theodore Roosevelt, for example—but who were not real collectors. It is always interesting to hazard a guess at a great man's personal likes by noting the titles in his library. In the past years I have bought other books from Washington's collection. There is *The History of America* by William Robertson, in two volumes, Brown's *Civil Law, Inland Navigation,* Jenkinson's *Collection of Treaties,* eight volumes of the *Political State of Europe,* a four-volume course of lectures by Winchester on the *Prophecies That Remain to Be Fulfilled*—in this last Washington wrote: "From the author to G. Washington." These are a heavy literary diet, somewhat one-sided when placed next to *Epistles for the Ladies,* which was also his. Each volume has the signature on the title page—"George Washington"—with his armorial bookplate pasted inside the front cover. There were doubtless book borrowers in those days, too, whose memories and consciences might be jogged at sight of the owner's name. Another, a gift to Washington, is a collection of poems "written chiefly during the late war," by Philip Freneau, one of the few very early American poets whose work has survived. On the title page in Freneau's hand, with his signature, is written: "General Washington will do the author the honor to accept a copy of his poems, as a small testimony of the disinterested veneration he entertains for his character."

The books belonging to Martha Washington are few, merely because she was not a great reader, and the common-sense title of the one book of hers which I have—*Agriculture of Argyll County*—would lead one to think of her as a practical woman rather interested in rural activities.

The collecting passion is as old as time. Even book collecting, which many believe to be a comparatively recent development, can be traced back to the Babylonians. They, with their passion for preserving records on clay tablets, could hardly go in for all the little niceties, such as original paper boards or beautifully tooled bindings, but they were collectors nevertheless.

Among the early individual book collectors such colorful names as Jean Grolier, De Thou, Colbert, and the Cardinals Richelieu and Mazarin shine forth. Jean Grolier, a collector of the late fifteenth and the early sixteenth century, now considered the patron saint of modern book collectors, showed unusual vision in selecting his books. Though many libraries of that time are both remarkable and valuable, their worth varies. But every collector is keen to possess a Grolier volume, and at each sale the prices increase. He evidently read what he selected, and his taste showed that he had education and discernment. Aldus Manutius, the most famous printer of that day, dedicated books to him and printed certain works for him on special paper. Aldus was the first to popularize the small-sized book, and that is why many from the Grolier collection are easier to handle than the more gross volumes from other early libraries.

Grolier's generous disposition is indicated by the fact that he has either written in, or had stamped on the outside of the truly exquisite bindings, "Io Grolierii et Amicorum"—his books were for himself and his friends too. Many people have since copied this inscription on their bookplates. The Grolier family were book lovers, and his library was kept intact for three generations. Not until one hundred and sixteen years after his death was it sold, and although many were bought by other famous collectors, old records show that some disappeared entirely. It is just such knowledge that keeps the true bibliophile living in hopes—a long-missing Grolier might turn up anytime, anywhere.

About the time of the discovery of America a book came out called *The Ship of Fools,* by one Sebastian Brant. In it was an attack on the book fool: a satire on the passion of collecting, in which the author said that the possession of books was but a poor substitute for learning. That phrase which the layman reader asks the book collector so often with a smirk of condescension, "So you really read them?" undoubtedly originated then. The real book collector, with suppressed murder in his heart, smiles acquiescence, assuming an apologetic air for his peculiar little hobby. His invisible armor is his knowledge, and he has been called a fool so often he glories in it. He can afford to have his little joke. So much for this threadbare gibe.

Cardinal Richelieu, according to history, sought relaxation from the cares of state in his love of books. His huge library was got together in many ways. Sometimes he bought books; he sent two learned men on the road, one to Germany and the other to Italy, to collect both printed and manuscript works. Often he would exchange volumes with other collectors, and one can imagine the covert smile of satisfaction on this ecclesiastical politician's lips whenever he got the better of a bargain.

Of course there was always a way to get a rare work, whether the owner cared to part with it or not, by an off-with-his-head policy of intimidation. After the taking of La Rochelle the red-robed Richelieu topped off the victory by helping himself to the entire library of that city. Even though he was something of a robber, his ultimate motive was good—he planned to establish a reference library for all qualified students. Yet it was his nephew, the inheritor of his library, who carried out these plans posthumously. He willed it to the Sorbonne, with a fund to keep up the collection and to add to it according to the needs and progress of the times.

Cardinal Mazarin had the appreciation of books instilled in him from his boyhood, when he attended a Jesuit school in Rome. Following in the footsteps of the famous Richelieu, it was necessary to carry out many of his predecessor's policies. One of these was to weaken the French nobles, who ruled enormous country estates, by destroying their feudal castles. Thus Mazarin, a great but wily character, took his books where he found them. Eventually his library grew to be a famous one, which he generously threw open to the literary men of the day. Fortunately the men who followed Mazarin kept his collection intact, and today, in Paris, one may see the great Mazarin Library on the left bank of the Seine.

Colbert, first as Mazarin's secretary, and later a great political leader on his own account, also collected a fine library in perhaps a more legitimate manner than his patron. He arranged for the consuls representing France in every part of Europe to secure any remarkable works they might hear of. Colbert not only offered the use of his collection to such of his contemporaries as Molière, Corneille, Boileau, and Racine, but pensioned these men as well.

De Thou, also a Frenchman, of the latter half of the sixteenth and the early seventeenth century, had the finest library of his time. His thousands upon thousands of volumes included many bought from the Grolier collection, and collectors' interest in them has never lessened. De Thou was the truest type of book lover. He had not one but several copies of each book he felt a particular affection for; he ordered them printed on the best paper obtainable, expressly for himself. His bindings are richly beautiful, of the finest leathers, exquisitely designed. They are easily recognizable, as his armorial stamp, with golden bees, is on the sides, and the back is marked with a curious cipher made from his initials. Most of the contents treat of profound but interesting subjects. He was a real student and wrote an extensive history of his time in Latin. Here is an example of inherited passion for books. His mother's brother and his father were both book lovers.

It is a general belief that books are valuable merely because they are old. Age, as a rule, has very little to do with actual value. I have never announced the purchase of a noted old book without having my mail flooded for weeks afterward with letters from all over the world. Each correspondent tells me of opportunities I am losing by not going immediately to his or her home to see, and incidentally buy, "a book which has been in my family over one hundred years."

I receive more than thirty thousand letters about books every year. Each letter is read carefully and answered. There are many from cranks. But it is not hard to spot these even before opening the envelope, when addressed, as one was recently from Germany, "Herr Doktor Rosenbach, multi-millionaire, Amerika." Indeed, the greater number of letters about books are from Germany. One man in Hamburg wrote me of a book he had for sale, then ended by saying he also had a very fine house he would like me to buy, because he felt sure, if I saw it, his elegant garden would appeal to me for the use of my patients! Many people write me, after I have purchased a book at a high price, and say they have something to offer "half as old at half the price"!

Yet one out of every two thousand letters holds a possibility of interest. I followed up a letter from Hagenau not long ago, to discover—the copy was sent me on approval—a first edition of "Adonais," Shelley's lament on the death of Keats, in the blue paper wrappers in which it was issued. There are only a few copies known in this original condition. I bought it by correspondence for a reasonable price. It is worth at least $5,000. On the other hand, I have often made a long journey to find nothing but an inferior copy of a late edition of some famous work. I once heard of a first edition of Hubbard's *Indian Wars,* in Salem, Massachusetts. When I arrived there the family who owned it brought out their copy, unwrapping it with much ceremony from swathings of old silk. Immediately I saw it was a poor reprint made in the nineteenth century, although the original was printed in 1677.

But luck had not deserted me entirely that day. As my train was not due for an hour, I wandered about the city. In passing one of the many antique shops which all New England cities seem to possess by the gross, I noticed a barrow on the sidewalk before it. In this barrow were thrown all sorts and conditions of books. Yet the first one I picked up was a first edition of Herman Melville's *Moby Dick,* worth about $150, which I bought for $20.

Speaking of this copy of *Moby Dick* reminds me of another; a more valuable one, which I prize in my private library. One day about five years ago John Drinkwater, the English poet and dramatist, and I were lunching at his home in London. Talking of books and the ever-interesting vicissitudes of collecting them, he told me of his *Moby Dick,* found one day, by chance, in a New York bookstore for but a few dollars. It was a presentation copy from the author to his friend Nathaniel Hawthorne, to whom the book was dedicated, and had Hawthorne's signature on the dedication leaf. When Mr. Drinkwater told me of this I became restless; I wanted this copy as much as I had ever wanted any other book, and there was nothing for me to do but tell him so. I offered him twenty times what he had paid for it, and to my surprise and delight he generously let me have it.

Why age alone should be thought to give value to most collectible objects, including furniture, pictures, and musical instruments, I don't know. However, it is a great and popular fallacy. The daily prayer of all true collectors should begin with the words "beauty, rarity, condition," and last of all, "antiquity." But books differ from other antiques in that their ultimate value depends upon the intrinsic merit of the writer's work. A first edition of Shakespeare, for instance, will always command an ever-increasing price. The same is true of first editions of Dante, Cervantes, or Goethe. These writers gave something to the world and to life—something of which one always can be sure.

Very often the greatness of an author, the value of what he has written, is not realized until years have gone by. Vital truths are sometimes seen more clearly in perspective. A first folio of Shakespeare's *Comedies, Histories and Tragedies* was sold in 1864 to the late Baroness Burdett-Coutts, who paid what was considered an enormous price—£716—for it. Yet only fifty-eight years later my brother Philip bought the same folio for me at Sotheby's in London for £8,600, Shakespeare's writings having increased in value more than twelve times in a little more than half a century.

The fallacy of thinking that age is of major importance in judging a book should be corrected by every book lover. Age? Why, there are many books of the fifteenth century which command small prices in the auction rooms today, while certain volumes brought out a decade ago are not only valuable but grow more so with each passing year. A first edition of A. A. Milne's *When We Were Very Young,* printed two years ago, is already more precious than some old tome, such as a sermon of the 1490s by the famous teacher Johannes Gerson, the contents of which are and always will be lacking in human or any other kind of interest.

The inception of any great movement, whether material or spiritual, is bound to be interesting, according to its relative importance. The Gutenberg Bible, leaving aside the question of its artistic merit and the enormous value of its contents, as the first printed book is of the greatest possible significance. But it so happens that this wonderful Bible is also one of the finest known examples of typography. No book ever printed is more beautiful than this pioneer work of Gutenberg, the first printer, although it was issued almost five hundred years ago. It has always seemed an interesting point to me that printing is the only art which sprang into being full-blown. Later years brought about a more uniform appearance of type, but aside from this we have only exceeded the early printers in speed of execution. Enormous value is added to some of these earliest books because they are the last word in the printer's art.

The first books printed on subjects of universal interest are the rarest "firsts" of all for the collector. These include early romances of chivalry, of which few copies are found today. They are generally in very poor condition, as their popular appeal was tremendous, and they were literally read to pieces. They were really the popular novels of the period. The ones which come through the stress of years successfully are extremely rare. For instance, there are the Caxtons.

William Caxton was the first printer in England and the first to print books in the English language. When he brought out the second edition of Chaucer's *Canterbury Tales* in 1484, with its fascinating woodcut illustrations, it was literally devoured by contemporary readers. This and other publications of Caxton were very popular— he evidently had a good eye for best-sellers—and now a perfect Caxton is difficult to find.

One of the finest Caxtons in existence is *Le Morte d'Arthur* by Sir Thomas Malory, published in 1485. This perfect copy, this jewel among Caxtons, sold at the dispersal of the library of the earl of Jersey in 1885 for £1,950, approximately $9,500. Now this is an excellent example of a book increasing in value for its pristine, perfect state as well as for its alluring contents. Twenty-six years later it brought $42,800 at the Hoe sale. It is now one of the treasures adorning the Pierpont Morgan Library.

The first editions of books which have that quality so glibly called today sex appeal, such as Boccaccio's *Decameron,* and his *Amore di Florio e di Bianchafiore*—a wicked old romance of the fifteenth century, truly the first snappy story—are firsts of which there are but few left for our edification. They are extremely precious to the collector, no matter what their condition. The first book on murder; the first book on medicine or magic; the first Indian captivity; the first music book, the first newspaper, the first published account of lace making, or the comparatively modern subject, shorthand—the first book on any subject marking the advance of civilization is always valuable.

One of the rarest and most interesting books is the first sporting book, *The Book of Hunting and Hawking,* printed at St. Albans, in 1486, by an unknown man, called, for convenience of classification, the Schoolmaster Printer. Women were sports writers even in those days, for this record was written by a woman, Dame Juliana Barnes, sometimes known as Berners. A copy was sold in the Hoe sale in

1911, for $12,000, to Mr. Henry E. Huntington, who formed one of the few great collections of the world. Nearly all of the few existing copies of this work are now in this country. Another one, the Pembroke copy, which I now own, sold for £1,800 in 1914. As it is the last one that can ever come on the market, heaven only knows what it is worth today. Like some other famous firsts, it has several novel merits, being one of the first books to contain English poetry and the first English book to be illustrated with pictures printed in color. This and Walton's *The Compleat Angler* are the two greatest sporting books of all time. Yet because there are more copies of the latter in existence, a fine copy of the first edition in the original binding is worth not more than $8,500 today.

Another tremendously rare book is the much read *Pilgrim's Progress*. No work, with the exception of the Bible, has enjoyed greater popularity all through the years than this powerful, imaginative, and moral tale. I have almost every edition of it, in every language. A best-seller for years after the author's death, and a very good seller today, too, the early editions were really read to bits. So it is hardly surprising that only six perfect copies of the first edition exist. A few months ago a copy sold at Sotheby's in London for £6,800. The most beautiful one in existence is that famed copy I purchased eighteen months ago from Sir George Holford. I believe if one of the half-dozen perfect first editions were offered in public sale today, it would easily bring from $40,000 to $45,000.

About five years ago the illness of an English barber's wife brought to light a first edition of *Pilgrim's Progress* which was in good condition, except that it lacked two pages. In the little town of Derby lived this barber, daily plying the trade of his ancestors. Between the lathering and the gossiping he found little time and inclination to read, but sometimes when business was not so brisk as usual he listlessly ran through a small stack of books which he inherited along with the shop. Old-fashioned in text, some with odd pictures, and leaves missing, he thought them rather funny and occasionally showed them to customers who shared his amusement. One day someone suggested the books were interesting because they were old and—following the popular fallacy of which I have spoken—must be valuable. He had heard of a man who once paid two pounds for a book!

But the barber shrugged his shoulders and said he had plenty to do without chasing about trying to sell old, worn-out books. Then came a day when his wife took to her bed and the doctor was hurriedly sent for. While waiting for him the barber tried to think of some way he might amuse his wife. As he went into the shop his eyes fell first upon the books on a low shelf. When the doctor arrived he found his patient's bed loaded down with books, and she was reading a copy of *The Pilgrim's Progress*. The doctor was a lover of books in a small way; he felt there was something unusual about this copy. He insisted it should be sent to Sotheby's in London for valuation. Even then the barber believed he was wasting both time and money.

Finally Sotheby's received a package accompanied by a letter, painstakingly written in an illiterate hand, with small *i*'s throughout and guiltless of punctuation. He was sending this copy, he wrote, because a friend was foolish enough to think it might be worth something. Of course it wasn't. He had inherited it from his people, and his people were poor. They couldn't have had anything valuable to leave him. If, as he believed, it was worthless, would they please throw it away, and not bother to return it, or waste money answering him? I don't know what his direct emotional reaction was when they replied saying his old book was worth at least £900—more than $4,000—and that they would place it in their next sale. Perhaps he was stunned for a time. Anyway, weeks passed before they received a rather incoherent reply. I happened to be in London when it was sold, and I paid £2,500—about $12,000—for the copy. I later learned that the barber was swamped for months with letters from old friends he had never heard of before, each with a valuable book to sell him.

As collectors grow older, they find it is better to buy occasionally and at a high price than to run about collecting tuppenny treasures. There is seldom any dispute about the worth of a rare book. Many collectors, however, feel collecting has a value other than monetary; it keeps men young, and as the years pass it proves to be a new type of life insurance.

The late Mr. W. A. White of New York, until his death a few months ago, was as vigorous at eighty-three as he had been thirty years before. He combined a quality of youth with his extraordinary knowledge of books and literature. His wonderful library would take away the load of years from a Methuseleh. Even to read over the partial list of his treasures, which was recently published, would have a distinctly rejuvenating effect. Mr. Henry E. Huntington was another successful man who practically gave up his business interests to devote himself to the invigorating pastime of book collecting. He collected so rapidly that no young man could follow in his steps! Even my uncle Moses grew younger and younger as he sat year after year surrounded by books.

Rare books are a safe investment; the stock can never go down. A market exists in every city of the world. New buyers constantly crop up. The most ordinary, sane, and prosaic type of businessman will suddenly appear at your door, a searching look in his eye, a suppressed tone of excitement in his voice. Like the Ancient Mariner, he takes hold of you to tell his story—for he has suddenly discovered book collecting. And if it happens to be at the end of a very long day, you feel like the Wedding Guest, figuratively beating your breast while you listen. He returns again and again, enthralled by this new interest which takes him away from his business. If he is wealthy, he already may be surfeited with luxuries of one sort or another; but here is something akin to the friendship of a charming and secretive woman. He takes no risk of becoming satiated; there is no possibility of being bored; always some new experience or unexpected discovery may be lurking just around the corner of a bookshelf.

Potch

BY LEO ROSTEN

Among the score of books Leo Rosten wrote, he is probably best known for
The Joys of Yiddish *and* The Education of H*Y*M*A*N
K*A*P*L*A*N. *Rosten considered the story of Potch—which first ap-*
peared in Look *magazine in the 1950s and later in his 1970 collection,*
People I Have Loved, Known or Admired—*to be one of his own fa-*
vorite pieces. Nearly everyone has had an experience like the one Rosten
writes about, an experience that sets one on a course through the world
of words, ideas, and books. One of the editors of this book, in fact, marks
his own entry into that world with his first reading of this piece.

We called him Potch, and he was as unprepossessing as his nickname: a sallow, humorless gnome of a boy who plunged me, at ten,
into the greatest moral crisis of my life.

Potch, who was given to sucking air and muttering odd maledictions, was not popular. He was never part of our "gang." He had no
athletic skills, no dreams of glory on gridiron or diamond, and
seemed actually to dislike the noble, shining hours we spent on soft-
ball, basketball, handball, "pinners." No one wanted Potch when we
chose up sides for Run, Sheep, Run or Prisoner's Base or Shoosh,
which was what, in Chicago, we called punchball, played right out

in the streets, with a manhole cover as home plate—and without a bat: you hit the ball with your fist.

Potch was a loner, skinny, moody, without luster. He was so non-popular that he did not even compete in our daily tournament of loyalty, each boy screaming out his own All-Time All-Star Baseball Team at the top of his lungs. Nor did Potch, upon seeing a man with a beard, spit into his left palm and jam his right fist into it, pronouncing the proper abracadabra that, we all knew, exorcised (or, at least, slowed up) the faceless demons who lurk around any familiar with a beard.

We never invited Potch to undergo the mysterious rites, performed in a cellar, of initiation into our secret club, whose sole function was to perform mysterious rites of initiation in a cellar. And whenever our volcanoes of adoration erupted, and we extolled the relative splendors of the Rover Boys or Tom Swift, the intrepid Nick Carter or the peerless Frank Merriwell, Potch merely made muffled, gargling sounds and drifted away. He never read anything, so far as we knew; and we (well, two of us anyway) were absolutely fanatical, insatiable addicts of print.

The only noteworthy thing about Potch was that he always seemed to have spending money, and more of it than any of the rest of us. I once saw him take a whole two-dollar bill out of his pocket. To me, whose allowance was five cents a week, this bordered on the supernatural.

We used to talk about Potch in front of the corner delicatessen, marveling over his readiness to buy a ten-cent bologna sandwich or a root beer, a Hershey bar or piece of halvah whenever he felt like it. And we came to the only conclusion possible to explain so staggering "a stash of mazuma" (that's the way men of the world talked on my block): Potch had not inherited a fortune, since his mother was still a laundress and his father had long since been buried by a fraternal order; clearly, Potch worked at some secret, lucrative part-time job and was well along the road to becoming a millionaire.

But what sort of a job could a callow schoolboy hold? We swiftly deduced that a job never mentioned, never even hinted at, was probably shady, possibly unlawful, perhaps even sinful. We tried not to show our envy. We failed. Potch came to enjoy an unvoiced prestige among us.

Once, Potch bought chocolate phosphates for five of us, and "Stomach" Ginsberg, who on a penny bet would eat matches, gravel, pencils, paper, etc., laughed, "Hey, Potch, watchado—robba bank or sumpin?"

Potch paused, blinked, and tossed noncommittal "Khoo!s" and "Flggh!s" around his throat.

"Well, Jesse James, didja?"

At that moment, Potch must have realized the aura he had acquired in the minds of his peers; a glow spread beneath his pastiness, like watercolors fanning out from a blot, and he grinned and brought out, "Pfrr . . . khnug . . . woonchoo liketa know!"

It was the first time I had seen him approximate a smile, and I saw that he was missing a tooth on each side of his mouth. He looked like a dog—not a good dog, a mutt. But there was all that money. . . .

Once, Potch and I were alone, spinning our tops one flaming afternoon in July, moving like sleepwalkers, hearing our sweat splat on the burning sidewalk, and I said, "Hey, Potch, no fooling—where do you get all your dough?"

He produced various facial twitches, made several rabbity squeaks, then gargled: "Hanh . . . Presents! Presents fmy birt'day!"

"Oh," I said. "When was your birthday?"

"Khroo . . . Skng . . . Las' March. . . . But you gotta remember I got fordy—fifdy uncles 'n' aunts! An' some of 'em live way far t'hellangone an' back, so it takes time, you have to figure, for alla my presents t'get here."

I did not know what to think, so I donned the liberating wings of fantasy. I thought of my book heroes, especially the great Jimmy Dale, a socialite by day, a Robin Hood at night, who outwitted the finest police brains of the time. Jimmy Dale was a one-man Corrector of Injustice, self-appointed Punisher of Greed and Chicanery, a noble, saintly Redresser of life's inequities, the law's blindness, the helplessness of innocents. Jimmy Dale wore an opera cape and mask as he made his midnight rounds, concealing his ropes and "burgalizing" equipment beneath the voluminous carapace. Ah, Jimmy Dale: his wit, his agility, his intrepid courage and blazing virtue—what more could you ask in an idol?

But Potch? Holy macaroni! Jimmy Dale was as handsome as Apollo, and Potch was a dish of oatmeal. Jimmy Dale was as courageous as Ajax, and Potch was "ascared" of mice. Jimmy Dale was as nonchalant as the Scarlet Pimpernel; Potch was only pimpled. Jimmy Dale wore tuxedos and was a paragon of sophistication; Potch, to put it in a nutshell, was a shmendrick and a klutz.

Still, I comforted myself with the uplifting thought that Potch was just beginning his career; if Fate only gave him a fair shake of the dice, a long and glorious career of crime might stretch beyond the springtime of his delinquency. In my mind, I even converted Potch's deficiencies into boons. Since he was so small and skinny, he could become a human fly. I could see him scaling walls, shinnying up pillars or down rainpipes, crawling across balconies, pulling himself up parapets, leaping with cat-footed sureness from rooftop to rooftop on moonless nights, forcing open skylights, windows, transoms, ventilators, jimmying open doors, prying back iron bars, outwitting locks, chains, bolts, burglar alarms—all without leaving so much as the scratch of a fingernail to betray him—to reach at last the baronial bedroom of Throckmorton Spondulix, where Potch would glide to the safe secreted behind a Raphael Madonna, the safe in which the fabled Star of Samarkand reposed, and, with a knowing smile, breathing softly, without a vestige of his youthful Phtrr!s and Shlgg!s, would proceed to apply his genius to the tumblers, seducing them into revealing their magic numbers by the superhuman sensitivity of his fingers on the dial. . . . And then Potch—Potch?! The whole luminescent edifice collapsed. It was crazy. It was ludicrous. It was impossible. You might as well cast cross-eyed Ben Turpin in the role of Don Juan, or ZaSu Pitts as Juliet.

One afternoon, as I was stretched out on my bed reading *The Red-Headed Outfield*, I heard a soft tap-tap-tapping at my window. I rolled over. Potch was crouched on the porch like the Hunchback of Notre Dame, his face screwed up.

"Hey, boychik," he whispered hoarsely, be quiet no one should hear. ". . . Krrr . . . Flmm . . . I wanna ask a favor."

"C'min," I said.

"Tru da window?" he protested.

"Sure." I raised it.

"Na, na!" He shot nervous glances around. "How's about you c'mon out?" He signaled to me vigorously and snaked his way down the back stairs.

I climbed out of the window and followed him and sat down on the bottom step. He was standing over me now, looking down, unaccustomed to being taller, sniffling, then began to dance around in crazy circles, straining his neck and jerking his arms about in a new repertoire of tics. "So I had a birt'day yestiday!" he cried. "So my uncle and aunts and, boy, maybe one hunnerd tousand other relations from all over hellangone give me presents, see? So many presents you can't even count 'em up. So they're piled up in boxes an' I can't hardly squeeze in the goddam bedroom me and my brother use, it's so crowded. Yeh. Phrr. Nyaa . . . So I remember you got a bedroom. Alone. Right?" He kicked imaginary time bombs off the sidewalk. "So I figure—how about me bringin' over some boxes, and leave 'em in your closet, for maybe one, two weeks? Whaddaya say you hold somma dem boxes, huh?"

"Well," I said, "I guess so, but—what's in them?"

"Like I *told* you. Presents." He looked harassed and swallowed air and scratched at his neck. "Well, what's in all dem boxes is actually nuttin excep'—books."

I gulped. "Books?"

"Maybe two hunnerd. But I don't have no place for books an' I ain't gonna read 'em, for cryin' out loud, so we just pile 'em up in your closet, see, and . . . phtrr . . . krsh . . . you hold on to 'em, huh? Just till I take 'em away."

My heart was knocking a sizable hole in my ribs. The unbelievable vision of two hundred books resting in my closet made me delirious. "You'll leave them, Potch—I mean the books—in my closet?"

"Yeh. Glawk. Chrr. Why not?" He rubbed his fingers on his shirt like Jimmy Valentine. "Just till I take 'em away."

"Why'll you take 'em away?" I asked, already too greedy.

"To sell them. Jeeze! . . . Chlog . . . I take away maybe six, ten at a time . . . to peddle, thassall."

I tried to keep the hammering out of my voice. "While the books are in my closet—Potch, you wouldn't mind if I read them?"

"I have to sell dem books!" he cried, hopping up and down. "Prsh! Shkr! They have to be bran' new."

I shouted, "I can wrap a towel or something around each book I read! No one'll know anyone even opened up a book!"

"Pipe down," he moaned. "You wanna tell the whole goddam neighbahood?" He rolled his eyes and waggled his head in the throes of indecision. "Damn books have to be absolutely clean, I'm tellin' ya!"

"There won't even be a spot on 'em!" I exclaimed with a fervor never exceeded on Kedzie Avenue. "Not one crease—or scratch even. I promise! Ask any of the guys—"

"Don't you ask no guys! This is just between you and me only. . . . Thrrp . . . klup . . . strr . . . So, okay. I'll bring over da boxes. I'll come up the back, like just now, an' shove 'em t'rough ya window." He sniffed and snaffled, and one eye twitched and teared up. "Hey, your old lady! . . . While I'm deliverin' the merchandise, you better see your old lady is busy in the kitchen or someplace, huh? . . . Knrr . . . Flggh . . . Old ladies stick their nose in everyt'ing!"

"I'll say," I warmly agreed. "Don't worry. She's in the front."

And so, in five separate trips, Potch carried cartons (not boxes) up the back stairs, soft of tread, but puffing and whirring away. He wiggled the cartons through the window onto my bed, then crawled in and placed each one in my closet. The cartons were clean, brown, and sealed. "You open up a box real careful," he whined. "You read a book don't even touch it, for luvvah Mike!"

"Holy smoke!" I feigned disgust at his unconfidence. "I told you I'd be triple careful!"

"Hanh . . . krr . . ." He disappeared down the steps, a ferret.

The moment Potch left, I dashed into the kitchen, opened a drawer stealthily, found a knife, and scurried back to my room. Silently I closed the door. I moved a chair under the knob with care and, my throat crowded with unfamiliar muscles and organs (my tongue seemed to have fallen into my larynx), I carefully cut along the divided top of the first carton. Slowly, I bent the covers back. Eldorado blazed before my eyes: there, in pristine, shiny, illustrated jackets, were books—a row, a line, a jeweled chain of them.

I washed my hands and took a pillowcase and reverently removed all the books from the first carton, using the pillowcase as a glove, spreading the books out on my bed, devouring the titles with my eyes. I repeated this ritual with the second carton, and the third, and the fourth—until over a hundred precious volumes shone their glory on my bed and dresser and desk. I resavored the titles, one by one, feasting on the names that glittered such promise and invitation. I must have done this for half an hour, like a gourmet prolonging the pleasure of caviar, then carefully placed all but one of the golden trove back in their unworthy containers.

Then I wrapped a fresh towel around my first choice and turned to page one. I was instantly transported beyond time, beyond space, beyond matter, beyond immediate sensation of the immediate, glossless world, far out into the kingdom of print, the only kingdom in which the humblest traveler can find his throne.

The first line (can I ever forget it?) was: " 'Crack!' went the bat." These were scarcely surprising words, need I add; in those days, boys' fiction began with an instant hurdle over introductory nonsense to plunge you smack into the center of breathless crisis: " 'Pow!' came the sound of Bob Sterling's boot against the pigskin." " 'Look out!' shouted the frantic engineer." " 'On your marks . . . set . . . Bang!' rang out the gunshot." Not even "Call me Ishmael" could have sent the blood racing through my veins so.

For three days, in the morning before breakfast, in the afternoon after school, from after supper until my eyes ached with fatigue, I read. I read and read and read.

On the third day, I heard an ominous tapping on my bedroom window and saw Potch's furrowed brow and vapid eyes above the sill. He was kneeling on the back porch, and he held up a large brown paper bag. "Gimme eight," he croaked.

My heart sank. I went to the closet, hating him: I had read only six books. Undiscovered worlds were slipping forever beyond my ken. I got the six books I had read and tried to select two more with the least enticing titles, but Potch was *krechtzing* and "phtrr"ing his impatient gibberish. . . . I handed the books through the window, two by two, suppressing my bitterness. He stuffed them into his bag and tiptoed off, trailing his rumblings and snufflings.

I was not caught short again. I now realized that I had to consume the books in the closet faster than Potch, an enterprising salesman, could retrieve them. And I did. I read earlier in the morning, and at the breakfast table, and after school (racing the four long blocks home each day), and after supper, and farther into the night. To explain my temporary resignation from the primal horde, my non-availability for Skoosh or "pinners" (what New Yorkers call "stoop ball," in which you threw a rubber ball at a flight of stairs, aiming for an edge so that you might catch the returned ball on a fly, for five points, instead of on a bounce, for one), or the hectic exchange of baseball stars' pictures, or the aimless, exquisite, interminable dawdlings at which the genius boy shows such genius—I explained my staggering renunciation of these ecstasies to my pals with a mish-mash of excuses: I had to sweep out the cellar; a cousin was arriving from Moldavia; I had to stock up coal for the stove; my bike needed emergency readjustments on the "New Departure" brake that worked by reversing the thrust of the foot pedals. The coarse pleasures of sport and play were renounced; I entered the divine sanctuary of reading.

Behind my bedroom door, I soared away each day—on great adventurings with the insidious Dr. Fu Manchu and fearless Henry Ware, brave Dave Porter, gentle Penrod, priceless roly-poly Mark Tidd. I lived in a haze of unutterable bliss, made drunk by deeds of valor at Chickamauga and ninth-inning rallies (score 3–0, bases loaded, our hero at bat) and last-minute touchdowns for God and Yale. I chortled over the inspired pranks of the Prodigious Hickey and the Tennessee Shad, matchless Doc Macnooder and Hungry Smeed and Skippy Bedelle. I saw hand-to-hand combat against the shifty-eyed Boxers in Peking and ran down treacherous natives on the Amazon. I joined patrols against the howling Berbers screaming "Allah!" and trapped skulking guerrillas in the steaming Philippines. Down a most precious and magical cascade of words—by Zane Grey and Sax Rohmer, Booth Tarkington, Burt L. Standish, Joseph Altsheler, and their immortal peers—I was borne from intrigue in Singapore to vigils in Tangiers, from Apache massacres to high crime in Mayfair or small-town deviltries or long, cold nights on the Chisholm Trail. Was ever any boy more blessed?

But—a nasty, nagging unease gnawed at me in my paradise of print. Those two hundred volumes. . . . In our neighborhood, a boy might receive a book for his birthday. Maybe two books. Possibly three. But two hundred? . . . And if Potch's books were presents, I could not help wondering, why were they in sealed cartons? And why didn't Potch keep them somewhere in his own house? I had to confront the insistent, unremovable suspicion (how I tried not to) that Potch wanted to conceal the books from his parents. And why would anyone do that? . . . I twisted and turned and dodged to keep from colliding with the awful, dreadful, unevadable possibility that the books were (oh, dear God, don't let it be!) stolen.

For a month, I pushed that horrendous thought away with ever-new, ever-more-ingenious rationalizations. After all, I was not the one who had stolen two hundred volumes. And they had been pur-

loined without the slightest knowledge, aid, comfort, or encouragement from me. And they had come to me clearly represented by
their possessor as presents. And Potch surely had a right to lend,
store, or sell his own presents. . . . But . . . and still . . .

I was too young to know what being accessory to a crime (before
or after) meant; but some basic moral sensor kept bleeping that it
was wrong to reap the fruits of thievery; and wrong not to ask Potch,
at least, if he had stolen the books; and wrong not to consult someone—my father, my mother, our gym teacher, a policeman. . . .

I did none of these. To ask Potch himself, however subtly, was to
run the unbearable risk of learning that what I feared was true. And
if it was true, I could not read on so happily, however skillful the rationalizations to soothe however gullible a conscience. . . . And if I
asked Potch and it was true, Potch would bring no further loot to
my bedroom! . . . And if it was not true, he might demand that I return his entire cache at once, in proper retaliation for being so unworthy a beneficiary.

There was no answer, no solution, no sop, no deliverance. What,
then, did I do? I read faster.

I finished the last book not more than an hour before Potch came
for the last volumes of his booty. He put them in a suitcase. The suitcase was new. So was Potch's cap. So were his mittens. So was his fob.
So was the pearl-handled knife that fell out of his pocket . . .

If a book is worth reading, it is worth buying.

—JOHN RUSKIN

"Damn it! Wait your turn!"

A Good Time to Start
a Book Club

BY AL SILVERMAN

*The Book-of-the-Month Club, founded by Harry Scherman in 1926, is
the oldest, and still the largest, book club in America. In this excerpt
from the introduction to his 1986 book,* The Book of the Month: Sixty
Years of Books in American Life, *Al Silverman briefly recounts the history of the club through the mid-1980s.*

Harry Scherman picked a good time to start a book club. It was
1926 and Hemingway was posing for a photograph with Joyce,
Eliot, and Pound at Sylvia Beach's bookstore in Paris. Scott Fitzgerald was in Paris, too, with Zelda, waiting for *The Great Gatsby,* published the previous fall, to take off.

It seemed like a good year for everyone. Calvin Coolidge said so.
The stock market was booming, and nobody was poor, and only the
Lost Generation seemed disillusioned. But that was okay, too; for
the Lost Generation, as the critic John K. Hutchens said, it was "creative disillusionment."

Popular art flourished in 1926 and, in some cases, became high
art. Rudolph Valentino made his last film, *Son of the Sheik;* Buster
Keaton starred in *Battling Butler;* Lillian Gish played Hester Prynne
in a Swedish film of *The Scarlet Letter;* Ronald Colman was Beau
Geste and John Barrymore was Don Juan. Martha Graham did her

first dance solo at New York's 48th Street Theater, and Henry Moore's "draped figure" was undraped for the public.

It was a vital year for books, too, though not quite as exciting as 1925 had been. The literary flow that year must have persuaded Harry Scherman to undrape his creation. In addition to *Gatsby*, the list of novels published in the United States included Theodore Dreiser's *An American Tragedy*, John Dos Passos's *Manhattan Transfer*, Virginia Woolf's *Mrs. Dalloway*, the English translation of Thomas Mann's *Death in Venice*, Liam O'Flaherty's *The Informer*, and new novels by Ellen Glasgow and Willa Cather. Pound wrote, "It is after all a grrrreat litttttttterary period."

The *r*'s and *t*'s would have to be shortened for '26. The harvest was less rich and the poet Rilke had died. There were a lot of popular best-sellers, including Edna Ferber's *Show Boat* and Anita Loos's *Gentlemen Prefer Blondes*. There was also an array of nonfiction best-sellers that could be smuggled onto today's best-seller list and nobody would know the difference: *Diet and Health;* a new edition of *The Boston Cooking School Cookbook* by Fannie Farmer; *Why We Behave Like Human Beings; Auction Bridge Complete;* and *The Story of Philosophy* by Will Durant. In that first year of the Book-of-the-Month Club's life, only two books of the month were best-sellers: *Show Boat* and John Galsworthy's *The Silver Spoon*. Not chosen as books of the month but recommended to the charter members of the Club were *The Story of Philosophy* and *The Sun Also Rises*.

Durant and Hemingway, as no other authors, thread their way through the sixty-year history of the Book-of-the-Month Club. Today, new generations of members are buying *The Story of Philosophy* as their parents and maybe their grandparents did—more than 300,000 copies have been distributed to members since 1960 alone. And Durant's massive fifty-year undertaking, *The Story of Civilization,* accomplished in partnership with his wife, Ariel, is one of the most popular "premiums" of the Club. In book-club terminology, a premium is a book (in this case eleven books) that can be had for a minimal price by anyone willing to enroll in the club. Over the years a lot of people have been willing.

As for Hemingway, what began in 1926 remains alive in 1986. In February of 1926 Hemingway came to New York and switched publishers. Scribner's was willing to publish his novel *Torrents of Spring,* a parody of Sherwood Anderson; Hemingway's first publisher, Boni &

Liveright, had turned it down. In April of that year, just as the Book-of-the-Month Club was emitting its first infant squeals, Maxwell Perkins of Scribner's was reading the manuscript of *The Sun Also Rises.* And Hemingway, the man who, the French said, had "broken the language," was on his way. In 1986, Hemingway's last, unpublished novel, *The Garden of Eden,* became a "Book of the Month."

Over the years Hemingway's effect on the Club and its members has been pervasive in various ways. In 1985 Elmore Leonard, the Raymond Chandler of our time, spoke at the Detroit Institute of Art, a lecture sponsored by the Club for its members in the Detroit area. Leonard, who established his literary reputation late in life, told of BOMC books coming into the house, beginning in 1937. His older sister had joined the Club, and Leonard began to grab the books. He remembered reading *Out of Africa, The Yearling,* Carl Van Doren's *Benjamin Franklin, Captain Horatio Hornblower, Native Son, Darkness at Noon, The Moon Is Down*—all BOMC Selections—and, he told the audience that night, "the novel that would eventually get me started as a writer, *For Whom the Bell Tolls.*" Some years later he reread the novel, this time, he said, "to use the book as a text that would teach me how to write."

If the middle 1920s had a distinctiveness, beside prosperity, it was this: Entrepreneurs of the word had captured America. DeWitt and Lila Acheson Wallace founded the *Reader's Digest* in 1922; Henry Luce and Briton Hadden started *Time* in 1923; Henry Seidel Canby became founding editor of the *Saturday Review of Literature* in 1924; Harold Ross created *The New Yorker* in 1925. And, in 1926, Harry Scherman invented the book club.

Scherman was a word man. He always believed in the power of words to change people's lives. This was a belief that turned into a vision, a vision of an organization that could reach out to a vast and varied and interested and untapped reading public.

Born in 1887 and reared in Philadelphia, Scherman quit the Wharton School at the University of Pennsylvania to come to New York to work for an advertising agency. He had a bent for advertising, particularly mail-order. He was a brilliant copywriter and idea man.

In 1914 Scherman, with Charles and Albert Boni and Maxwell Sackheim, formed the Little Leather Library. These were miniature classics bound in sheepskin. Scherman persuaded the Whitman Candy Company to enclose a book in every one-pound box of chocolate. The venture was too successful—more than 40 million copies of these miniature classics were produced, and they exhausted the market. But Scherman was ready to move on. His next idea was to distribute the best new books being published—books that would be chosen by an independent and eminent board of literary experts, books that would be sent through the mail across the country. It would be the first such organization in the English-speaking world.

The first announcement appeared in the February 13, 1926, issue of *Publishers Weekly,* the book-publishing community's bible then as it is now. It described a plan "to solicit subscriptions to an A-Book-a-Month program." In April of that year "A Book a Month" was launched as "The Book-of-the-Month Club." The first book was *Lolly Willowes,* a first novel by an unknown British writer, Sylvia Townsend Warner.

It was not by accident that the original board of judges should choose a new author rather than a surefire name as the Club's first Selection. As Scherman wrote years later, the Club has "provided that swift accumulation of renown which is the most valuable support and encouragement a working writer can have." The Cinderella example of Scherman's swift accumulation of renown came in 1936.

Margaret Mitchell was a writer none of the Club's judges had ever heard of. When *Gone with the Wind* came to them for discussion, the debate was lively. There were some doubts about the characterization and the quality of the writing. One judge admitted that it was "a page turner," but he wasn't sure if other readers would like it well enough to turn the pages. In the end the board felt that the book would do. The Club released *Gone with the Wind* just before its publication. Still little known, it received a polite but underwhelming reception from members. But becoming the book of the month did something for the book and the author. The following letter from Margaret Mitchell to Harry Scherman, dated June 20, 1936, ten days before publication date, explains what it meant to the author.

Atlanta, Ga. June 20, 1936 Dear Mr. Scherman;
    Thank you so much for your letter. I was very glad to get it, not only because of the flattering sentiments you expressed but because I have been wanting to write to the Book of the Month Club and did not know who to address. I wanted to thank the Ed-

itorial Board from the bottom of my heart for selecting my book. It was quite the most exciting and unexpected thing that ever happened to me, so exciting and unexpected that I did not believe it true and told no one for three days (my husband was out of town at the time and I waited for his return to discuss the matter). Then I cagily told a friend on the *Atlanta Journal* that Mr. Brett, Jr. of The Macmillan Company had evidently taken leave of his senses for he had written me the most remarkable letter and it did not seem possible that the Book of the Month Club had really picked me. Then my friend said that I was the So-and-soest fool she had ever heard of to know such news for three days and keep it from my own old newspaper and she rushed the news into print, accompanying it with the world's worst picture. And I quaked, thereafter, fearing there had been a mistake somewhere and that you all would denounce me as an imposter.

I had had the manuscript knocking around the house for so many years, never even trying to sell it, so when Mr. Latham bought it my excitement was naturally great. But when I heard that you all had selected it, it was too much to be borne and I went to bed and was ill, with an ice pack and large quantities of aspirin. And your letter, telling me that it was the unanimous choice, has made me so proud, that it has taken great strength of character not to go back to bed again! I thank you all, so very, very much. I have never had anything happen to me that was as nice.

I hope to come to New York sometime in the Autumn and I hope to meet and thank in person the members of the Board. Henry Seidel Canby's article about the book in the Bulletin was enough to turn a harder head than mine and Dorothy Canfield's review in the *Ladies Home Journal* was most flattering. I suppose I shall have to put my prejudices in my pocket and read the Russians, Tolstoi and Dostoyevsky, etc. And probably Thackeray and Jane Austen, too. Yes, I know it sounds illiterate of me but I never could read them. But when people are kind enough to mention them in the same breath with my book, I ought to be able to do more than duck my head and suck my thumb and make unintelligible sounds. Heaven knows, this "up-country" Georgia girl never expected to get in the same sentence with them!

Sincerely,
(signed)
Margaret Mitchell
(Mrs. John R. Marsh)
4 East 17th Street N. E.

The Scherman method worked from the beginning. By the time the Club turned twenty-five, in 1951, 100 million books had been sent into the nation's households. Scherman felt that less than 10 percent of that number would have made it into readers' hands if it hadn't been for his invention. But some critics worried about the standardizing effect that such a massive distribution of preselected books would have on America's reading habits. In his challenging essay "Masscult and Midcult," Dwight Macdonald criticized the Book-of-the-Month Club for what he felt was its tendency to water down and vulgarize high culture. On the other hand, Carl Van Doren said, "A good book is not made less good or less useful by being put promptly into the hands of many readers." Harry Scherman was a pragmatist, and a populist, when it come to reading. He understood that there would always be that gulf between Macdonald's High Culture and popular culture, but he also felt that the two sometimes merged and, anyway, that a bridge existed between the two and that people could walk back and forth as they chose. Which is what Book-of-the-Month Club members did then and do today.

"If you are to deal with or think about the American people en masse," Scherman wrote in 1966, "you can trust them as you trust yourself. You can trust their consuming curiosity about all the quirks and subtleties of human existence; you can trust their fascination with every colorful aspect of history; you can trust their immediate response to good humor and gaiety, but also to the most serious thought; you can trust their gracious open mindedness, forever seeking new light upon their troubled but wonderful world. Whoever may have good evidence about that world, and whatever it may be, here is proof that the thoughtful people of this country will give him the audience he deserves."

Harry Scherman died in 1969 at the age of eighty-two. Clifton Fadiman, the senior judge of the board at the time, remembered Scherman as full of "goodness and generosity." The publisher Bennett Cerf called Harry Scherman "the happiest man I know."

"Trust them as you trust yourself." That became the philosophy of the first editorial board assembled by Scherman. And it is the abiding watchword of the Club to this day. But what kind of audience deserved that trust? Scherman talked about "the thoughtful people." That was close to George Saintsbury's "general congregation of decently educated and intelligent people." Those standards fit the Scherman era, but since then the world has become more complicated, and more perilous. Today, Clifton Fadiman says, members are looking for books that will satisfy "the serious American interest in self-education. They want books that explain our terrifying age honestly." The newest member of the editorial board, Gloria Norris, opened it up even more. "I think one reason we've kept members for so long is that we respect their possibilities."

The Club has had eighteen judges in its sixty years. Five of them— Amy Loveman, Basil Davenport, Lucy Rosenthal, David Willis McCullough, and Gloria Norris—rose from the ranks of the Club's editorial staff. These wise and learned men and women were in the forefront of the search for books that would strike their hearts and would therefore be likely to pierce the hearts of the reading public.

But when the Club was founded, Harry Scherman felt that it was important to find literary figures with established reputations—for his first board. "You had to set up some kind of authority," he said, "so that the subscribers would feel that there was some reason for buying a group of books. We had to establish indispensable confidence with publishers and readers." Scherman chose well: Henry Seidel Canby, Dorothy Canfield Fisher, William Allen White, Heywood Broun, Christopher Morley. White was the editor of the *Emporia* (Kansas) *Gazette* and represented the values of middle America. The New York newspaper columnist Heywood Broun spoke for urban America. The witty and sophisticated novelist Christopher Morley looked for "what literature is most intended to be, entertainment, surprise, and delight."

But the two most influential figures, as you will note by their contributions in this volume, were chairman Canby and Miss Canfield. She was a woman of high moral values and determined taste. She was also the most conscientious reader on the first board. Robert Frost sums up her character in these pages, but it can be said that her standards were exacting. A novelist herself, she tended to focus on the accuracy of image, the unity of plot, the depth of characterization. She didn't like books that seemed "soft and arranged." She looked for books that exhibited "value, truth, and literary skill."

It was Canby, a Quaker, who shaped a board that acted on the Quaker system of concurrence—that is, the judges arrived at a sense of agreement about their enjoyment of a book or its importance. No concurrence, no Book of the Month. At least once, the spirit of concurrence worked against Canby. In his *American Memoir* he recalls holding out for John Steinbeck's *The Grapes of Wrath*. Alas, he couldn't get any of his colleagues to concur. More recently, in 1985, John K. Hutchens, a member of the board since 1964, a loving and gentle man with a hard-rock Montana integrity and a deep sense of balance in his judgment of books, lost his heart to a novel called *Heart of the Country* by Greg Matthews. It was about a half-breed, hunchbacked buffalo hunter, and Hutchens called it "one of the best books on the old West I've ever read." Another judge, David W. Mc-Cullough, was almost as enthusiastic. He mentioned its faults but said, "I think it's a great, strong book." But two of the other judges felt just as passionately the other way. No concurrence. The book became an Alternate, not a Selection.

Even through this debate, however, the spirit of concurrence prevailed. Clifton Fadiman once explained the process. "In all the time I have been with the Club I have never heard a judge defend himself, only the book in question. Because we know that the book and author under discussion are more important, for the moment, than our prejudices, oddities, life-slants."

Harry Scherman was always proud of the system he had worked out for selecting books. But he remembered one book that got through the net—*The Caine Mutiny*—"because our first reader's reaction happened to coincide with the original unexcitement on the part of the publisher." He also recalled how *Darkness at Noon*, another book that arrived without the publisher's "excitement," was discovered by its first reader at the Club and passed on to the judges, who made it a Selection. Over the years, inevitably, worthy books were missed, some that were to become classics. *Man's Fate* didn't make it, nor did *Under the Volcano* or *All the King's Men,* though all of them received favorable reviews in the *News*. No Faulkner novel became a Book of the Month until his last book, a minor work called *The Reivers,* perhaps because one judge confessed that he always giggled when reading Faulkner. Yet many other books by little-known writers who became well known were taken, including Richard Wright's *Native Son* and *Black Boy,* Koestler's *Darkness at Noon,* Orwell's *Animal Farm* and *1984,* J. D. Salinger's *Catcher in the Rye,* and, more recently, Toni Morrison's *Song of Solomon* and John Irving's *The World According to Garp.*

Lest you think that books are picked by the Club when they become winners, you should know that manuscripts are submitted six months or more before publication. The Club's readers and judges don't have the benefit of hindsight. They must make their decision long before the fate of the book in the marketplace is known. Will the judges make the book a Selection? Will it become an Alternate? Will it be ignored? The readings, the reports, the debates, and the passion that a reader has for a book—these are all elements that go into the final decision. Incidentally, when we talk about "Selection," sometimes called "Main Selection," it is the Book of the Month, the book picked by the outside judges. An Alternate is a book that has been selected by the editorial readers who work inside.

In the early days, Selection was all. More than 50 percent of the members took the Selection. But they didn't have much choice because only one or two Alternates were offered along with the Selection. The last Selection to reach 50 percent acceptance was *Crusade in Europe* by Dwight D. Eisenhower. That was in 1948. Today the Club offers a dozen new Alternates in each issue of the *News,* along with the Selection and a backlist of 125 books, most of them quite recent. Club members, that family of intelligent book readers grown more intelligent and sophisticated in their reading tastes over the years, now make their choices from a rich variety of possibilities. So much for masscult.

When the original judges died or retired, they were replaced by others of similar stature. They included John P. Marquand, author of *The Late George Apley* and other novels about the Brahmins of Boston and its environs; John Mason Brown, the eminent drama critic of the *Saturday Review of Literature;* Paul Horgan, the novelist, critic, and historian of the West; and Gilbert Highet. Highet served from 1954 until his death in 1978. He was the most erudite of all the judges—a writer, critic, teacher, raconteur, classicist, translator, and radio commentator. He once began a lecture to his Columbia students by saying, "I was reading Toynbee this morning while shaving." He had a habit that annoyed some publishers: he would correct galleys of their books and send them back to be worked on. It was said that he could start, finish, and correct an entire galley while hanging on to a subway strap on his way home.

The current members of the board are Clifton Fadiman; John K. Hutchens; Wilfrid Sheed, the critic, novelist, essayist, baseball and cricket fan; Mordecai Richter, the Canadian novelist and saturnine humorist; and David Willis McCullough and Gloria Norris, both former editors of the Club and both writers. It is a harmonious group, still operating on the principle of concurrence.

Of all eighteen judges in the Club's history, none has had more impact than Clifton Fadiman. None has served longer. "Kip" is in his forty-second year as a judge. But it is not so much his years of service that count as how Fadiman has used those years. He is a man of high energy who looks years younger than his age. He acts even younger. He is a cultured man, one who loves books—though not uncritically—and who can't stand to be without a book to read. In his understated way he exerts a patriarchal influence on the board's deliberations. He is never without an opinion, but he is also an accomplished listener. He manages to see whatever point of view a colleague might put forth, not that he always agrees with it. His own pronunciamentos are voiced with a persuasive combination of wit, authority, and, if tactically necessary, self-deprecation. Once, discussing a novel of some soap-opera dimensions, Fadiman allowed that he rather liked the book. He excused himself with these words, "I'm by far the most sentimental of us and should be watched with suspicion." Here is a sample of other judgments pronounced by Fadiman at board meetings:

- On a book about Mount Everest: "I think we should take it because it's there."
- On a contemporary novel: "It has no center. What it has is a lot of wonderful periphery."
- On a volume of William Shirer's memoirs: "One should never reach the age of eighty because by then you realize your life is not worth a good goddamn."

Here Fadiman was making a judgment on himself as an octogenarian and not on his fellow octo, William Shirer. And of course it was a judgment at odds with the facts. For Fadiman's whole life has been one both of reflection and engagement, and of constant self-scrutiny. In 1983 he wrote a letter to Gloria Norris, who was then the Club's editor-in-chief, about the novel *The Name of the Rose:*

> Clearly, I admired the book enormously. But through pride I assumed that my admiration of it followed from my superior taste

and knowledge. I should know that at my age such superior taste and knowledge are shared by hundreds of thousands of my fellow Americans. The book is now a bestseller. I said, "This remarkable novel will sink without a trace." I also said, "It's the kind of book our culture will automatically reject." Unless we assume that the bestsellerdom merely reflects a kind of snobbery, we must conclude that while my judgment of the book was correct, my judgment of its appeal was ludicrously at fault. There is only one deadly sin and all the others follow from it: Pride.

Let every man, if possible, gather some good books under his roof, and obtain access for himself and family to some social library. Almost any luxury should be sacrificed to this.

—WILLIAM ELLERY CHANNING

Invasion of the
Book Envelopes

BY JOHN UPDIKE

*John Updike is the author of more than three dozen books, including
novels, short stories, poems, essays, criticism, children's stories, and a play.
In this short essay—which originally appeared in* The New Yorker *in
1981 and later in his 1983 book of essays and criticism,* Hugging the
Shore—*he paints a dire, if tongue-in-cheek, scenario of the obliteration
of the human race by book envelopes.*

Small puddles of gray fluff had been appearing for years on office
floors and in the vestibules of suburban homes, but no one paid attention. An occasional book reviewer or mail clerk showed up in
city-hospital out-patient clinics bearing the tiny double marks of
"staple stab" all over their thumbs, but it never made the newspapers. It was not until the iron-gray fluff was augmented by a ubiquitous snow of magnetized white plastic pellets and entire secretarial
staffs were incapacitated with digital cuts and sprained wrists suffered while wrestling with thread-reinforced strapping tape that the
full scope of the horror dawned upon the public—by which time the
plague was far advanced. The book envelopes and their deadly, drift-
ing spore were everywhere.

From what dying star had they been launched into space, and
upon what deserted patch of our planet had they made their unwit-

nessed landing? Northern New Jersey seemed the best guess. No one could remember when they had not existed, when books had been simply wrapped in brown paper and string, like everything else. At first, the envelopes had parted with their contents easily, releasing what seemed a negligible spattering of dull-colored matter as innocuous as the woolly beige corymbs maple trees drop in the spring. Then their staples seemed to lengthen and to become baroquely tenacious in shape, so that only a prolonged struggle pried open the limp brown pods, with a proportionately lavish dissemination of the ominous fluff. People began to notice the book envelopes piling up in corners of their basements and garages, with no recollection of who had put them there. The post offices, in a move whose dire significance was grasped only in vain retrospect, began to sell the things—disarmingly named "mailers," after a civic-minded, prize-winning author of the era—over the counter, in every precinct and hamlet. The infiltration had spread to the top levels of government and soon contaminated the entire globe.

Distracted by tension abroad and economic malaise at home, the nation did not concern itself with the strangely swelling bales being unloaded by "banana boats" in New Orleans and Galveston and "macadamia freighters" along the vulnerable, already fad-ridden West Coast. A mutant third species of book envelope entered from Japan, lined with a plastic bubble-paper that children in their innocence loved to pop, releasing odorless vapors into the atmosphere. Paid experts pooh-poohed any correlation between bubble-paper and acid rain. Canada, long regarded by the anti-envelopment underground as a refuge, ceased to be so when André Jiffy was elected prime minister and ordered the border stapled shut.

Within the tormented maze of the U.S. Postal Service regulations was born the rumor that strapping tape had become obligatory, rendering each envelope impervious to mechanical attack. All fourth-class mail, the lifeblood of an educated citizenry, now traveled back and forth unopenable. Drifts of fluff reached knee-high into the Rockies. The president and his joint security chiefs had themselves shipped to Bimini via UPS, and over the radio rustling, muffled spokesthings declared the country to be sixty percent recycled fibers and entirely under the rule of a tan, pre-stamped junta, in a variety of handy sizes.

Somewhere near the dotted Mason-Dixon Line, the last human voice expired, crying, "Pull here!"

*Let your bookcases and your shelves be your
gardens and your pleasure-grounds. Pluck the
fruit that grows therein, gather the roses, the
spices, and the myrrh. If your soul be satiate and
weary, change from garden to garden, from
furrow to furrow, from sight to sight. Then will
your desire renew itself and your soul be
satisfied with delight.*

—JUDAH IBN TIBBON

"It's $37.50 until December 31. Thereafter $50.00,
and to some people we might not sell it at any price."

My Friends

BY PETRARCH

I have friends, whose society is extremely agreeable to me: they are of all ages, and of every country. They have distinguished themselves both in the cabinet and in the field, and obtained high honors for their knowledge of the sciences. It is easy to gain access to them; for they are always at my service, and I admit them to my company, and dismiss them from it, whenever I please. They are never troublesome, but immediately answer every question I ask them. Some relate to me the events of past ages, while others reveal to me the secrets of nature. Some, by their vivacity, drive away my cares and exhilarate my spirits, while others give fortitude to my mind, and teach me the important lesson how to restrain my desires, and to depend wholly on myself. They open to me, in short, the various avenues of all the arts and sciences, and upon their information I safely rely, in all emergencies. In return for all these services, they only ask me to accommodate them with a convenient chamber in some corner of my humble habitation, where they may repose in peace: for these friends are more delighted by the tranquillity of retirement, than by the tumults of society.

Norman Mailer's
Ten Favorite American Novels

1. *U.S.A.*, John Dos Passos
2. *The Adventures of Huckleberry Finn*, Mark Twain
3. *Look Homeward, Angel*, Thomas Wolfe
4. *The Grapes of Wrath*, John Steinbeck
5. *Studs Lonigan*, James T. Farrell
6. *The Great Gatsby*, F. Scott Fitzgerald
7. *The Sun Also Rises*, Ernest Hemingway
8. *Appointment in Samarra*, John O'Hara
9. *The Postman Always Rings Twice*, James M. Cain
10. *Moby-Dick*, Herman Melville

W. Somerset Maugham's Ten Greatest Novels

In 1948 the British novelist wrote Great Novelists and Their Novels, *which contained the following list of what he considered the ten greatest novels ever written. He acknowledged in the introductory essay that "to talk of the ten best novels in the world is to talk nonsense," but he went on to analyze what made these novels great in a short essay that became required reading for any would-be novelist. It is difficult to believe that anyone embarking on reading these ten books would not come out of the experience a changed person.*

1. *Tom Jones,* Henry Fielding
2. *Pride and Prejudice,* Jane Austen
3. *The Red and the Black,* Stendhal
4. *Old Man Goriot,* Honoré de Balzac
5. *David Copperfield,* Charles Dickens
6. *Wuthering Heights,* Emily Brontë
7. *Madame Bovary,* Gustave Flaubert
8. *Moby-Dick,* Herman Melville
9. *War and Peace,* Leo Tolstoy
10. *The Brothers Karamazov,* Fyodor Dostoevsky

The Bible Through the Ages

BY BEN D. ZEVIN

Ben Zevin was the president of World Publishing, a fine general-interest publisher and the largest Bible publishing house in the world. He was a lifelong student of the history of the Bible and Bible publishing. This talk was given in 1955 to the Rowfant Club, Cleveland's celebrated bibliophilic society, and included in William Targ's fine 1955 collection, Bouillabaisse for Bibliophiles.

Until quite recently, as time is measured, it was dangerous to have anything at all to do with publishing the Bible. Heresy might lurk in the phrasing of a marginal gloss or, worse, in a typographical error inadvertently left uncorrected in the published book. The biographies of those connected with the early history of the English Bible—printers, translators, sponsors—are rare which do not end suddenly in martyrdom at the stake or tell of long periods spent in the prisons of the Lancastrian or Tudor kings. John Wycliffe, first of the giants among the translators of the Bible into English, did manage to die of natural illness, suffering a fatal stroke in his sixties; but in 1428 his bones were dug from the consecrated ground in which they had lain for nearly half a century and were burned and scattered on the waters of the river Swift. In the less vindictive era of the Stuarts two centuries later, the printers who permitted an edition of the

Bible to pass through their hands with Psalm xiv beginning "The fool hath said in his heart there is a God" got off merely with having the entire edition confiscated and the imposition of a fine of £3,000, no mean sum even today.

But time works great changes. Long gone are the surreptitious days when a Tyndale must flee from England to Hamburg, from Hamburg to Cologne, from Cologne to Worms with his translation or with a few salvaged printed sheets, when plans must be made to hide the printed edition in sacks of grain to be smuggled across the Channel. The accent in supervision of the press has shifted from orthodoxy in religion to orthodoxy in morals (and, in some parts of the world, in politics), and the Bible today has greater relative freedom of circulation than it has ever known. More Bibles are in circulation now than at any previous time, and as always there are never enough.

The compulsion to circulate ever more and finer Bibles is irresistible. Everyone who deals with the Bible understands that. The minister in the pulpit, the theologian in his study, the professor in the seminary—they grasp it instantly. So do those whose contribution in widening the influence of the Bible is on a different plane—the printer at the case, the colporteur, the bookseller, the bibliophile, the publisher. The Bible gives rise to a universal hunger in those who work with it: to improve it, to make it finer, to bring the physical thing—word, phrase, book itself—nearer to its spiritual content.

That feeling—an emotion comparable to the one motivating the great artists, the composers, the creators in any field—springs from the Bible itself. The painter visualizing a Madonna, the sculptor liberating from a block of stone one of the heroic Old Testament figures, the musician seeking sweet melody and new harmony to match the words of a psalm—these are moved to creation by realization of the Bible's own nature. They draw, and have drawn, inspiration from the Bible, a book that has been made known to them more intimately by printing. The process is a continuing one. It works deeply on all who read the Bible, and, perhaps, most deeply on those whose vocation stems directly from the Bible. It is no accident, no wonder, that the Bible stands as the first printed book, the best printed book, the most printed book. It is not chance that makes the Bible the book most translated, most sold, most given away. No outward pressure has been necessary in making it the most widely read and most often read book.

Historians and scholars are in agreement that the Bible has saved the Jews from extinction or assimilation. The Jews had been a long time writing it. More than five hundred years went into the fashioning of Genesis. The Prophets were active in the centuries when the kingdoms of Israel and Judah flourished. In the eighth and seventh centuries B.C., their work culminated in the stirring messages immortalized in the books of the greatest of them. These men left their distinctive mark in the Bible, a way of thought and expression that has influenced philosophers and writers ever since. As their greatest achievement, they established the monotheistic definition which distinguished first Judaism, then Christianity. Amos, Hosea, Isaiah—these and their like conceived the oneness of God and His perfection. From them came the moral ideas that make the Bible supreme among the works guiding man's conduct.

The writing of the Old Testament took perhaps a thousand years. Writing the New Testament took about fifty years, principally in the last half of the first century A.D. All came down through the years in Greek, for in the third century B.C. a group of Jewish scholars at Alexandria, seventy-two according to tradition, had translated the Old Testament into Greek. This version, known as the Septuagint, formed the base from which all later versions of the Christian Bible derived. The name Bible, itself, originally meaning in Greek "the books, the writings," came to mean "the Book, the Scriptures."

The authorship of the New Testament is better defined than that of the Old Testament. The authors of the latter were anonymous, writing for no other reason than to preserve the traditions and the way of life of a people proud in its knowledge. Authorship was not definitely ascribed. It therefore came about that the portions of the Law were attributed to Moses, the Psalms to David, the Proverbs to Solomon, all heroes of national tradition. But more definitely, rather than less, the authorship of much in the New Testament is ascribed to Paul. So, too, with the Gospels of Matthew, Mark, Luke, and John, though biblical scholars are not as sure of all portions of these books as they are of the Pauline Epistles. However, the writers and rewriters are fairly well recognized by biblical historians; the anonymity of Old Testament writings is not characteristic of the New Testament.

Until some three hundred years after the birth of Christ, there was no assurance that both Testaments would be included in the Bible. The moot point was the Old Testament emphasis on monotheism.

Origen, a Christian leader of the third century, more than any other individual swung the weight of Christian opinion toward maintenance of the monotheism conceived by the writers of the Old Testament. Thereafter no thought of abandoning it arose.

In the second half of the fourth century, there began the first authoritative translation of the Bible into a language other than Hebrew and Greek. This was the Latin translation by Jerome. There had been an earlier anonymous translation into Latin, but with much variation among its copies. Jerome's was a masterwork, commissioned by Pope Damasus I, whose secretary he had been. It took fifteen years before the translation was completed in 405. It became known as the Vulgate, though apparently this name was not applied to it until the thirteenth century, when Roger Bacon used the term. Jerome was a thorough scholar who took the hard way to achievement. For his translation of the Old Testament he went to Hebrew, the language from which the Septuagint had derived.

The Vulgate met a mixed reception. Some of Jerome's scholarly contemporaries did not like his rendering of certain passages. They were all for literality; he had proceeded in the path deemed best by subsequent translators, hewing to the meaning rather than the literal translation. Jerome was long dead before the Vulgate was in general favor, which did not come for the better part of two centuries. But once acceptance came, it was effective; for a thousand years the Vulgate was the one Bible available to the peoples of Western Europe.

They came to revere it, but one could hardly say they knew it. Under the circumstances then existing, that was impossible. Every copy of the Bible had literally to be copied by hand. Beautiful copies were made, but production in quantity was simply not possible. Though copying, illuminating, and other duties involved in the preparation of manuscript copies became the lifework of many people connected with monasteries and universities, supply never could catch up with need. Nevertheless, the admiration, or, better, adoration, of the Bible caused its contents to become more or less familiar; in all lands, peoples became acquainted in their own language with parts of the Bible if not the whole. In England, Caedmon, Cynewulf, Bede, Alfred, Aelfric, and Orm stand out as translators or paraphrasers of parts of the Bible; later the miracle and mystery plays were to bring alive the biblical stories and characters in the colloquial language of the people.

What each nation needed was a scholar to make a complete translation, a scholar like Jerome. But only from the Church and through Church training could such scholars come, and as the Church grew powerful, the leaders at Rome were less inclined to favor uninstructed reading of the Bible. In consequence, popular yearning for the Bible was met along other avenues, notably by means of the arts, especially the drama. These were to serve until the spread of printing from movable type coincided with the Reformation at the end of the fifteenth century and the beginning of the sixteenth.

Prior to Gutenberg's invention, there had been no great progress made in bringing the Bible into English, in spite of considerable efforts. The ninth-century endeavors in Anglo-Saxon were partial and incomplete. John Wycliffe in the fourteenth century had greater success. He was more than a scholar; he was, as has been said of him, an ecclesiastical statesman. A philosopher and theologian, he was an acknowledged leader among his contemporaries at Oxford. In the sense in which the word was used in the Reformation, Wycliffe was a reformer; his ideas were very much those preached by John Huss, who, thirty years after Wycliffe's death, died at the stake in Prague for heresy. Wycliffe, perhaps, was fortunate in being among the first of the translators.

Some at least of the Wycliffe English translation of the Bible was done by an aide, Nicholas Hereford, and four years after Wycliffe's death the whole work was revised by another, probably John Purvey, who also had been his aide. The Wycliffe Bible was for a hundred years the only English translation. The reform movement of which Wycliffe was the forerunner spread throughout England in the years that followed his death. And despite the forcible suppression of the Lollards, as the followers of the movement were called, well over 150 manuscripts of Wycliffe's Bible still survive.

The half century from 1450 to 1500 saw the invention and spread of printing from movable type. It was in this period also that the Byzantine empire fell, and with the taking of Constantinople in 1453 there came into Western Europe a flood of scholars from the East, men versed in Hebrew and Greek, carrying with them manuscripts invaluable to biblical scholarship. Students in Western Europe suddenly were granted the vision of new horizons, and there arose the scholarly aspect of that revolution in outlook we call the

Renaissance, the "New Learning" that came to digest more fully the meat on which the Scholastics had chewed so long—and so vainly.

Properly enough, the first "book" resulting from the invention of printing was a Bible, the forty-two-line edition of the Vulgate prepared by Johann Gutenberg at Mainz sometime before 1456. There may perhaps have been as many as three hundred copies printed of this masterpiece, esteemed by admirers of the printed word as the most beautiful book ever printed, a work in which printing seems to spring fully perfected from nothingness in one magnificent leap.* Forty-six copies only have survived of the two-column folio, only twenty-one of them complete, some on vellum, some on paper; thirteen are in the United States, and of them only five are perfect. The story of the resurrection of the Gutenberg Bible, after François Guillaume de Bure recognized its importance when he came upon a copy in 1763 in the Mazarin library, is however not a part of the history of the Bible in English and must be passed over here.

But Gutenberg's Bible was the first, and others followed. During the half century from 1450 to 1500, some 130 separate editions were published. In 1466 the first Bible in a modern tongue, German, was issued; before the turn of the century the Hebrew Bible had been printed; in 1516 the Greek New Testament of Erasmus was issued at Basle. A new era was in sight, not only for scholars, but for all the people as well.

The William Tyndale Bible, the basis of today's Bible in the English language, cost its producer his life. The Reformation was in full swing, but the new orientation was still too new to save Tyndale. Tyndale was publicly executed as a heretic, as Huss had been a century earlier.

Like Wycliffe, Tyndale was a scholar, though in no sense as renowned a figure. Whereas Wycliffe had many other interests, Tyndale had virtually a single objective, and that was to put the Bible within popular reach. In his hopeful days, talking to a theologian, he said: "If God spare my life, ere many years I will cause a boy that driveth the plough shall know more of the scripture than thou dost."

---

*The Constance Missal has some support among students as an earlier book than the Gutenberg Bible. The claim is based primarily on the crudity, and at the same time the similarity, of the typography of the Missal as compared with the Gutenberg Bible, it being argued that the forty-two-line Bible is too fine a production to be the very first book and that other books must have preceded it. One of three known copies of the Missal is now owned by the Pierpont Morgan Library of New York.

Tyndale's encouragement came only from layfolk; in clerical and official circles he was discouraged. Finally he realized that if he were to bring out a Bible for all to read, he could not do it in England. He went to Germany, where, after completing his translation of the New Testament and being forced to move hurriedly with what sheets had already been printed, he published a scholarly if tendentious New Testament in 1526. To this he added the Pentateuch in 1530 and the Book of Jonah in 1531, issuing his final revision of the text in 1535. The influence of Tyndale's Bible has been immeasurable. It has been said that 80 percent of the language of our English Bible is still Tyndale's.

Tyndale was doubly unfortunate; not only had he opposed the leading ecclesiastics, but he had offended Henry VIII, and that probably was why the king let events take their course. Arrested in Belgium, Tyndale was condemned as a heretic, strangled, and burned at the stake. At his martyrdom, Tyndale prayed, "Lord, open the King of England's eyes."

While he was in prison prior to his execution, Tyndale became a Hebrew scholar. But the Old Testament was not in his thoughts when he first decided upon translating the Bible; his whole zeal was in providing his fellow countrymen with an English version of the New Testament. His main sources were the Greek text by Erasmus and Martin Luther's German translation, which itself stemmed from Erasmus. These two versions preceded Tyndale's by only a few years, Erasmus's in 1516, Luther's in 1522.

Erasmus was near the end of his days when he published his text, not only in Greek but also (in 1519) a translation in Latin. Doubtless Erasmus looms so large in biblical history because he was the great scholar and teacher of the era. His materials were meager. Available to him were only a few Greek manuscripts, none earlier than the tenth century. Historians write that the one he most relied upon was of about the fifteenth century, virtually in his own era. It seems reasonable to say that Tyndale could do what he did only because Erasmus had done what he did.

Had Tyndale been slightly more the politician, or sycophant, he might have saved his life and yet realized his zealously pursued objective to put an English-language Bible within easy reach of whoever wanted to read it. Indeed, within a year after Tyndale was executed, the same Henry VIII who had not lifted a finger in Tyndale's behalf gave his approval to a Tyndale-like venture.

Henry had renounced his allegiance to the papacy, and in 1535 a parliamentary act declared him the supreme head of the Church of England. The unfavorable view by Rome of uninstructed Bible reading no longer was consequential to the British ruler. But he had to be approached sensibly. Tyndale had been so confident of the rectitude of his course that he did not bother to be diplomatic.

Miles Coverdale was a different sort of person. He employed tact to serve his ends. Coverdale, an Austin friar, was a contemporary of Tyndale. They had been together as students at Cambridge, advanced within their respective priestly fields at comparable speeds, are said even to have worked briefly together on Tyndale's Bible. While Tyndale was in prison, Coverdale began to work on a translation of his own. He was neither as scholarly as Tyndale nor as hard a worker. He made a translation of the entire Bible without much effort, making use of Tyndale's work, and Luther's, along with the Vulgate and the Swiss-German Bible of Zwingli, and with little attempt to go back to original sources. His own contribution was a greater felicity of expression.

That Coverdale won success instead of death may be attributed to two factors: the reform climate had come to England, and Coverdale smoothed a path for himself with flattery. He dedicated his translation to King Henry VIII and "his dearest just wyfe, and most vertuous Pryncesse, Queen Anne." Coverdale's Bible has the distinction of being the first complete Bible to be printed in English and, in the edition of 1537, the first to be printed in England, the 1535 printing being either from Zurich or Marburg.

There ensued now a veritable flood of editions. Coverdale's Bible, despite his diplomacy, had not received the king's authorization. But the popularity of Tyndale's work made it apparent to both king and clergy that, in some form at least, an official Bible needed to be licensed. So, in 1537, there appeared, by "the Kinge's most gracyous lycence," what is known as Matthew's Bible. Thomas Matthew was the pseudonym of John Rogers, who had been an associate of Tyndale and who, seemingly, was Tyndale's literary executor. For Matthew's Bible included new translations, undoubtedly by Tyndale, of the Old Testament books from Joshua through Chronicles in addition to Tyndale's Pentateuch and New Testament and Coverdale's Ezra to Malachi and Revelations. Almost baldly, the work of the executed scholar became the accepted version. In 1539, Richard Taverner's revision of Matthew's Bible was issued; but the objections to Matthew's version which had led to the revision were not fully answered, and in the same year Coverdale produced what came to be known as the Great Bible. Essentially a combination of Coverdale's earlier work and Tyndale's version, this Bible, sponsored by Thomas Cromwell and then by Archbishop Cranmer, was authorized by the king to be read in churches. Thus, three years after Tyndale was martyred, the essence of his work had the accolade of the very men who were responsible for his execution.

The Great Bible went into another edition within a year, issuing in 1540. The revision was popularly called Cranmer's Bible, the name deriving from a long introduction written by the archbishop. That was the last biblical version undertaken by Coverdale at home. He rose high in the Church of England but fell from royal grace, and from freedom, when the Roman Catholic Queen Mary came to the throne in 1553. Coverdale was imprisoned, released after a year, and then fled to Geneva. There he, William Whittingham, John Calvin, John Knox, and others produced by 1560 what came to be known as the Geneva Bible.

The Geneva Bible was for many years, until the King James Bible attained its own popularity, the popular version. It was the first English Bible to be printed in roman type, the first to use italics for those words interpolated into the text for smoother English reading, the first to divide chapters into verses. Its language was accurate and readable, and it rapidly won a wider reading than any of its predecessors. The Bible of the Nonconformists, the Geneva Bible—known also as the "Breeches Bible" (so called from the translation of Genesis 3:7, "They sewed fig leaves together and made themselves breeches")—was the Bible brought to America by the settlers of Massachusetts and Virginia. It was reprinted nearly two hundred times by 1644, by which year the King James Version had taken full hold.

Though the Geneva Bible was the preferred version until the King James Version came out early in the seventeenth century, it had some successors prior to the 1611 translation, principally the Bishops' Bible, a revision of the Great Bible under Archbishop Parker's direction, and the Douay Bible.

The latter, the Roman Catholic translation, was out of the main current of English Bible translation, though it had a definite influence on the translators of the King James Version. Translated by members of the Catholic College, the New Testament was issued in 1582 at Rheims, the Old Testament in 1609–1610 at Douay.

For centuries the Latin Vulgate had been the only text available to the Roman Catholic clergy, who frequently stumbled when they had to render English translations during their sermons. The ancient dislike of putting the Scriptures into the "barbarous language" of everyday use still existed. But the Reformation had introduced a new factor. The Roman Catholic cause was suffering for lack of an English version of the Bible, and, conversely, the Protestant cause was gaining by having just that. Thus, the Douay Bible, a direct translation from the Vulgate, whose text had been established in the Clementine edition of 1592.

James I came to the English throne in 1603. Nearly a century had passed since Tyndale had begun his struggle to put an English version of the Bible into everyone's hands. At the price of his life, he had succeeded, succeeded so very well that, if at the turn of the seventeenth century there was a problem in Bible reading, it stemmed from a multiplicity of Bible versions, not from a paucity. More translations surely were not needed. The need seemed to be for agreement on one, for a standard English version.

Historians are not wholly agreed where the impulse came from that resulted in the King James Version. That a standard English Bible was needed was well recognized in England. The situation at the close of Elizabeth's reign and at the beginning of King James's was unsatisfactory because the two versions then in greatest use were, in effect, competitive. The Bishops' Bible, regarded as more or less authoritative, was used in the churches. The Geneva Bible was preferred by people for use in their homes.

Circumstances seemed to point to a revision. There even had been introduced in the Parliament during Elizabeth's time a measure described as "an act for the reducinage of diversities of Bibles now extant in the English tongue to one settled vulgar translated from the original." Not the change in English rulers, but the course of events and circumstances seemed to bring about a climate favorable for producing an official standard work. In 1604 King James called the Hampton Court Conference of churchmen to resolve High

Church and Low Church differences, and at this conference came action. To the suggestion that there be a new translation, King James commented that he had never seen a Bible well translated into English, and of all he deemed the Geneva Bible to be the worst.

The king's slur on the Geneva Bible, essentially the Puritan Bible, may not have been unwelcome, for its popularity among the laity had not been shared by the churchmen. In consequence, some time later the king appointed, so history relates, fifty-four "certain learned men" to proceed with the work, though records produce the names of only forty-seven. All on the list were renowned scholars, mostly from Oxford and Cambridge Universities, the dean of Westminster, Dr. Lancelot Andrewes, heading the list. Scholastic attainment was the main qualification of these men. They were not chosen for attitude or rank, apart from the rank of scholarly competence; High Church and Puritan leaders alike were selected. Militant Puritans, however, were not included.

Three years passed in organizing a beginning. The entire group of scholars was divided into six smaller groups. One from Westminster, headed by Dr. Andrewes, was made responsible for the translation of the Pentateuch and the rest of the Old Testament from Joshua to II Kings. A Cambridge group, led by Edward Lively, was made responsible for I Chronicles to Ecclesiastes; Dr. John Harding of Magdalene College headed an Oxford team assigned the major prophets, Lamentations, and the minor prophets; another from Cambridge, supervised by Dr. John Duport, worked on the Prayer of Manasses and the rest of the Apocrypha; another from Oxford, led by Dr. Thomas Ravis, was given the Four Gospels, the Acts of the Apostles, and the Apocalypse; another from Westminster, headed by the dean of Chester, Dr. William Barlow, took the rest of the New Testament.

The translators had guidance in the form of a set of fifteen specific rules, sometimes attributed to Bishop Bancroft. The translators were to use the Bishops' Bible as their principal guide and were to use the common rather than the Latin forms of proper names and the commoner meanings of words in general. However, the older forms were to be used for ecclesiastical words—church rather than the Puritan congregation—and there were to be no marginal notes except to clarify an unavoidable awkwardness in the translated text or to indicate a cross-reference. Special rules were laid down for cooperation among the translators; authority was apportioned within the groups;

bishops were advised to request suggestions from their clergy; a special group was established to decide on meanings where a word might be subject to several interpretations. As a modification of the rule giving precedence to the Bishops' Bible, the several existing English Bible versions were listed to which the translators could turn in instances where the preferred text was faulty. All in all, the rules were wisely drawn, providing a framework in which scholars could work without hobbling, overspecific restrictions. A final editing was done by Bishop Bilson of Winchester, and by Dr. Miles Smith, who wrote the Preface.

Begun in 1607, the work was completed in 1611. The editors had approached and accomplished their task with humility, as the Preface bore out: "We never thought . . . that we should need to make a new Translation, nor yet to make of a bad one a good one . . . but to make a good one better, or out of many good ones, one principal good one."

That prefatory statement accurately described the accomplishment. King James had voiced the recognized need when he called for a rewriting; he had appointed an exceptionally qualified editorial group, and they had done, as would be said nowadays, a good job. They disregarded the king's slur on the Geneva Bible, and what they found to be worthy of choice in it, they chose. Nor did they fail to be influenced by the Douay New Testament. They approached their task with a free, high mind, bent on making the best of the much that was available.

Expectations for success had been great, and the result was not disappointing. The King James Bible stands as the great monument of English prose. It was written in the period—Elizabethan still, though some discern in Jacobean English a mellowing of the raw youthfulness of the earlier decades—when the language was at the peak of its vitality, and in this translation the vigor of the language is evoked to the full in expressing thoughts for which it alone, in its flexibility, color, and cadence, is the capable tool. As a result, the influence of the King James Version can be felt strongly in the further history of English. The balanced rhythm of the short biblical verses, the use of Anglicism rather than Latinism when the choice among words arose, the shunning of obscurity in favor of clarity of meaning, the figured poetical phrasing, all can be traced in the great writers in English through the centuries that have followed.

More errors were discovered in printing than in translation. One not subsequently corrected was the use of "at" when "out" was meant in Matthew 23:24. Thus arose the oft wrongly employed "straining at a gnat." Almost 150 years were to pass before this fine biblical translation appeared without an excess of printer's errors. In the interim there were many editions, and most of them managed to win labels derived from the mistakes they contained. The very first printing of 1611 is known as the "He Bible," because of its use of "he" in Ruth 3:15; the second printing, the "She Bible," corrects this to read "and she went into the city." When, in 1631, twenty years after the first edition, the Seventh Commandment was affirmatively printed, reading "Thou shalt commit adultery," the edition promptly was named the "Wicked Bible." Comparable errors in other editions caused such appellations as the "Vinegar Bible," due to a printing error of Vinegar for Vineyard. This, a folio edition by John Baskett of Oxford, has been called "Baskett's Basket full of errors" because of its many typographical errors. Other similar slips of the printer's stick and proofreader's eyes have been memorialized in the "Leda Bible," in which there was used an initial letter showing Leda and the swan which had been intended for an edition of Ovid, the "Unrighteous Bible," which states "that the unrighteous shall inherit the kingdom of God," the "Wife-Hater's Bible," misprinting "wife" for "life" in Luke 14:26, and many more.

The immediate acclaim which greeted the King James Version was perhaps the main reason for its being thought of as having royal authorization, but this was not the fact. Nevertheless, it became known as the Authorized Version, and the title was never disputed. One of its predecessors, the Great Bible, had been authorized; another, the Bishops' Bible, contained the words "Authorised and appointed to be read in churches," but there was no mention of authorization on the title page of the 1611 publication. The phrase used was "Appointed to be read in Churches," and this was understood to mean that the Bible had been printed by the king's printer with the approval of the king and the bishops. Perhaps this is splitting hairs, but biblical historians make much of the fact that the King James Version, known over the centuries as the Authorized Version, never was formally authorized. Its superior merits won for it a position as high as authorization could have brought, and even higher than authorization could have won had the translation been less successful.

The best testimony to its success has been its vitality over the centuries. Many translations have been made in an attempt to supersede the King James Version, but none has supplanted it. During the greater part of the three centuries between 1611 when the King James Version appeared (the Revised Version came out in the late nineteenth century), and the mid–twentieth century when the controversial Revised Standard Version was issued, more than one hundred translations were published.

Within a half century of the issuing of the King James Bible in England, the book was printed in the American colonies—but not in English. In his missionary zeal, the Reverend John Eliot thought he could make better progress if he had a Bible that the Indians could understand. But the Algonquian Indians he worked among possessed no written language. So the Reverend Mr. Eliot learned their spoken language, established a symbology so that it could be reduced to print, and, with the help of a London printer and London machinery sent to New England to do Eliot's bidding, produced in 1661 the New Testament and in 1663 reissued it in combination with the Old Testament. This Indian Bible, printed at Cambridge, Massachusetts, was the first edition of the Scriptures in any language to be printed in what became, a little over a century later, the United States of America.

The Eliot Bible was not the first book printed here. The Bay Psalm Book, biblical in nature, preceded it by twenty-one years. But it was eighty years after Eliot's complete Bible was printed before a Bible in a modern European language appeared: in 1743 Christopher Saur of Germantown, Pennsylvania, reprinted Luther's German Bible in a quarto of 1,272 pages. And Saur's Bible antedates the first complete English Bible printed here by thirty-nine years, though a New Testament was printed by Robert Aitken of Philadelphia in 1777. It was Aitken also who printed the complete Bible of 1781–1782, a duodecimo of which fewer than forty known copies have survived. This Bible is distinguished as the only one ever authorized by Congress. Other Bibles followed: the first Catholic Bible in 1790, the first translation in English of the Septuagint in 1808, the bowdlerized Bible of Noah Webster in 1833, the only translation of the whole Bible by a woman—Julia E. Smith of Glastonbury, Connecticut—in 1876.

The time came when in the United States the printing of Bibles soared to figures which would have appeared fantastic to John Eliot, missionary to the Indian. More than ten million copies of the Bible in whole or part are now annually printed here and sent worldwide. Translations of both Old and New Testaments are now made in 184 languages; of the New Testament alone, in 227 languages. Nothing more significant could be stated regarding the Bible as an influence in the world.

Since the day of Gutenberg no era has been without an outstanding Bible printer. There is an irresistible compulsion to harmonize the inspired content with exceptional printing. Someone always bows to that compulsion, and it is reasonable to forecast that no future age will fail to produce a printer notable for his Bibles.

John Baskerville is a good example. He had been a clergyman's servant, exhibited a skill in penmanship which attracted his employer, became a teacher, then a businessman, made a fortune, and by the time he was fifty could afford to indulge in a hobby. That hobby was printing. He designed his own type, had presses built to special specifications, ordered paper to his own requirements, made his own ink. He did all this because he was a perfectionist; the best available was not good enough. He spent seven years in experimentation before publishing his first book. His greatest production was the folio Bible printed under the auspices of Cambridge University in 1763—it won the reputation of being one of the most beautiful printed books in the world. The edition was 1,250 copies, but barely half sold at the price of four guineas per copy, about twenty dollars, a fairly high price almost two hundred years ago. Baskerville sacrificed the remainder to a London bookseller.

Another exceptionally beautiful Bible, perhaps the most beautiful between Baskerville's of 1763 and its own date of 1903–1905, is the Doves Press Bible, which takes its name from the press which issued it. The partners in the Doves Press in England, T. S. Cobden-Sanderson and Emery Walker, were typographical artists and enthusiasts. As had printers before them, when they determined to produce something incomparable, they turned to the Bible.

In the 1930s there came the Oxford Lectern Bible, designed by Bruce Rogers, the most important figure in the field of fine printing in the United States. This superb edition of the King James Bible was specially commissioned after it became known that the librarian of King George V had reported his failure to find a lectern Bible suitable for the king to present to a church.

When the World Publishing Company, a leader in American Bible publishing, obeyed that recurrent printers' impulse, the most natural procedure was to seek the aid and guidance of Mr. Rogers. The type in the Bruce Rogers World Bible is Goudy Bible, the first use of a face named for the late Frederic Goudy, a great type designer. But Mr. Rogers gave it his own orientation, adapting it from Mr. Goudy's Newstyle, and with characteristic modesty named it for Goudy rather than for himself.

The Bible is timeless. Man's adoration of the Holy Scriptures is reflected in the works of artists of every age and in every field of endeavor. In all the arts, fine and applied, there has ever been a continual striving to interpret the Bible's inspiration through art and craftsmanship. In no field has this been more true than in printing. For in printing we deal not with an interpretation of the Bible—as in music, painting, and sculpture—but with the Bible itself, the very Word. In this work, the printer will ever strive to match in zeal the great masters from Gutenberg to Rogers, as he endeavors to give into mankind's hands the greatest of all inspirational works, in the most perfect form possible.

Aldus Manutius

BY WILLIAM DANA ORCUTT

It is fitting that this essay about one of the most important people in the history of the Book should be written by a man who was himself the author of some of the most beautiful books about books ever published.

The great figure in the whole history of the Book is Aldus Manutius, whose claim to fame comes not only from his work as a printer, but also from the profound effect of his scholarship upon the learning of the world, and his successful efforts to preserve the Greek classics to posterity. He was born at Bassiano, a small town in the Romagna, in 1447, his baptismal name being Teobaldo, from which came the abbreviated, Latinized form by which he will always be known. The Manucci were a noble Tuscan family.

The young Aldus, as a student, early showed a distinct tendency toward learning, and at Rome and Ferrara he distinguished himself, particularly in the classics. Having mastered Latin, he studied Greek under the famous Guarini of Turin. At Ferrara he formed a devoted friendship with a brilliant fellow student, Pico della Mirandola, prince of Carpi, from which association may be directly traced his later steps in life. It was through this friend's influence that, when Aldus completed his studies at Ferrara, he became tutor to the two young sons of Pico's sister at Carpi; it was from meeting at Carpi the accomplished Greek scholar Adramyttenos, a refugee from Constantinople, that the full beauty of the Greek language burst upon him; it was from his work in instructing his youthful charges in Greek from manuscript textbooks that he received his vision of what it would mean to the scholarship of the world if these same manuscript classics might be multiplied by means of the new invention of printing; it was through the sympathetic and financial assistance of the princess of Carpi that he received his backing when he established himself in Venice, to translate his vision into practical expression.

Beyond all this, the years at Carpi developed Aldus into an all-round, cultured gentleman. The atmosphere in which he lived was so charged with appreciation of the beautiful that life unfolded in such a way as to make upon him an indelible impression.

While the tutor was under the influence of these surroundings, examples of the new art of printing fell into Aldus's hands—volumes printed perhaps by John of Spires or Nicolas Jenson in Venice. They came to him as a direct message, almost as a command, to abandon his happy environment and, during his remaining years, to apply his scholarship and experience to extending the world's horizon of learning through the now accessible medium of the printed book. "I have resolved," Aldus wrote, "to devote my life to the cause of scholarship. I have chosen, in place of a life of ease and freedom, an anxious and toilsome career. A man has higher responsibilities than the seeking of his own enjoyment; he should devote himself to honorable labor. Living that is a mere existence may be left to men who are content to be animals. Cato compared human existence to iron: when nothing is done with it, it rusts; it is only through constant activity that polish or brilliancy is secured."

Aldus at once outlined his vision to the princess of Carpi, and he found in her a regretful but a sympathetic listener. After all these years, it was a wrench for both of them to terminate the delightful relations which had always existed; but the young princes had grown up, and Aldus had really completed his work at Carpi. So the princess encouraged him to proceed with his ambitious plans and promptly offered to supply him with a modest financial background, to which her brother Pico and her two sons later generously contributed. That Aldus fully realized his obligation is shown in a letter, written years later to a friend who asked for a discount on an order for books: "I cannot give you these at a reduced price, because they belong to me in common with several other persons."

The princess and Aldus discussed the details, and the plans rapidly matured. It was important for the embryo printer to place himself where manuscripts were most available, and where he could receive capable editorial assistance. This made the selection of Venice inevitable. Starting with the notable collection of Greek and Latin manuscripts which Cardinal Bessarion had bequeathed to the Venetian Republic on his death in 1474, no city was richer in potential material. Venice was also the center of a large Greek colony, including many who were well educated and fully competent to assist Aldus in his ambitious undertaking. It was in Venice, therefore, that Aldus settled, about 1488.

Aldus approached the art of printing with seriousness and with a full comprehension of the difficulties involved. There were the type letters to be designed and cut, the compositors to be taught, the editors and correctors to be assembled, the manuscripts to be selected, and last, but by no means least, provision to be made for the sale of his volumes. It required much courage for the young tutor voluntarily to abandon his delightful surroundings and to embark upon a career in an almost untried field, obviously full of pitfalls, and demanding for success much beyond the scholarship and enthusiasm which were his undoubted assets.

In those early days a printer expressed himself in the design of his type as much as in the quality of his workmanship. Aldus was not content simply to copy what other printers before him had done. His Roman face, it is true, was based upon the same handlettering as Jenson's, but he introduced originality by cutting small capitals to use with it, which no one else had ever thought of doing. Then it occurred to Aldus that the inclined, cursive handwriting of Petrarch would make an excellent type, so he had it translated into metal and called it "Italic."

The art of printing, as such, would never have appealed to Aldus if it had not offered him an opportunity to produce his beloved classics. Several of the great Latin authors had already been printed, but at this time Greek books had been issued in only four places: in Milan in 1476, in Vincenza in 1483, in Venice in 1484, and in Florence in 1488. Esop, Theocritus, Hower, and Socrates were the only Greek classics which had ever been printed in the original; and even these were composed in Greek type which was incomplete in the matter of capitals, breathings, and accents. Of his predecessors, Sweynheym and Pannartz, Vindelin of Spires, Nicolas Jenson, and Erhardus Ratdolt had introduced Greek characters in their books, but none except Bartolomeo di Libri and Leonicus Cretensis had attempted to print a complete book in Greek. Aldus felt that he had a clear field before him, and he settled down to prepare himself to embrace his opportunity.

Gradually the Aldine Press began to shape itself. Aldus established himself in the old Campo S. Paternian, now the Piazza Manin, in Venice, near the church of S. Agostino. Here he set up his presses, organized his business, gathered together his staff, and made his home. Besides casting his own type, Aldus had to manufacture much of his material—the printing ink, for instance, being made upon the premises. Most of his paper came from the famous Fabriano mill, which is still in existence—"hand linen [so the old records run], made of pure linen and hempen rags beated in pieces by dint of wood, and made stiff with glue got from boiled hides." At its height, the Aldine Press, including Aldus's family, housed thirty-three souls, embracing the editors, the proofreaders, the compositors, and the pressmen. True to his ideals, Aldus permitted no word to be spoken within the limits of the establishment except in the Greek tongue.

As against its many advantages for a printer, Venice presented one serious handicap—it had no university. In other cities the early printers drew freely upon the professors for editorial assistance and depended upon the universities to absorb a considerable number of printed volumes. Aldus was forced to retain learned editors upon his staff and to summon them from distant places.

The personnel naturally changed from time to time. His chief compositor, fellow editor, friend, and most important collaborator was Marcus Musurus, a Cretan. Musurus was also a friend of Pico della Mirandola, and Aldus had first met him at Carpi. His labors were of the greatest value to the overworked head of the Aldine establishment, and Aldus always recognized his debt of gratitude. In 1502, upon the recommendation of Aldus, Musurus was asked by the Venetian Senate to occupy the chair of belles lettres at the University of Padua, where his lectures, repeated in Venice, attracted wide attention. "Scholars hasten to Venice, the Athens of our day," wrote Aldus, "to listen to the teachings of Musurus, the greatest scholar of the age." It was from the handwriting of Musurus that Aldus took the design for his Greek characters.

The chief corrector for the Greek proof was John Gregoropoulos, of Candia. Theodore Gaza, from Athens, was numbered among the most useful editors Aldus had. Johann Reuchlin, the famous scholar of Heidelberg; Hieronymus Alexander and Pietro Bembo, both of whom later became Cardinals; Scipio Carteromachus; and the great Erasmus of Rotterdam were proud to be numbered among his associates and advisors. Erasmus put through the press the Aldine editions of Terence, Seneca, Plutarch's *Morals,* and Plautus, while Gaza devoted himself chiefly to the great five-volume Aristotle. Erasmus is said to have made himself unpopular with the loyal Musurus by criticizing the meager table set by the financially harassed Aldus. The Cretan retorted by remarking that Erasmus "drank enough for the triple-bodied Geryon, and did the work of only half a man."

The greatest obstacle encountered by Aldus in preparing for his Greek publications was the lack of Greek lexicons and grammars. It was obvious that these had to be written and printed before editors could prepare the copy for the compositors and before the correctors could revise the proof after the copy had been put in type. About 1480 a Greek refugee named Constantine Lascaris had compiled the first Greek lexicon ever issued, published in Milan, which stands as the first work of a living writer printed in Italy. Aldus found this to be hopelessly inadequate, but he made of it an excellent basis for a revision the author now undertook, under his supervision. This was the first book printed at the Aldine Press. Then Aldus called upon Gaza to prepare a Greek grammar, and this was issued during the following year. Undismayed by the manifold duties which overwhelmed him, Aldus himself prepared a Greek-Latin dictionary that immediately became the standard. It passed through many editions and was honored by being pirated by the Giunta, famous printer-publishers in Florence, who even copied the famous Aldine mark of the Dolphin and Anchor.

The patience and restraint of Aldus during these five tedious years of preparation show the character of the man. Other printers might issue texts filled with errors, using incomplete fonts of Greek type, but not Aldus. He tested out his material with Musaeus's *Hero and Leander* in 1494, but his first real example of what he could do was the great Aristotle in five volumes, which appeared during the years 1495–1498. As an expression of affection, Aldus dedicated this splendid work to his former pupil, Albert of Carpi.

Aldus came into the story of the Book at exactly the right time. We have noted how much the world owes to Italy for the spontaneous and extraordinary evolution of the printed book in the fifteenth century. We have seen how Venice quickly became the center of the new art, but it is even more important still to understand that it was the happy cooperation of the entire country that produced the final result. The humanists were scattered all over Italy and dominated the intellectual life of the period: in Florence they were devoting their energies to discovering manuscripts, founding libraries, and encouraging the study of the Greek language; in Naples they elevated the standard of learning by their constructive criticism; in Rome they brought learning nearer to the people by accurate translations; in Mantua and Ferrara a definite system of education was begun; in Venice the results of all this labor were made permanent, being given to the world in printed form.

Thus it is to Italy as a whole rather than to any single Italian city that the gratitude of the world is due for the benefaction of the Book. The contribution in each center was vital, but it was the splendid coordination of all that regained the culture of antiquity, classified and interpreted it, and then turned it over in its entirety to all Europe. No finer instance could be found to exemplify the humanistic creed we have already studied: "to hold oneself open to receive truth unprejudiced as to its source; and, having received truth, to give it out again, made richer by one's personal interpretation."

There was no more ardent humanist than Aldus. He appreciated to the full the service his fellow humanists of the preceding century had rendered to the world by preserving the classical manuscripts. His was to be the privilege of giving these precious gems of thought an eternal permanency. He pondered over the sudden antagonism exhibited by the great Italian princes to the development of the new art and quickly sensed its true significance. He watched an intellectually shackled people awake to the astonishing realization that these gems of thought, hitherto available only to the wealthy overlords, were now within their reach. It was an amazing revelation, and the spontaneous response on the part of the masses was so enthusiastic that it became terrifying to those who had previously counted upon their ignorance as essential to easy government. The man in the street, hitherto compelled to study argument merely by means of pictorial design, was now able to make himself as familiar with the vital problems of the day as those who had considered themselves his masters; and with this new knowledge came a self-reliance which the princes knew would eventually destroy their prestige and power.

Aldus made application to the Venetian government for protection in the publication of his Greek volumes, and, when a monopoly for twenty years was granted, this became the first copyright in history. Just how valuable this concession was, and how it operated, is difficult to understand, as we find other printers, such as Calliergi, issuing Greek volumes in Venice long before the expiration of this period.

In his Aristotle Aldus demonstrated the ability of the press to produce a machine-made book of sufficient attractiveness to compete against the written volume. Other volumes, such as the Plato, were even more beautiful, and some were deemed worthy of being embellished by the art of the illuminator. Aldus might easily have curried favor with the princes and wealthy collectors by confining himself wholly to expensive publications, but this would have been in direct violation of his vision and a prostitution of his purpose in coming to Venice, He never wavered in his determination to produce volumes in Latin, Greek, and Italian—well made, but at so low a cost that anyone could purchase. "I will never desist from my undertaking until I have performed what I have promised," he declared, "always unmindful of expense, however great, and equally regardless of labor, even were I to live in ease and affluence."

The first volume in the Aldine classics was the *Bucolics* of Virgil, issued in 1501 at a price of about fifty cents a volume. This was promptly followed by a long list of Latin and Italian authors. The Greek series opened with the Sophocles of 1502. These were set in the first Italic type ever cut.

It was a curious and happy turn of the wheel that brought about the use of this newly cut type, based upon the handwriting of the father of humanism, in the Aldine classics, which were destined to fulfill Petrarch's fondest dreams for the preservation and dissemination of the humanities!

The type was cut for Aldus by Francesco da Bologna, of the celebrated Griffo family. The small, compact form of this design found immediate favor. Its condensed nature enabled the printer to compress his subject matter into a smaller number of pages and thus reduce the cost. This led Aldus to drop the quarto format and to issue his volumes in octavo size, which innovation immediately proved so popular as to create a revolution in bookmaking. The smaller volumes could be carried in the pocket, were cheaper, and were more available for everyday use. Aldus was granted a monopoly in Venice for ten years on all books issued in this form.

Few realize how immensely popular the Italic face became in the sixteenth century. In Italy, France, and even in England this cursive design became the fashionable vernacular type, and it was used in volume after volume. In the seventeenth and eighteenth centuries, the tide again turned toward the Roman face, the Italic being used only for emphasis or for proper names.

Eager to make the most of his monopoly in Greek publications, Aldus pushed the work forward with hectic enthusiasm, the editors and the correctors working on the copy at the same time that the earlier forms were being printed on the press. In those days, no printer had sufficient type to set up a whole volume at a time. As soon as enough type was composed to constitute a form of four or eight pages, it was run off on the hand press. Then the type was distributed, reset, and the procedure was repeated.

"My days and nights are devoted to the preparation of material," Aldus writes. "I can scarcely take food or strengthen my stomach owing to the multiplicity and pressure of business. With both hands occupied, and surrounded by pressmen who are clamorous for work, there is scarcely time even to blow my nose."

As a result of this haste many of these early volumes were set up directly from the original manuscripts. When one realizes that Homer was the only great Greek author who had been issued in printed form prior to Aldus, and recalls that Aldus gave to the world for the first time printed editions of Aristotle, Plato, Thucydides, Xenophon, Herodotus, Aristophanes, Euripides, Sophocles, Demosthenes, Lysias, Echines, Plutarch, and Pindar, he may appreciate the stupendous contribution made by this great printer to scholarship. And except for the effort of Petrarch in the fourteenth century, and his fellow humanists in the fifteenth, many of these manuscripts would have been irrevocably lost before Aldus had the opportunity to multiply them!

The publications of Aldus include about one hundred titles issued during twenty years in about two hundred and fifty volumes. Taking into account the difficulties presented by the fact that the art of printing was still in its infancy; that each of these titles was produced from manuscript copy; and that from 1509 to 1511 Venice was so harassed by war that business was almost at a standstill, Aldus may be credited with the most tremendous and important accomplishment in the whole history of publishing.

Aldus felt the lack of inspiration which would have come from intellectual contact with university surroundings, so with characteristic energy he undertook to supply this signal lack in the completeness of Venetian life. This, in 1550, took the form of the Neo-accademia Nostraan Academy, which should be to Venice what the famous institution established by the Medici had been to Florence. The special object of this organization was to assimilate the knowledge of the classical literature of Greece and to become more familiar with it. One of the basic rules of the Academy was that the members must speak nothing but Greek among themselves, or submit to a fine. When the sum thus collected was sufficient, the members indulged in a banquet. Aldus himself was the first president of the organization, and the members included readers and correctors of the Aldine Press, priests and doctors, the cultured nobility of Venice, Padua, Rome, Bologna, and Lucca, Greek scholars from Candia, and even the great Erasmus from Rotterdam.

The Academy proved useful and stimulating to Aldus. On certain fixed days the members examined new Greek manuscripts and passed judgment on the desirability of their publication, taking as their measuring stick the service such texts might render to scholarship. In a way, this was a revival of the Academy founded by Ptolemy Philadelphus in 300 B.C., and a more recent parallel would be the functions exercised by the delegates of the Clarendon Press of Oxford, England. Aldus had hoped that the Venetian Academy would assume greater responsibilities by exercising its influence upon arts and sciences in general, and had the life of the indefatigable founder been longer spared, his ambition might have been gratified.

A letter written by Lorenzo of Pavia in 1501 to Isabella d'Este, marchesa di Mantora, gives an interesting glance into the business of the Aldine Press at that time. The marchesa was a cultured noblewoman, who took particular interest in the work of Aldus. Seeking to secure examples of his work, she commissioned Lorenzo to secure them for her, and this letter, freely translated, is a report of his experiences in fulfilling his commission:

> You have expressed the desire, illustrious lady, to obtain large-paper copies of Virgil, Petrarch, and Ovid. At this moment the Virgil is the only one I can secure, and I send it to you. The Petrarch is not yet completed, but it will be finished in ten days. The delay is due to a lack of the fine paper—it has been with difficulty that they secured the small amount required for the Virgil. Your copy of the Petrarch will be selected sheet by sheet, so that you shall have the most beautiful of all the copies. This is the more assured because this volume is issued by Aldus in collaboration with Pietro Bembo, who is wholly devoted to Your Ladyship. It is Bembo who secured the manuscript, which Petrarch had written with his own hand, as a pattern for the types. I have actually held this manuscript in my hands! It belonged to a Paduan, who copied each letter with such care that the type exactly matches the written characters. I will send the volume to you as soon as it is printed. Aldus and Bembo wish the first copy to be yours. They say that this will be for them the best of auguries.
>
> Immediately after the Petrarch they will print the Dante, and after that, the Ovid, which will be begun, I think, about the end of September; but the Dante will be started within twenty days. I have been asked to look about for some good hempen paper, of high quality and pure white, not too thick in one spot and too thin in another. The difficulty is to find paper of good enough quality. They tell me that the price of the Virgil and Petrarch will be not less than five ducats each.

Aldus considered the matter of the sale and distribution of his books his most serious business problem. Bookselling as an organized trade was unknown prior to 1550, and the printer-publisher of the fifteenth century was largely dependent upon personal correspondence with scholars who were interested to purchase his product. In those days, as now, the real business of books was hampered by casual and insincere flutterers around the flame of learning. Aldus had no patience with such as these:

"Nearly every hour," he writes, "comes a letter from some scholar, and if I undertook to reply to them all, I should be obliged to devote

day and night to correspondence. Then, through the day, come calls
from all kinds of visitors. Some wish merely to give a word of greeting; others want to know what there is that is new; while the greater
number come to my office because they happen to have nothing else
to do. 'Let us look in upon Aldus,' they say to one another. Then
they loaf about and chatter to no purpose. Even these people with
no business are not so bad as those who have a poem or something
in prose (usually very prosy indeed) which they wish to see printed
with the name of Aldus. These interruptions are now becoming too
serious for me, and I must take steps to lessen them. Many letters I
simply leave unanswered, while to others I send very brief replies;
and as I do this not from pride or from discourtesy, but simply in
order to be able to go on with my task of printing good books, it
must not be taken unkindly. . . . As a warning to the heedless visitors
who use up my business hours to no purpose, I have now placed a
great notice on the door of my office to the following effect: 'Whoever thou art, thou art earnestly requested by Aldus to state thy business briefly and to take thy departure promptly. In this way thou
mayst be of service, even as was Hercules to the weary Atlas. For this
is a place of work for all who may enter.' "

There was another side to this correspondence which must have
been gratifying to the busy printer. Purchasers of books looked upon
Aldus as a benefactor of mankind and freely expressed their appreciation of the privilege of buying. Urbanus, for instance, a highly educated monk, wrote Aldus in 1505: "May the blessing of the Lord
rest upon thee, thou illustrious man. The high regard in which you
are held by our Brotherhood will be realized by you when you learn
that we have ordered (through the House of Fugger in Augsburg) a
group of your valuable publications, and that it is our chief desire to
be able to purchase all the others. We pray to God each day that He
will in His mercy long preserve your life for the cause of good learning. Our neighbor, Mutianus Rufus, the learned Canonicus of
Gotha, calls you 'the light of our age,' and is never weary of relating
your great services to scholarship. He sends you a cordial greeting, as
does also Magister Spalatinus, a man of great learning. We are sending you with this four gold ducats, and will ask you to send us
(through Fugger) an Etymologicum Magnum and a Julius Pollux,
and also (if there be money sufficient) the writings of Bessarion, of
Xenophon, and of Hierocles, and the Letters of Merula."

There were other rewards that came to the overburdened Aldus. "I cannot tell you what joy I experienced," he wrote a friend, "when I learned that in the great city of Brescia the most distinguished men were devoting themselves passionately to Greek literature. This truly surpasses all that I hoped when I undertook the publication of Greek texts. This passion has increased, day by day, while arms have contended against books, not only in Italy, but in Germany, in France, in Pannonia, in England, in Spain, and wherever the Latin tongue is known. My joy makes me forget my fatigue, and my ardor is redoubled to come more and more to the aid of all students, and especially of the youth born at this period of the renaissance of letters."

The reference made by Aldus of arms contending against books recalls the frequent interruptions caused by the wars of 1500, 1506, 1510, and 1511, in which Venice was directly involved. During these periods the universities north of the Alps had to discontinue their classical instruction because soldiers in the passes prevented the Aldine classical texts from being transported from Venice to their destination.

The piratical reprints of the Aldine volumes annoyed Aldus even more than the wars. The copyrights secured from the Venetian government gave protection only within the limits of Venice itself. The printers of Paris were guilty of this piracy to some extent, but those of Lyons, particularly the famous house of Giunta, were the chief offenders. Aldus would not have minded so much the filching of the text, but when the unscrupulous printers ventured to copy his types and his original style of typography, and sold their counterfeit copies as the product of the Aldine Press, his indignation knew no bounds. "These fraudulent volumes, printed and sold under my name," he declares, "prejudice friends of letters to my sorrow and discredit. The paper is inferior, and even has a foul odor; the type characters are defective, and the consonants do not align with the vowels. It is by their imperfections that you may distinguish them."

No printer's mark is better known than the famous Anchor and Dolphin of Aldus. Its origin goes back to the medals of imperialistic Rome struck for Vespasian and for Domitian. Pietro Bembo presented one of these medals to Aldus, who adopted the device, adding the words *Festina lente,* which he found in Augustus. The dolphin stands for speed in execution, and the anchor for firmness in deliberation. Sir Thomas Browne translates the slogan, "Celerity contempered with cunctation."

The most important rival of Aldus in Venice was the establishment formed by Nicolas Blastus and Zacharias Calliergi, devoted exclusively to the production of Greek volumes. Both these men were Cretans, Blastus being a man of wealth and culture, while Calliergi was a printer. The partnership was an expression of national pride: exiled from Greece, these patriotic sons endeavored to keep alive interest in Greek literature. In spite of the rivalry, the relations between this press and Aldus were not only friendly but intimate. Aldus saw in the work of Calliergi a real contribution to Greek learning, and he welcomed the competition. Marcus Musurus, the chief associate of Aldus in the Aldine Press, was also a Cretan, and between him and Blastus existed the closest friendship. Aldus went so far as to include the Calliergi volumes in his catalogue, offering them for sale side by side with his own.

The extent to which the Cretan national pride carried these exiles is shown by the impassioned appeal, written by Marcus Musurus, which appears at the beginning of the *Etymologicum* printed by Calliergi in 1499: "Let no one be astonished at the spirit of the Cretans," he declares, "since it was Minerva herself who, at the command of Jupiter, taught the Cretans the beauties of the art of printing. It was a Cretan who cut these punches; it was a Cretan who devised the accents, and a Cretan who joined them to the letters. It was a Cretan who cast this font of letters in lead; it was a Cretan, whose name is synonymous with victory [Nicolas], who bore the expense of this volume; and he who now celebrates its glory is a Cretan."

Marcus Musurus and Nicolas Blastus were voluminous correspondents, and frequently the subjects discussed were of present interest. Musurus shared Aldus's disgust of those book lovers who declined to loan him their precious manuscripts to be used as copy at the Aldine Press. In one of his letters Musurus writes:

> The lack of books, my very dear Nicolas, is a great misfortune for every one, and particularly for those who burn with a desire for self-instruction and are unable to procure books because of their lack of means. This is the fault of the manuscript collectors, who accept self-praise and glory from their possession, and keep them for themselves alone, depriving others of the fame and glory which would come through their use.

Aldus married Maria, the daughter of an earlier Venetian printer, Andrea de Torresani, in 1498, and became the father of three sons and a daughter. Manutius, the eldest, became a priest at Arola, Antoninus was a librarian at Bologna, while Paulus entered the Aldine Press. Alda, the daughter, was educated in a convent at Carpi, and in his will her father bequeathed her 300 ducats if she remained with the Sisters and 600 ducats if she married. She chose the latter alternative and became the wife of a Mantuan named Cato.

At the time of Aldus's death, Paulus was too young to assume charge of the business, so Andrea de Torresani combined his own printing establishment with the Aldine Press. Previously, Andrea had purchased the type and presses which Nicolas Jenson had left, so the consolidation brought added historic luster to the already world-famous plant of Aldus. Working with Andrea were his two sons, Francesco and Federico.

It was during this period that Jean Grolier became interested in the Aldine Press. From this association Grolier became an outstanding figure in the world of books in Italy and later in France. He succeeded his father as treasurer of the Duchy of Milan in 1510, when thirty-one years old. Having already developed a passionate and an understanding love for books, he sought out the famous establishment of Aldus and became acquainted with the great scholar-printer. Later, Grolier came to know Andrea de Torresani and formed a warm friendship with Francesco. He became the patron of the press, sending manuscripts to be printed, loaning money at eventful crises, and in general fulfilling the role of good angel. As a result, many of the Aldine publications are dedicated to Grolier, and one copy of every book was especially printed on vellum for this fastidious collector.

In a letter Grolier wrote to Francesco, when sending him the manuscript of Budeus's *De Asse* for publication, the Frenchman gives instructions which reveal his familiarity with the basic principles of good bookmaking:

"You will care with all diligence," he writes, "O most beloved Francesco, that this work, when it leaves your printing shop to pass into the hands of learned men, may be as correct as it is possible to render it. I heartily beg and beseech this of you. The book, too, should be decent and elegant; and to this will contribute the choice of the paper, the excellence of the type, which should have been but little used, and the width of the margins. To speak more exactly, I should wish it were set up with the same type with which you printed your Poliziano. And if this decency and elegance shall increase your expenses, I will refund you entirely. Lastly, I should wish that nothing be added to the original or taken from it."

Grolier is perhaps better known from his bindings than from his association with the printing of books. The famous inscription IO GROLIERII ET AMICORUM, stamped on the covers of his volumes, expresses this book lover's understanding of what a book should be—not a treasure to be acquired and hoarded, but a joy to be shared with others. In his library of some eight thousand books Grolier had several copies of the same title, so that no one of his friends need be deprived of the pleasure which he himself secured. "You will owe nothing to books," Erasmus wrote Grolier, "but in the future, books will give you an eternal glory."

Paulus Manutius assumed charge of the Aldine Press when he was eighteen years old, but he was unable to combine, as his father had, his undoubted scholarly attainments with the business necessities. Paulus was particularly interested in Cicero and devoted his lifetime to preparing commentaries to this author's works, which were published after his death. Paulus was in poor health during most of the years he struggled with the problems of the Aldine Press, and later at Rome. In 1570 he writes pathetically to his son Aldus, "Scholarship and industry have never brought me rest or fortune. I pray God that you may be better favored." But the younger Aldus had no yearning for his grandfather's honors. Gradually the affairs of the press ran down, and it passed out of existence at the close of the sixteenth century.

The death of the great Aldus occurred on February 6, 1515, while he was in his sixty-eighth year. Measured by human standards, in spite of the fact that he died a poor man, the sum total of his accomplishments seems incredible; yet Aldus himself considered his labors wholly incomplete. Gutenberg had conceived the idea of printing books and had proved it practical. Fust and Schoeffer, Sweynheym and Pannartz, John of Spires, Nicolas Jenson, and Erhardus Ratdolt had each in his turn contributed to what had gone before, and thus prepared the way for Aldus; but no one of these great figures had visualized the relation which the new invention bore to learning or to the civilization of the world. They were satisfied if their books compared favorably with the manuscripts they imitated and found a limited sale among the wealthy book-collectors and well-to-do students and professors. Aldus, assuming that quality was an inherent element of bookmaking, sought, in the selection of his titles, and in the low price of his volumes, to make knowledge universal. His books were but the vehicles conveying wisdom to those who craved it. To Aldus, each author remained a prisoner so long as he existed only in manuscript form, and in multiplying the classics so that all the world might read, the great printer felt himself nothing less than a liberator of faithful souls in bondage.

The great contemporaries of Aldus combined at his death to do him honor. Musurus, Reuchlin, and Erasmus declared that he had accomplished more for the spread of learning and for the development of literature than all the scholars of his period. His fellow printers acknowledged without question his supremacy as a master artist-printer. No one can again contribute so much to the external and internal advancement of the Book because that much is not now left undone. Even as a pioneer, he established so high a standard that no one has surpassed his work, even with the aid of modern mechanical improvements—and it is a question whether any printer has yet equaled the quality and taste shown in the Aldine masterpieces.

Raphael Regio, professor of the humanities in Venice at the time, delivered the funeral oration over the body of Aldus lying in state in the old Church of S. Paternian. The casket rested on a catafalque banked high with choice editions of the volumes he had created. These tangible evidences of the devotion of a lifetime form the ever-living monument to the continuing benefaction of his greatness.

Benjamin Franklin's Epitaph

In 1729, drawing on similar epitaphs written by others, the young printer Benjamin Franklin composed this epitaph for himself. Franklin did not, however, instruct that it be used on his grave, which actually bears only his name and that of his wife.

The Body
of
Benjamin Franklin, Printer
(Like the cover of an old book,
Its contents torn out,
And stript of its lettering and gilding,)
Lies food for worms:
Yet the work itself shall not be lost,
For it will (as he believed) appear once more
In a new
And more beautiful edition,
Corrected and amended
by
The Author.

The Collector

BY WILLIAM TARG

Bill Targ's remarkable career in publishing included his heroic support of Mario Puzo in the writing and publishing of The Godfather. *A man of wide interests and a lover of life, Targ's 1975 memoir,* Indecent Pleasures, *is one of the great publishing memoirs. This is a chapter from that rollicking book.*

The Virus

The book collector's virus attacked me early in life. I was never to recover; in fact, the malady became aggravated with the years. It was in my eighteenth year, while working at Macmillan, that a friend introduced me to a Dickensian character who owned a coffee shop near our office on the South Side of Chicago. One day this man—some devilish instinct prompting him, no doubt—handed me a thick paper-bound catalog of rare books. I had never seen one before. He told me he collected Trollope, but there were other books in the catalog that might interest me. It was issued by Maggs Brothers of London, a quarto volume, expensively printed and lavishly illustrated. Some plates were in color.

I spent many nights studying its contents (I didn't buy anything from it, of course), but I resolved that I must have more of the catalogs which Maggs so invitingly offered in a list on the back cover. I wrote that firm and before long found myself a regular recipient of their catalogs. As each new one arrived, my sense of guilt increased. I felt like a con man, for I could not afford to buy any of the books they offered. But I did read the catalogs and came to learn something of old books and bibliography and a great many other related things.

Like some small nimble mouse between the ribs
Of a mastodon, I nibbled here and there.

I suppose I became insufferable because of the odd smattering of knowledge I was acquiring. I became, overnight, an "expert" on Elizabethan literature, color-plate books, rare medical and scientific works, books on exploration, history, and such. I became a repository of information relating to incunabula and early printing. Points and variant bindings became my daily diet. At eighteen I was talking glibly about Dickens in "parts" and Scott in "boards," about trial issues and the 1865 *Alice.* The vocabulary of the bookbinder became mine, and I rolled on my tongue such phrases as "silk doublures" and "gilt dentelles." The Maggs catalogs became, over the years, my university. And of course, I scrounged catalogs from other dealers in Europe and at home. Ultimately, I began to order books from them. Packages with foreign stamps began to arrive, and is there any excitement to compare with the opening of a fresh parcel of books? It was inevitable as funds became available that my library began to expand, from cheap subscription sets and twenty-five- and fifty-cent bin books, until it boasted of press books, modern first editions, Beadle Dime Novels, fine bindings, small runs of books by such then favorites as G. K. Chesterton, Lafcadio Hearn, James G. Huneker, Theodore Dreiser, and others, plus a number of books about books (one of the first I read was Pearson's *Books in Black or Red*). Gradually, the subscription sets and bin books were eased out of the house. I was a collector. I was always broke!

And of course my collection of book catalogs grew, and I have never ceased regarding them with special affection. Eugene Field termed it "The Malady Called Catalogitis." I can only add for emphasis that catalogs, and books about books, are the backbone of any good collector's library. They are the fuel that keep the bibliophilic temperature at boiling point, or near it.

As a footnote to my Maggs Brothers catalog experience, thirty years after getting my first one, I made my first trip to London. I proceeded at once to Maggs Brothers, 50 Berkeley Square. I won't attempt to relate the sense of exhilaration and aroused sentiment that was generated within me as I entered the doors of this establishment. My wife stood at the foot of the stairs leading to their door and aimed her camera at me. The snapshot, with the Maggs plaque behind me, is one of the precious mementos of my first European trip.

I visited many other London bookshops—shops whose names were as old friends to me through numerous catalogs I had received over the years. And I bought books from many of them, none of which failed to give me satisfaction.

A book collector has friends everywhere. The bookseller from whom you buy books is, more frequently than not, your friend. There is a bond between you that transcends the commercial transaction. For you've established *something* (call it rapport) between you that is personal, almost spiritual if you will. He understands your interests and your needs and the compulsion which brings you to him. (And let it be freely admitted, his magnet is as compelling to the bibliophile as the bar is to the boozer.) The bookseller becomes inextricably identified with you, your library, your intellectual life.

First Principles: Collect What You Like

Collecting the great names, the milestones of literature, is child's play; all it takes is a checkbook and some indoctrination. But collecting a young, fledgling author—that's the game!

Did you ever hear of, or read any of, the poems of Patti Smith?

Well, one day, while browsing at Gotham Book Mart, I picked up a copy of a pamphlet entitled *Seventh Heaven*. I was attracted by the photograph of its author, a young woman who looked as though she had just come in out of the rain, or just back from a swim. I began to read the poems in her little book, which was published by Telegraph Books in 1972, and was instantly taken by them. One of the two people the book is dedicated to is Mickey Spillane, one of my favorite authors. So I bought it.

Later, I acquired other works by Patti Smith, pamphlets called *Witt* and *Kodak* and a four-page thing entitled *One of Us Is the Stronger—Early Morning Dream*. She also published, in holograph reproduction, *Devotions to Arthur Rimbaud,* a broadside which ends up with the words "He was so damn young." Someone described her voice and delivery as a "quivering quickness, like the quail that lights down so fast you almost miss."

Gotham had a party for Patti and I went, bringing along my various Patti Smith artifacts. I met her, I found her enchanting. Shy. Self-effacing. Embarrassed by all the attention. She inscribed each of my books and the Rimbaud broadside. I let her borrow my Parker fountain pen, which, I told her, Samuel Beckett had used to inscribe my *Waiting for Godot.* She genuflected and kissed the pen.

Patti Smith appeared at Max's Kansas City and elsewhere, but I missed her "act." I want to continue reading her poetry and shall buy each booklet as it appears. Someday I will be able to say I recognized her talent way back—that's collecting. If she doesn't become famous, no harm. I empathize with her and her poems. I hope you make the discovery one day.

One day, in a long coffee-shop visit with Patti, I learned of her deep interest in flying saucers; of her ability to see and sense the proper placing of a word beside its destined mate; that she once listened to a half-hour discourse by a tortoise—all of which I earnestly believe. She understands, too, a great deal about the sexuality of extraterrestrials and other arcane matters. She will surely write (based on a deep regard for William Burroughs's writings) a major novel, and I hope to serve as her editor.

Closeup of a Collector

Carl Sandburg, in his *Lincoln Collector,* has much to say about collecting, and in particular, about that prototype of the great collector, Oliver R. Barrett.

Sandburg tells this anecdote about Charles Gunther, the candy manufacturer–collector, and Barrett—an anecdote which offers a classic portrait-in-miniature of the true collector:

In another session, when Barrett saw a manuscript in the handwriting of Robert Burns—the verses of "Auld Lang Syne"—he said, "I want this 'Auld Lang Syne.'" Gunther replied, "I know how you feel, I went over to England and I got it and I had to pay a lot of money."

Barrett: "I want it now. You know how it *feels* to have it, and I *don't* know how it feels."

Gunther: "I will sell you this 'Auld Lang Syne' and you write out the receipt and put in the receipt that any time I want it, I can buy it back at the same price."

Barrett took it home. A week later Gunther was on the phone, saying: "Bring back the 'Auld Lang Syne.' You know, I haven't been able to sleep. I hear the waves of Lake Michigan pounding at night and I think about it. I walk down Michigan Avenue thinking about it, and now it is gone and I am not going to last many years. Let me have it back."

The World's Greatest Book Collector

When I was visiting with Ben Glazebrook of Constable in 1966, he mentioned an upcoming book that pulled me up short. It was a one-volume condensation of the five-volume work on Sir Thomas Phillipps (*The Phillipps Studies*) adapted by Nicolas Barker.

The prospect of publishing, for Putnam's, the story of the unparalleled account of the most fanatically dedicated book collector in all history was a great prospect. I was delighted to learn, on reporting the project to Walter Minton, that he was all for publishing the book, although he held out little hope for sales or profit. (The virus had reached him!)

Phillipps was the ultimate bibliomaniac. He said somewhere that he wanted to own one copy of *every book printed*. He was the illegitimate son of a rich Birmingham merchant and was never allowed to see his mother. Lawrence Clark Powell conjectures that this was the cause for his bibliomania—an unfulfilled need for affection. Whatever the reason, he was insatiable. He filled two large mansions with books and priceless manuscripts. No one knows how many printed books he finally did get to own. He begrudged his wife the space occupied by her dressing table—because it could have accommodated another bookcase. I believe, in the end, he had more than 60,000 manuscripts which be cataloged. In today's terms, his library could be valued at perhaps a hundred million dollars, possibly more. He often neglected to pay his bills and sent some booksellers into bankruptcy (or to the madhouse).

Bookseller, librarian, publisher, collector—all will respond to this fantastic story. The man was detestable, personally. But so admirable in his genius for collecting. If you can find a copy of this now out-of-print book, treat yourself to something *recherché*.

I believe I have some of Phillipps's genes in my makeup; alas, what is lacking is his income. He was damnably rich.

Book Collecting for the Smart Money; or, What the Disillusioned and Bewildered Stock Market Speculator Can Turn to for Solace, Culture, and Some Profit

A publisher I know told me, in utmost seriousness, that anyone who couldn't take a complete break from his daily interests was suffering from soggy brains.

I disagree. Editors and publishers do read manuscripts after hours; they also see authors and fellow publishers socially, at home. Somehow, I think they should have decent libraries, *aside* from the usual reference miscellany, the haphazard stuff assembled over the years. I mean they should have a *collection,* put together with plan and purpose, a cohesive collection.

The investment factor is also there, and that is, in part, why the following article was written. It first appeared in *New York* magazine (November 11, 1974) in somewhat modified form, when the subject of inflation and investment was on everyone's mind; when a president was up for impeachment and a secretary of state was double-talking and making protests over accusations such as wiretapping and other indelicate behavior; when it *appeared* that only gold had an intrinsic value and bread was going to cost a dollar a loaf. It was a time of fear and depression—talk, and stocks were unpopular and going to hell. The article was also intended to indicate what was going on in the rare-book world, and I wrote it with the hope that it would suggest as well a perfect escape hatch for the troubled, escape from the routines and pressures of work and the rigors of social life.

As a rare-book watcher for over three decades, as well as a some-time collector, I've come to a few drastic conclusions. One, that the possession of a rare book beats owning a deflated stock certificate. Also, that there's no contest when the choice is between curling up with a good book or a Wall Street engraving. However . . .

If you're going to take to books with the single crass purpose of making money, then please turn to another page. The prospect of lending voice to the sole practice of making money out of bibliophily gives me the horrors. This is not my intention here.

What I want to enunciate here are a few not-too-well-known facts about rare books and collecting. First, rare book prices are skyrocketing in America, England, and France; literary "stocks" (which include autographs and manuscripts) have gone inflationary, and the climb appears to continue steadily Everestward.

First editions are *in* among many hundreds of college and university libraries where collections of rare books are being avidly assembled. Scholars use them! The emphasis appears to be on contemporary literature as well as the milestones of the past. The great rarities will soon be out of circulation because of institutional buying. (Where does one find a first-issue copy of Whitman's *Leaves of Grass* or Rimbaud's first little book, *Une Saison en Enfer*, which he published at his own expense—as did Whitman? Or Camus's first book, *L'Envers et l'endroit*, printed in Algiers in 1937?)

It's plain to see that it's folly to sell one's books in haste.

A home library of, say, 1,000 good first editions could represent a pretty impressive estate or nest egg for any modest family. And what glorious reading!

"How do you know it's a genuine first edition?" That's the most common question asked by book owners. There is no simple answer; there are many rules and guidelines, and also many variations and contradictions, and publishers do not have a uniform style for indicating first editions, alas. Some trade publishers will indicate "First Edition" or "First Impression" on the copyright page. But not always. Some publishers put reprint information on the copyright page, which quickly answers the question as to whether it is a first edition. Some publishers put the publication date on the title page, then remove it in reprintings. In short, bibliographies must be consulted, as well as booksellers. Instinct and rule of thumb are called into play. In the end, your memory and rule-of-thumb sense will guide you. A bookseller will of course guarantee any book he sells to you.

If you have a wall or shelf of books at home, take down and examine those by famous authors such as Steinbeck, Hemingway, Tennessee Williams, and others—books you bought when the books were first published. The chances are that some of them are first editions—that is, if you bought them around the time of publication. The books which seem to you to be first editions should then be checked out through rare booksellers' catalogs, bibliographies, guides, and auction records. Use the public library as much as possible. Catalogs are valuable guides.

Don't expect your bookseller to be on tap for endless questions; to earn his attention and service you must first prove yourself a customer and a reasonably serious collector. If you simply badger him with questions and fail to buy, you'll alienate him quickly. Courtesy and good business manners must prevail. Remember, the bookseller has rent to pay and an overhead. Don't bring in boxes and bundles of books for appraisal; if you want to sell them, ask for an offer. If you think you can get free appraisals, guess again. No professional dealer will hold still for that. Many dealers charge a fee for appraisals and properly so; what they have to offer is a lifetime of experience and study.

What is a rare book and what is it worth? How high is up? The first question is easily answered: A book is rare when the supply is short and the demand long. Its value is what one is willing to pay for it in a competitive market. Often, a rare book is rare by virtue of its limited first printing. If one hundred copies were printed and most of them landed in institutional collections, the chances are the price will be prohibitive.

For example: James Joyce's *Ulysses* (Paris, 1922), one of 100 copies, signed by the author, bound in blue paper wrappers as issued, could have been bought for around $1,500 in 1964. Today it would cost you anywhere from $7,500 to $10,000 (a copy sold for $8,000 at auction in February 1975) if you can locate a copy. In 1935 the Limited Editions Club reprinted the book and got Joyce to sign around 250 copies. The book was issued at $15 plus $5 for the autograph. Today the book fetches $1,500, $2,000, or more.

Hart Crane's great poem, *The Bridge* (1930), was issued in Paris, with 50 copies on Japan vellum, signed, at about $50. Today it is probably a $1,500 to $2,000 book; and the American trade edition, issued the same year, is also a great rarity and may very well be in the $500 area.

On a personal note: Nine years ago my wife, Roslyn, expressed the desire to buy me a present. I suggested that a book would be very nice and proposed that we visit John Fleming's ducal book emporium on East 57th Street in New York. As an old devotee of Doves Press books, I asked if there were any in stock. Fleming showed us a few titles, including Emerson's *Essays,* one of 25 copies printed on vellum. The price was $225. My wife generously bought it for me

In 1974, a copy of the Doves *Emerson* on vellum was sold for $2,600, at the Parke Bernet auction gallery in New York. (Paul Getty, Jr., was the buyer.) Shortly after the sale, Fleming encountered my wife and asked her if she thought I would care to sell my copy of the book back to him. He suggested that his customer might pay $3,000 for it. Of course we wouldn't sell the book. But we were pleased with the "appreciation" this little book enjoyed in some nine years—an appreciation unheard of in Wall Street.

Do you like Robert Lowell's poetry? You might—he's possibly our best living poet. Anyway, if you want to collect him you'll be interested to know that his first book, *The Land of Unlikeness,* published in 1944 at around $2, might cost you $1,000 today—more if inscribed. William Faulkner's first book, a little volume of poems entitled *The Marble Faun,* printed (not published) in 1924 at about $1.50 a copy, now costs between $3,000 and $5,000, depending on whether it has the original jacket and is inscribed by the author.

Samuel Beckett's famous play *Waiting for Godot* was published in Paris, in 1952. It was first written and published in French, and its title is *En Attendant Godot.* There were 35 copies printed on a paper called Velin; it retailed for about $25 when published. Today, a copy, if available, would fetch around $5,000. Ezra Pound's first book, *A Lume Spento,* printed in Venice in 1908, brings around $7,500 today. It was privately issued and first offered for a few dollars—or given away to friends.

Are there many commercial stocks with comparable histories of growth?

And what about that "sure thing," gold! Eh?

Here's another interesting rarity: John Hawkes, one of our *finest* novelists, issued a small paper-covered booklet of his poems in 1943; it was entitled *Fiasco Hall.* It could have been bought at that time for $1. Dealers are currently offering it for $250. A "fiasco" in reverse.

There are more collectors for such first editions than there are books available. Every collector of Stephen Spender would love to own a copy of his first, privately printed book. Spender himself printed it on a crude hand press. It was called *Nine Experiments by S.H.S.* and was issued in Hampstead, England, in 1928. About 18 copies were made and I've never seen a worse piece of book printing. A copy of this book would bring well over $5,000 today, and alas, no Spender collection can be complete without it.

As a collector, my personal preference is in the poetry area, and I've been watching the price climb on certain key books by Auden, Betjeman, Eliot, Plath, Marianne Moore, Robert Frost, W. C. Williams, Dylan Thomas, Allen Ginsberg, and others. A fine copy of Eliot's *Prufrock and Other Observations* (London, 1917) might bring over $1,000 today; likewise Robert Frost's *A Boy's Will* (London, 1913). Certain key French books, in particular Baudelaire's *Le Fleurs du Mal* (1857), with the six suppressed poems intact (a black tulip if there was ever one), might bring a few thousand dollars today. Wallace Stevens's *Harmonium,* published by Knopf in 1923, with the striped boards binding in dust jacket, might justify a $200 price today if you can locate a copy. A fine but tough poet to collect, William Carlos Williams is worthy of any serious collector's attention, provided he has the funds and patience to follow the labyrinthian paths leading to a complete collection. Of course there is no more difficult author to collect in his entirety than Samuel Beckett—but the course is worth the time, money, and energy. Poets and playwrights—a broad collection in these two fields—are highly recommended to new collectors; poetry is enjoying a renaissance today, with more works being published than ever, and many of the new poets are top-notch. Happily, they are finding favor (and pleasant loot) on university campuses.

(Speaking of poetry, the monumental *Leaves of Grass* by Walt Whitman [Brooklyn, 1855] was cataloged by Dawson's of London in January of 1975 at £5,500 [or around $13,500]. There aren't too many copies of this book [in its first-issue binding] lying around.)

Does a book have to be ancient to be valuable? As you can see above, the answer is no, definitely not. Age has nothing to do with dollar value. Allen Ginsberg's two books of poems, both issued in paper wrappers in 1956 (one was mimeographed on board a ship), *Siesta in Xbalba* and *Howl,* are rarities; the first may be worth about $500 today, and *Howl* might fetch $150 today. It was published at 75¢. Norman Mailer's novel *The Naked and the Dead,* published in 1948, is currently offered for $150 in the paper-covered advance copy. Thomas Wolfe's *Look Homeward, Angel*, with its dust jacket intact (1929) brings between $250 and $350 today. There are numerous titles from many areas of literature published during the past fifty years which bring premiums of 100 percent to 1,000 percent and more over their publication price. To repeat, supply and demand plus "collector's condition" determine the price. A book without its dust jacket could be worth up to 50 percent less. It is part of the book regardless of logic; so never throw a jacket away, and when you read a first edition, remove the jacket first so that you don't soil or tear it. And please read all first-edition copies with care. Keep the book as clean and close to the original condition as possible. No soup stains on the pages; no dog-eared pages; no glass rings on the cover or jacket. Don't open your books carelessly so that the spine is cracked. Handle a rare book gently—as a delicate and valuable object. And—don't lend your first editions to anyone.

The literary explosion in America, brought on in part by the so-called paperback revolution, explains the widespread interest in books. The book clubs (club editions are *not* first editions) have helped to heighten the possessive interest in books. The auction sale record prices have animated many newcomers. Students and young executives are learning something about the pleasure (and status) of a good home library cum collection. Some of them are listening to the siren songs emanating from the auction rooms, and they're responding.

More and more, we see shelves with books as background decor in newspaper and magazine advertisements. *A house without a library is not a home.* And books are so easy to acquire. The taste for books and reading is leading more and more to collecting, and once the step is taken, the investment factor rears its beautiful bead. And when this happens, rules of the game must be studied and followed. It can take years to master the intricacies, not to mention the vocabulary, of the hobby. But it's all great fun, and all it takes is a love of books.

How and what type of book to collect? The answer usually is: Buy the books and authors you like best. But of course if your taste runs to soap-opera fiction and nonbooks, forget it. Quality is the prime consideration in collecting—in collecting anything, for that matter. The author must be gilt-edged. Schlock literature may be fun but will get you nowhere in the investment sense. There are no hard and fast rules, and each season turns up surprises. Many of the "beat" writers, the "outsiders," and avant gardists of not too long ago, who were suspect insofar as durability goes, have won their permanent place in the "market." Among the notable ones are Jack Kerouac, Michael McClure, Gregory Corso, William Burroughs, and others. And let us not forget the perdurable Henry Miller. Michael McClure's seminal play, *The Beard,* issued in pictorial wrappers, small folio size, in Berkeley, California, in 1965, may one day become a major collector's item. Today it is worth around $40.

And then there are many exciting comparative newcomers such as Richard Brautigan, John Gardner, Thomas Pynchon, Harold Pinter, Robert Creeley, John Barth, Gary Snyder, Kurt Vonnegut, Jr., LeRoi Jones (Imamu Amiri Baraka). These are all worthy of the collector's attention, and some of their books are already way out of reach.

As for the modern solid-gold standbys, I cite at random: F. Scott Fitzgerald, John Steinbeck, Truman Capote, Robert Frost, Theodore Roethke, Anaïs Nin, Sean O'Casey, William Saroyan, Robinson Jeffers, Graham Greene (his first book, *Babbling April* [Oxford, 1925], might cost you around $400 today), Richard Wright, Katherine Mansfield, Randall Jarrell, Nelson Algren, Tom Wolfe, Richard Wilbur, James T. Farrell (his Lonigan and Danny O'Neill series are, with Dreiser's novels, among the best novels of our century), and so many others—they will all give the reader immeasurable pleasure and satisfaction in the collector's sense.

There are several levels of book collecting. The top plateau (where collecting is really "a sport of kings") comprises the deepest blue of blue chips: manuscripts, incunabula (books printed prior to 1501), literary and typographic milestones of the sixteenth and seventeenth century; high spots of literature such as Boswell's *Life of Samuel Johnson,* Gibbon's *Decline and Fall of the Roman Empire,* Jane Austen's *Pride and Prejudice,* etc. Then there are the great examples from the fine presses: the Doves, Kelmscott, Ashendene, Gregynog, Grabhorn, and other presses. First folios of Shakespeare, Caxtons, early examples from the press of Aldus, illuminated manuscripts, Elizabethan literature, colonial American and Western Americana rarities—all of these are for the serious, long-view collector, and invariably, they are surefire investments. A single leaf from the Gutenberg Bible (I bought one for $500 about twelve years ago) now brings around $4,000 or $5,000—if you can locate one.

Then there are the first editions of Dickens, Thackeray, Melville, Poe, Hawthorne, Shelley, Byron, Keats, Coleridge, Wordsworth, Whitman, Twain, Thoreau, etc., etc. These authors' books are always in demand, particularly so when signed or inscribed. Autograph material by any such authors—and that includes all important contemporary writers—is also in our category of good investments. Good holograph letters and manuscripts by notable writers as well as celebrated public figures are spiraling upward each year. (What would you pay for a letter from Charles G. Rebozo to Richard Nixon relating to gambling casino or real estate matters? Or a love note to Jackie, signed "Ari"?)

Specialization is recommended to new collectors. Concentrate on an author or category. There are many collectors who now buy only *first books* of famous writers. Others want everything an author has produced, including the ephemera and juvenilia—and in the case of playwrights, theatre programs and posters. Do not confuse a rare book collection with a library.

If you have very limited funds and can only spend five or ten dollars a week, I'd suggest buying first editions of the new poets, as published. It just happens that some of the best writing today is coming from poets such as Erica Jong, Muriel Rukeyser, Adrienne Rich, Anne Sexton, Denise Levertov, Diane Wakoski, Sandra Hochman. If you want to concentrate on an *established* living author, I'd recommend Albee or Tennessee Williams. (Either will present plenty of challenges.) If you like critics, try collecting the first editions of Edmund Wilson. The field is wide open, and in the end, it's fun to collect the authors you admire and enjoy reading. Your taste will prove your collecting judgment in the end. Unless you have an unlimited bank account—and even if you have—make a plan; don't collect at random. Don't look for bargains. If a book is truly rare, the price you pay today will probably look like a bargain five years from now. A signed copy of James Joyce's *Ulysses* will not get cheaper; nor will Marianne Moore's first book, *Poem;* nor Sylvia Plath's *Bell Jar,* which she published under the pseudonym of Victoria Lucas in London, in 1963; nor Hemingway's *Three Stories and Ten Poems.* And then there is in our midst a man who is as close to genius as one can come, Edward Gorey, writer and artist, whose little books are being bought up like the proverbial hot cakes. He may provide one of the most delightful single categories for a collector who wants to concentrate on one subject. He is immensely gifted and also prolific, and each of his books is a jewel. Some of them are very modestly priced, i.e., under $10.

Wherever possible, get an author to sign or inscribe your book for you—provided he's an author of importance and the book is a first edition. If the author is willing to make notations or corrections in the text of the book, great—its value increases. An autographed copy can often double the value of a book, or certainly enhance its value since it becomes, ipso facto, a unique, one-of-a-kind copy, a personal or, possibly, an "association" copy. Don't write in your book (unless you are famous yourself) or underscore lines.

As an *example* of the importance of a famous author's inscription, Dylan Thomas's first book, *18 Poems* (London, 1914), in dust jacket and inscribed by Thomas, would fetch about $1,000; a copy without a jacket, not inscribed, about $400.

Keep your books away from windows or sunlight. Damp stains are to be avoided. A collection of value should be kept in a temperature-controlled room. Fragile books or booklets might be housed in slip-cases or acetate envelopes.

Reputable dealers will always guarantee their wares; they will also guide and advise you. Each has a good reference library for ready consultation. There are many reference works and collector's guides to study; and auction records are important. Here are a few reference books to consider: *A Primer of Book Collecting* by Winterich and Randall; *The Book Collectors Handbook of Values* by Van Allen Bradley; *American Book-Prices Current,* published annually; *Cold in Your Attic and Afore Gold in Your Attic* by Van Allen Bradley.

When a dealer knows you are serious about collecting, he will help you if you level with him and don't use him for comparative-price-shopping-around purposes. A dealer is your best bet for buying at auction. A beginner should avoid competing with the experts in the auction room. There is a lot of specialized knowledge to acquire. A careful study of dealer and auction catalogs is one good way to begin learning about books and values. A special brand of savvy is required—a savvy not comparable to stock market investing. Taste and a special kind of instinctive response and literary judgment are called for. Plus a willingness to stick your neck out—for a *new* Ezra Pound or T. S. Eliot or Faulkner; new ones are always coming along.

Who are the hottest authors, including those living, to bet on for the present and future in terms of lasting worth and dollar appreciation?

Here's my personal lineup, and don't ask for logic or literary evaluation. These authors appear frequently in rare-book catalogs and at the auction sales, and their key books are climbing in price each season, especially their *first books*. They are virtually all foolproof and, in opening the list with Samuel Beckett, I indicate my high regard for the Big Irish Writers, who, through season after season, prove to be the most favored of all.

My "top ten" are:

Samuel Beckett	(*En Attendant Godot*)
James Joyce	(*Ulysses*)
William Faulkner	(*The Marble Faun*)
William Butler Yeats	(*Mosada*)
Ezra Pound	(*A Lume Spento*)
Gertrude Stein	(*Three Lives*)
Ernest Hemingway	(*Three Stories and Ten Poems*)
T. S. Eliot	(*Prufrock and Other Observations*)
Tennessee Williams	(*Battle of Angels*)
Dylan Thomas	(*18 Poems*)

I would follow the above "top ten" with twenty superstar authors to consider next, if you are able to accommodate a broad range of authors:

Robert Frost	(*A Boy's Will*)
Edward Albee	(*The Zoo Story; The Death of Bessie Smith; The Sandbox; Three Plays*)
William Carlos Williams	(*The Tempers*)
Stephen Spender	(*Nine Experiments by S.H.S.*)
D. H. Lawrence	(*The White Peacock*)
W. H. Auden	(*Poems*, 1930)
Wallace Stevens	(*Harmonium*)
John Steinbeck	(*Cup of Gold*)
Gwendolyn Brooks	(*A Street in Bronzeville*)
Eugene O'Neill	(*Thirst*)

Henry Miller   (*The Tropic of Cancer*)
Hart Crane   (*The Bridge*)
F. Scott Fitzgerald   (*This Side of Paradise*)
Edward Gorey   (*The Unstrung Harp*)
James Baldwin   (*Go Tell It on the Mountain*)
Robert Lowell   (*The Land of Unlikeness*)
Sylvia Plath   (*The Colossus and Other Poems*)
Vladimir Nabokov   (*Lolita*)
Virginia Woolf   (*The Voyage Out*)
Marianne Moore   (*Poems,* London, 1921)
Katherine Mansfield   (*In a German Pension*)

(*Caution:* After each of the above author's name I've put a book title in parenthesis; the book is one of the author's key books, a landmark high-spot title; in its first edition each is scarce to *very* rare. It's unlikely that you'll find many of these books in New York bookshops at this time. So please don't harass booksellers by phoning and asking for *A Lume Spento* or the signed limited edition on vellum of Hart Crane's *The Bridge;* nor is it likely that you can find a first edition of Gertrude Stein's first book, *Three Lives,* by making a few phone calls. Some of these books are priced as low as $35 and others run into the thousands of dollars.)

The following additional list of modern authors from England, France, and America is also recommended to all collectors. While this is our tertiary list we don't mean to imply that any of them are of lesser importance in literary terms; they are all highly esteemed in the marketplace and among readers. And there are others, not included, who merit inclusion; but lack of space, in addition to a subjective selective system employed by this writer, determined the present group for present purposes.

James Agee	Saul Bellow	Willa Cather
Conrad Aiken	John Berryman	Louis-Ferdinand
Guillaume	Elizabeth Bishop	Céline
Apollinaire	Louise Bogan	Raymond Chandler
John Ashbery	Paul Bowles	Gregory Corso
Djuna Barnes	Ray Bradbury	Baron Corvo
Donald Barthelme	Albert Camus	e. e. cummings
Simone de Beauvoir	Truman Capote	Edward Dahlberg

James Dickey	Randall Jarrell	J. D. Salinger
Joan Didion	Erica Jong	Carl Sandburg
J. P. Donleavy	Carolyn Kizer	William Saroyan
H. D. (Hilda	Mary McCarthy	Jean-Paul Sartre
Doolittle)	Carson McCullers	Siegfried Sassoon
John Dos Passos	Claude McKay	Anne Sexton
Norman Douglas	Somerset Maugham	George Bernard
Lawrence Durrell	Arthur Miller	Shaw
Richard Eberhart	A. A. Milne	Edith Sitwell
Ralph Ellison	Anaïs Nin	Gary Snyder
E. M. Forster	Charles Olson	James Stephens
John Gardner	George Orwell	William Styron
Herbert Gold	St. John Perse	J. M. Synge
Edward Gorey	James Purdy	Allen Tate
Robert Graves	Mario Puzo	Kurt Vonnegut, Jr.
Graham Greene	Thomas Pynchon	Diane Wakoski
Dashiell Hammett	Adrienne Rich	Mary Webb
John Hawkes	Laura Riding	Eudora Welty
Joseph Heller	Theodore Roethke	Nathanael West
Lillian Hellman	Philip Roth	Thornton Wilder
Chester Himes	Muriel Rukeyser	Edmund Wilson
Christopher Isher-	Antoine de Saint-	Thomas Wolfe
wood	Exupéry	Tom Wolfe

(*Note:* The author cannot, will not, engage in correspondence relating to the buying or selling of rare books. Please consult a bookseller.)

Death of a Bookshop

When Scribner's on Fifth Avenue in New York decided to give up its rare-book department, it was a sad piece of news for me and, I'm sure, for other collectors. A lot of history was made in that store. Harold Graves, the last manager of the shop and successor to the famous David Randall, had the lugubrious job of liquidating the stock and closing the department in 1973.

David A. Randall (until his death in 1975 with the Lilly Library at Indiana University) joined the Scribner rare-book department in 1935 and ran the show until 1956. John Carter, bibliophile sui generis (I published his *Books and Book-Collectors* at World in 1957), assisted him from England. Between them the New York rare-book business hummed. Its reverberations were felt around the world. The shop handled *two* Gutenberg Bibles in its heyday. Randall reviewed and clobbered (and rightly so) one of my very early books, a rare-book manual; but I respected his judgment and superior knowledge too much to hold it against him. I liked him, too. Get a copy of Randall's book, *Dukedom Large Enough.* It's full of good book-collecting lore and vignettes of bookmen.

I don't know why Charles Scribner decided to give up the rare-book end of his very successful bookshop, "the cathedral of bookshops." Presumably it wasn't making enough money; I never asked him, since it is not my business to inquire. But I miss that part of his great store. I bought some of the best books and autographs I own from it, including my first edition of Coleridge's *Kubla Khan* (with *Christabel* and *The Pains of Sleep* [1861]). I also acquired some remarkable Thomas Wolfe letters from Scribner's. It was always a pleasure to step into its rare-bookshop door, to visit and browse. A shop like this should not have been allowed to die.

From the Journal: "A Thing of Beauty"

The acquisition of a first edition of Keats's *Endymion* (from Scribner's in November of 1971) enlivens my week. It begins: "A thing of beauty is a joy forever." When a line like that hits a poet, what can he do for an encore? Can I convey to my readers the excitement of reading that opening line from the first edition of this book of poetry? I'm sure most will not understand how one can work oneself up into a quiet state of hysteria over such an experience. Okay. But does it—could it—*mean anything* to you? Explore the notion.

The book has given me a sense of happiness, which is, I suppose, comparable to a sultan's having added a great beauty to his harem. Possessiveness is an evil, agreed—and the root of this evil is collecting. Why deny it—unless one has a plan to make the books and autographs available to the public, to students, to poets. Time will decide this. Meanwhile, I hold the book in my hand and wonder how many persons on this planet would share my feelings about the physical possession of this book by Keats. I hesitate to guess; the figure would probably depress me.

Keats was in his early twenties when he published this allegory dealing with ideal beauty. It was attacked viciously, and there are theories that the criticism helped to hasten his death. True or not, he died at twenty-six.

Another treasure acquired from Scribner's (on June 11, 1971) was a first-edition (first issue) copy of Walt Whitman's *Leaves of Grass,* published in Brooklyn in 1855. "Published" is not an accurate word—"printed" would be more to the point. It was received with indifference or scorn, except by Emerson, one of the few civilized Americans of the time. He *greeted* Whitman "at the beginning of a great career." Emerson knew.

The Whitman is one of my most treasured books, and though the price seemed a fortune at the time, it is, thanks to time, one of the great bargains in my collection. Every time I remove the tall, green slender book from its slipcase, to read a page or two, I have the feeling that I am touching the poet. It is said that he set some of the type, and he may have handled the very binding I am holding.

John Carter

I've mentioned John Carter elsewhere in this book, but an additional comment is not without purpose. I knew him from the time I had the pleasure of publishing one of his books, and a bit of his expertise rubbed off on me. At least so I like to think.

Carter, who died at sixty-nine on March 28, 1975, has a historic place in book-collecting history for having exposed Thomas J. Wise, the famous book forger. Together with Graham Pollard, Carter unmasked this heretofore eminently respected British bibliophile in a book entitled *An Inquiry into the Nature of Certain Nineteenth Century Pamphlets.* Published in 1934, the book was virtually a David vs. Goliath encounter. (My inscribed copy seems to be missing from my library, but I do have a letter from Wise written shortly before he died in disgrace.)

Carter had many distinctions; one not generally known is that he was an expert in the field of musical manuscripts. He unearthed many forgotten or "lost" scores, including the original score of Mozart's Haffner Symphony. He also loved and collected detective fiction.

Any student of book collecting, searching for a thesis or graphical subject, will find it in the life and works of John Waynflete

Carter. He was an ornament to society, to literature, to the fraternity of bookmen.

Lawyers and Literature

One of the noblemen of the legal profession in New York is Melville Henry Cane, a poet of talent and sensibility, who continues, in his nineties (he was born in Plattsburg, New York, on April 15, 1879), to write excellent poetry—and to practice law. He represented the interests of Sinclair Lewis, Thomas Wolfe, and other men of letters. O rare Melville Cane.

But unique among New York lawyers—and, alas, a man I never met—was John Quinn. He died in 1924 at the age of fifty-five. When I say unique, I mean just that. He was a self-made man, a lawyer who lived only from his earnings as a lawyer. This is not in itself unique. But the man was gifted with a special sight and artistic sense seldom found in a layman or a lawyer. His taste for art and literature was intense, and he spent all his spare time and money cultivating (the word is used in its best sense) writers, poets, painters— especially men of genius who had not quite arrived at universal recognition.

For example, he recognized T. S. Eliot, Synge, Lady Gregory, Ezra Pound, Joyce, and Yeats, as well as Picasso, Gauguin, Matisse, Brancusi, Rouault, Duchamp, and Rousseau when they were barely known in America—or elsewhere. He provided legal aid to James Joyce when Joyce ran into trouble with the serialization of *Ulysses;* eventually, Quinn owned the manuscript. (Rosenbach acquired it later at auction: a long and complicated saga.)

Quinn bought works by the great unknown artists and holograph manuscripts by writers who were yet to be recognized. He would give or lend money to artists in need and kept up a heavy correspondence with them. He was the ubiquitous patron, "the bravest and most serviceable patron of modernism of his time, and probably the greatest collector of modern art." Aline Saarinen called him "the twentieth century's most important patron of living literature and art." He favored, above all, the living Irish writers; Yeats's father called him "an angel."

A detailed biography of John Quinn, *The Man from New York,* was written by B. L. Reid. What is significant in this story is the fact that Quinn, whose livelihood depended solely on his daily appearance in his office or in the courtroom, had the time, the genius, the will, to partake of the best around him and to befriend men and women of genius through gifts, friendship, and old-fashioned patronage. In the process, he amassed an incredible private art and literary collection. Collecting is obviously an art, and the results depend on the passion, devotion, and seriousness of one's dedication to the pursuit.

Though Quinn remained a bachelor throughout his lifetime—and one might surmise that he had no time for romance or family—his biography reveals some curious documentation relating to his romantic affiliations. He was definitely not asexual. In this respect he reminds me of A. S. W. Rosenbach, who also never married, but who loved women only next to books. I suspect that if the choice had been put to him, Rosenbach would have preferred a copy of *The Bay Psalm Book* to the company of a beautiful woman. Possibly I underestimate him.

When you bet on the horse race, you bet for win, for place, for show. When you buy books, you buy some to read, some to own, and some for reference. You want to possess the books, you want to own them, you want to hold them. Perhaps you even hope that you will read them.

—LOUIS SZATHMARY

The Newark Public Library

BY PHILIP ROTH

Philip Roth, a native of Newark, New Jersey, has had one of the most re-
markable careers in American letters this century. This piece appeared in
his 1975 collection, Reading Myself and Others, *with the following*
note: "In February 1969, after riots had already destroyed much of
Newark's black slums, the City Council voted to strike from the city's
budget the $2.8 million required to finance the Newark Museum and
the Newark Public Library. Hundreds of Newark residents vehemently
opposed this move, which would have shut down two exceptional civic
institutions. In the face of the protest, the council eventually rescinded its
decision. My piece appeared on the editorial page of The New York
Times *about two weeks after the announcement of the budget cutback*
(1969)."

What will the readers of Newark do if the City Council goes ahead
with its money-saving plan to shut down the public library system
on April 1? Will they loot the stacks the way Newarkers looted ap-
pliance stores in the riot of 1967? Will police be called in to Mace
down thieves racing off with the *Encyclopaedia Britannica*? Will
scholars take up sniping positions at reference-room windows and
school children seize the main Washington Street building in order

to complete their term papers? If the City Council locks up the books, will library card holders band together to "liberate" them?

I suppose one should hope not. Apparently there must be respect for Law and Order, even where there is none for aspiration and curiosity and quiet pleasure, for language, learning, scholarship, intelligence, reason, wit, beauty, and knowledge. When I was growing up in Newark in the forties, we assumed that the books in the public library belonged to the public. Since my family did not own many books, or have the money for a child to buy them, it was good to know that solely by virtue of my municipal citizenship I had access to any book I wanted from that grandly austere building downtown on Washington Street, or from the branch library I could walk to in my neighborhood. No less satisfying was the idea of communal ownership, property held in common for the common good. Why I had to care for the books I borrowed, return them unscarred and on time, was because they weren't mine alone, they were everybody's. That idea had as much to do with civilizing me as any I was ever to come upon in the books themselves.

If the idea of a *public* library was civilizing, so was the place, with its comforting quiet, its tidy shelves, its knowledgeable, dutiful employees who weren't teachers. The library wasn't simply where one had to go to get the books, it was a kind of exacting haven to which a city youngster willingly went for his lesson in restraint and his training in self-control. And then there was the lesson in order, the enormous institution itself serving as instructor. What trust it inspired—in both oneself and in systems—first to decode the catalogue card, then to make it through the corridors and stairwells into the open stacks, and there to discover, exactly where it was supposed to be, the desired book. For a ten-year-old to find he actually can steer himself through tens of thousands of volumes to the very one he wants is not without its satisfactions. Nor did it count for nothing to carry a library card in one's pocket; to pay a fine; to sit in a strange place, beyond the reach of parent and school, and read whatever one chose, in anonymity and peace; finally, to carry home across the city and even into bed at night a book with a local lineage of its own, a family tree of Newark readers to which one's name had now been added.

In the forties, when the city was still largely white, it was simply an unassailable fact of life that the books were "ours" and that the public library had much to teach us about the rules of civilized life, as well as civilized pleasures to offer. It is strange (to put it politely) that now, when Newark is mostly black, the City Council (for fiscal reasons, we are told) has reached a decision that suggests that the books don't really belong to the public after all, and that what a library provides for the young is no longer essential to an education. In a city seething with social grievances there is, in fact, probably little that could be *more* essential to the development and sanity of the thoughtful and ambitious young than access to those books. For the moment the Newark City Council may have solved its fiscal problem; it is too bad, however, that the councilmen are unable to calculate the frustration, cynicism, and rage that this insult must inevitably generate, and to imagine what shutting down its libraries may cost the community in the end.

Why Does Nobody Collect Me?

BY ROBERT BENCHLEY

Robert Benchley was an essayist, humorist, and actor who invariably portrayed his life as a series of humiliations and frustrations. In this essay—which first appeared in The Colophon *in 1934 and was subsequently included in William Targ's excellent 1947 collection,* Carrousel for Bibliophiles—*he is true to form. In it, he questions why first editions of books by his friend Ernest Hemingway are valuable while his are not, when "I am older than Hemingway, and have written more books that he has."*

Some months ago, while going through an old box of books looking for a pressed nasturtium, I came across a thin volume which, even to my dreamer's instinct, seemed worth holding out, if only for purposes of prestige.

It was a first edition of Ernest Hemingway's *In Our Time,* the edition brought out in Paris by the Three Mountains Press in 1924, while Hemingway was just "Old Ernie" who lived over the sawmill in the rue Notre Dames des Champs. I knew that it must be worth saving, because it said in the front that the edition consisted of one hundred and seventy copies, of which mine was number thirty-nine. That usually means something.

It so happened that, a few weeks later, "Old Ernie" himself was using my room in New York as a hide-out from literary columnists and reporters during one of his stop-over visits between Africa and Key West. On such all-too-rare occasions he lends an air of virility to my dainty apartment which I miss sorely after he has gone and the furniture has been repaired.

More to interrupt his lion-hunting story than anything else, I brought out my copy of *In Our Time* and suggested that, in memory of happy days around the Anise Deloso bowl at the Closerie des Lilas, it might be the handsome thing for him to inscribe a few pally sentiments on the fly-leaf. Not, as I took pains to explain to him, that I was a particular admirer of his work, so much as that I wanted to see if he really knew how to spell.

Encouraged by my obviously friendly tone, he took a pen in his chubby fist, dipped it in a bottle of bull's blood, and wrote the following:

> To Robert ("Garbage Bird") Benchley,
> hoping that he won't wait for prices
> to reach the peak—
> > from his friend,
> > Ernest ("———") Hemingway

The "Garbage Bird" reference in connection with me was a familiarity he had taken in the past to describe my appearance in the early morning light of Montparnasse on certain occasions. The epithet applied to himself, which was unprintable except in *Ulysses,* was written deliberately to make it impossible for me to cash in on the book.

Then, crazed with success at defacing *In Our Time,* he took my first edition of *A Farewell to Arms* and filled in each blank in the text where Scribner's had blushed and put a dash instead of the original word. I think that he supplied the original word in every case. In fact, I am sure of it.

On the fly-leaf of this he wrote:

> To R. (G). B. from E. (———). H.
> > Corrected edition. Filled-in blanks.
> > Very valuable. Sell quick.

Now, oddly enough, I had never considered selling either book. I had known, in a general way, that a first edition of the Gutenberg

Bible would be worth money, and that, if one could lay hands on an autographed copy of *Canterbury Tales,* it would be a good idea to tuck it away, but that a first edition of one of Ernie's books could be the object of even Rabelaisian jesting as to its commercial value surprised and, in a vague sort of way, depressed me. Why are not my works matters for competitive bidding in the open market?

I am older than Hemingway, and have written more books than he has. And yet it is as much as my publishers and I can do to get people to pay even the list price for my books, to say nothing of a supplementary sum for rare copies. One of my works, *Love Conquers All,* is even out of print, and yet nobody shows any interest in my extra copy. I have even found autographed copies of my books in secondhand book shops, along with *My Life and Times* by Buffalo Bill. Doesn't *anybody* care?

What is there about me and my work that repels collectors? I am handsome, in an unusual sort of way, and speak French fluently, even interspersing some of my writings with French phrases. True, some of my copy, as it goes to the printer, is not strictly orthodox in spelling and punctuation, but the proof-readers have always been very nice about it, and, by the time my books are out, there is nothing offensive to the eye about them. And yet I have been told by hospital authorities that more copies of my works are left behind by departing patients than those of any other author. It does seem as if people might at least take my books home with them.

If it is rarity which counts in the value of a book, I have dozens of very rare Benchley items in my room which I know cannot be duplicated. For the benefit of collectors, I will list them, leaving the price more or less up to the would-be purchaser. All that I ask is that I don't actually lose money on the sale.

There is a copy of my first book, *Of All Things,* issued by Henry Holt in 1922. (Mr. Lincoln MacVeagh, who engineered the deal, is now ambassador to Greece, which ought to count for something.) It is a first edition, an author's copy, in fact, and has a genuine tumbler-ring on the cover. I have no doubt that it is actually the first volume of mine ever to be issued, and, as *Of All Things* has gradually gone into twelve editions since, it ought to be very valuable. Page 29 is dog-eared.

Love Conquers All (Holt, 1923) is, as I have said, now out of print, which makes my extra copy almost unique. I doubt very much if anyone else has an *extra* copy of *Love Conquers All*. It is a third edition, which may detract a little from its market value, but this is compensated for by the fact that it belonged originally to Dorothy Parker, who left it at my house five or six years ago and has never felt the need for picking it up. So, you see, it is really a Dorothy Parker item, too.

Pluck and Luck (Holt, 1924) was brought out later in a dollar edition for drugstore sale, and I have three of those in a fair state of preservation. One of them is a very interesting find for collectors, as I had started to inscribe it to Donald Ogden Stewart and then realized that I had spelled the name "Stuart," necessitating the abandonment of the whole venture. It is practically certain that there is not another dollar edition of *Pluck and Luck* with Donald Ogden Stewart's name spelled "Stuart" on the fly-leaf. Would a dollar and a quarter be too much to ask, do you think?

Faulty inscriptions account for most of the extra copies of *The Early Worm* (Holt, 1926) that I have lying about. It was during that period, and that of my next book, *Twenty Thousand Leagues Under the Sea, or David Copperfield* (Holt, 1928), that I went through a phase of trying to write humorous remarks on the fly-leaves of gift copies. Those copies in which the remarks did not turn out to be so humorous as I had planned had to be put aside. I have eighteen or twenty of these discarded copies, each with an inscription which is either unfunny or misspelled.

During what I call "my transitional period," when I changed from Henry Holt to Harper's and began putting on weight, I was moody and fretful, and so did not feel like trying to make wisecracks in my inscriptions. The recipient of a book was lucky if I even took the trouble to write his name in it. He was lucky, indeed, if he could read my name, for it was then that I was bullied into autographing copies at book-shop teas (this was my transitional period, you must remember, and I was not myself), and my handwriting deteriorated into a mere series of wavy lines, like static.

For this reason, I have not so many curious copies of *The Treasurer's Report* and *No Poems* hanging about. I have, however, a dummy of *The Treasurer's Report* with each page blank, and many of my friends insist that it should be worth much more than the final product. I don't know just how dummy copies rate as collectors' items, but I will be very glad to copy the entire text into it longhand for fifty dollars. Thirty-five dollars, then.

And now I come to what I consider the choicest item of them all—one which would shape up rather impressively in a glass case a hundred years from now. It is a complete set of corrected galleys for my next book (to be called, I am afraid, *From Bed to Worse*), which I had cut up for rearrangement before I realized that I was cutting up the wrong set of proofs—the one that the printer wants back. I haven't broken the news to the printer at Harper's, and I may never get up the courage to do so (printers get so cross), in which case the book will never come out at all. Would that be a valuable piece of property or not—a set of hand-corrected galleys for a Benchley item which never was published? And all cut up into little sections, too! A veritable treasure, I would call it, although possibly the words might come better from somebody else.

But, until the collecting public comes to its senses, I seem to be saddled, not only with a set of mutilated galleys, but about twenty-five rare copies of my earlier works, each unique in its way. Possibly Hemingway would like them in return for the two books of his own that he has gone to so much trouble to render unsaleable for me.

How Not to Care for Books

BY HOLBROOK JACKSON

The name Holbrook Jackson has been associated with bibliomania since the 1930 publication of his masterwork, Anatomy of Bibliomania—*recently republished under the title* The Book about Books. *Jackson collected and organized material from an incredible range of world literature, assembling virtually everything written about books until his day (which explains the archaic spelling in many of his quotations). This section is about the abuse of books.*

Next to persecutors, if I may distinguish them, are those neglectors, irreverent of careless handlers, bullies of books, who are not far behind them as destroyers. Swift compared libraries to cemeteries and as some authorities affirm that a spirit hovers over the monuments of the dead till the bodies are corrupted and turned to dust, so he believed a like restless spirit haunted every book, till dust or worms seized upon it. *Alas!* exclaims Janin, *'tis no wonder that these miracles of the printers are priceless,* for before reaching us they have escaped so many dangers, confronted so many obstacles: unhealthy homes, damp cellars, either too hot or too cold; fire and water. When Leland visited Oxford after the suppression of the monasteries, he found few books, only *moths and beetles swarming over the empty shelves.* It was no better at Cambridge, even in more recent times. *Nothing,* says Bradshaw, *could be more disgraceful than the way in which the manuscripts* of Bishop Moore's library, presented to the University by George I, *were literally shovelled into their places; and for the thirty-five years that followed the presentation the pillage was so unlimited that the only wonder is that we have any valuable books left.* Every library, especially those that are old and large, or small and neglected, breeds its own inimical flora and fauna, mould, bookworms, moths, *anthrene, vorilette,* bugs, mice, rats, the story of whose devastations would fell many volumes. In addition Janin enumerates such enemies as dust, children, kittens, hot greasy hands, *les sales mains d'Hermogenes,* and finally, *les imbeciles et les brigands qui di tiennent autour des trones, an changant la chanson:*

> Eteignons les lumieres,
> Et rallumons le feu . . .
>
> *Let's put out the lights,*
> *And stoke up the fire . . .*

Many authorities support him, extending his catalogue, as William Blades, who would add gas, bookbinders, houseflies, bugs, black-beetles, and servants; upon all of which he dilates at large. Rats and mice have doubtless browsed on books, growing fat if not wise. But sometimes their gnawings have been frustrated, as in that example, recorded by Bernard Shaw, of the MS. of his own first novel, *Immaturity,* which, rejected by publishers, lay neglected until part of it *was devoured by mice though even they had not been able to finish it;* but tough or tender, mice have no respect for either genius or masterpiece:

> *Ho, ho! Master Mouse! safe at last in my cage*
> *You're caught, and there's nothing shall save you from dying:*
> *For, caitiff! you nibbled and tore Shakespeare's page,*
> *When close by your nose Tupper's nonsense was lying.*

Because these enemies of books are so malign in themselves, and so hard to be removed, *prevention is better than cure;* and the best averter of such rebellious carriers of destruction is wise and constant use. When Sir Thomas Bodley was told by his Librarian James that some of his books were infested with worms, he replied: *I hope those little worms about the covers of your books come by reason of their newness, and that hereafter they will away.* For more to this end, see my Digression of Bookworms.

Most of these misfortunes come by neglect, which is in itself a negative ill-usage. All those misaffections which I have named are as weeds in the garden of books; dust, mould, maggots, bugs, moths, beetles, and the like are the zymotic diseases of books, and as devastating as the perils of direct attack and abuse. Petrarch gave a collection of books to the city of Venice, but many years afterwards they were found rotting away in a cellar: some had become mere dust, others were agglutinated by the damp into formless masses, but a few survived and are still preserved in the Ducal palace. The Library of Monte Cassino survived the desecrations of Lombard and Saracen only to rush destruction from neglect. When Boccaccio visited the monastery he found noble manuscripts scattered and disordered in a doorless loft reached by a ladder. The books were white with dust and whole sheets had been ripped out and margins cut away. Boccaccio wept at the sight and demanded of a monk how such precious volumes had been so ill-used. He was told that the brethren needed money and would cut out enough leaves from a Bible to make a little Psalter, which they would sell, and they raised more revenue by disposing of the blank margins for use as "briefs."

Yet dust, according to some authorities, is not in itself so damaging to books as the act of dusting them by unskillful or irreverent performers. Both Blades and Birrell stiffly maintain that *you should never dust books;* let the dust lie *until the rare hour arrives when you want to read a particular volume; then warily,* Birrell advises, *approach it with a snow-white napkin, take it down from its shelf, and withdrawing to some back apartment, proceed to cleanse the tome.* Blades has a terror of careless servants and rampant housewives conducting a Spring offensive, and if he admits that *books must now and then be taken out of their shelves, they should be tended lovingly and with judgment,* and he agrees with Birrell that *if dusting can be done just outside the room so much the better.* I am with these reliable authorities in both their strictures and advice, but neither they nor I are ignorant of the fact that it is not only frenzied domesticity which desecrates our temples in pursuit of dust; bookmen themselves are often perverse offenders, and not least among them our learned Dr. Johnson, as I have shown, but I will again recount the story for a caution, this time out of Birrell. When about to dust his books the Doctor *drew on huge gloves, such as those once worn by hedgers and ditchers, and then, clutching his folios and octavos, he banged and buffeted them together until he was enveloped in a cloud of dust. This violent exercise over, the good doctor restored the volumes, all battered, and bruised, to their places, where of course, the dust resettled itself as speedily as possible.* It is the good fortune of books that such methods have been superseded by the invention of that ingenious engine called the vacuum cleaner, although I must not omit to mention that cleanliness does not satisfy all bookmen, for there are some who regard dust on books as a mark of age, and therefore of distinction, much as connoisseurs will preserve with tender care the grimy encrustations on a bottle of an ancient and honourable wine. Such enthusiasts as these consider the dust of the library, together with that of the crematorium and of the churchyard, *as a measure sacred.*

But abuse more direct and deliberate has been as common in most times, from their use as a packing or tinder to the indignity of sanitary necessity, for although Gargantua discommends paper, and books as such are not named in his famous *torcheculatif,* their use in this wise is historically established and has become a byword in French *coprology. Avisez-y, doctes: parce que souvent d'espice, ou des mouchoirs de cul.* There are those also, as that old English aphorist, who go so far as to class the writer of abundance of Books with the begetter of *abundance of Children,* as a *Benefactor of the Public,* because he furnishes it with *Bumfodder and Soldiers.* I must perforce be indefinite in such a record, so shall only add one instance in which Carew Hazlitt tells us that not so long since, a copy of Caxton's *Recuyell of the Hystoryes of Troye* was found *hanging up in a water-closet at Harrogate;* part of it had already been consumed, but the remainder was rescued and *sold to a dealer in Manchester for thirty pounds.* Many times rashly and unadvisedly are good books destined to an indignity which might be deemed infamous and ridiculous for even a newspaper, and if I were disposed to enlarge this theme, here might easily be recalled many unsavoury tales from our own early literature, and I would go on with it, but as Grangousier advised Gargantua, it is a *dull theme,* so to wander on would be no joke, the curious in such business may look for more in Thomas Dekker, his *Gul's Horn-Booke,* Dryden's *Mac Flecknoe,* Swift, etc.

As *martyrs of pies* and victims of economy books have a long and tragical history. To recount how many have been so destroyed would make a long list. They have suffered I know not what in this wise; but I can give no more than a taste, as the example which Macray gives out of the notes of Rawlingson how that collector came by many rare documents which had been disposed of as rubbish. *I lately rescued from the grocers, chandlers, etc.,* he records, in 1755, *a parcel of papers once the property of Compton and Robinson, successively Bishops of London;* amongst them *remarkable intelligences relating to Burnet and the Orange Court in Holland in those extraordinary times before 1688;* and letters from Bolingbroke, Oxford, Ormonde, Strafford, Prior, and the Elector and Electress of Hanover. At another time, from a shop whether they had been sentenced to serve for supporting *pyes, currents, sugar, etc.,* he redeemed *as many as came to 12s. at 6d. per pound.* These included a collection of *ecclesiastical causes,* and the causes of Bishop Watson and the Duchess of Cleveland.

The history of books teems with such accounts, not only from past ages but from nearer our own times. The letters which James Boswell addressed to his friend the Rev. William Temple were discovered, about the middle of last century, by a clergyman, in the shop of a Madame Noel, at Boulogne. He observed that the article he had bought was wrapped in a piece of paper bearing English writing. His interest was aroused, and upon examination the paper proved to be part of a letter written by the biographer of Dr. Johnson. He made further inquiries and discovered a goodly parcel of letters by the same hand which Madame Noel had purchased from a hawker, who passed through that seaport twice a year supplying the tradesfolk with wrapping paper. The clergyman immediately secured the whole parcel, and the letters are now among the treasures of our epistolary literature. Another such rescue from the paw of the shopkeeper had a curious issue, if the tale D'Israeli tells of Barbosa, Bishop of Ugento, be true. In the year 1649, that ecclesiastic printed among his works a treatise, called *de Officio Episcopi,* which he obtained by having perceived one of his domestics bring in a fish rolled in a piece of paper which his curiosity led him to examine. His interest was immediately provoked and he ran out and searched the fish market until he found and secured the MS. from which the sheet had been torn.

Now and again in other circumstances of time and place whole libraries have been left to the risk of adventitious events, and some have suffered no further damage than dispersal, as the library formed by Edward Gibbon at Lausanne for the writing of his history of the *Decline and Fall of the Roman Empire.* Mary Berry tells how she saw this library when she visited that city, in 1803, where it still remained, although, as I have shown in its place, it had been bought by Beckford seven years earlier. *It is,* she says, *of all libraries I ever saw, that of which I should most covet the possession; that which seems exactly everything that any gentleman or gentlewoman fond of letters could wish.* The books were under the care of a Mr. Scholl, a physician of that place, and were all clean and in good condition. Several years before Beckford had packed up 2,500 out of 10,000 volumes, intending to send them to England, but they still remained there in their cases. In 1818 they were seen by another traveler, Henry Matthews, *locked up in an uninhabited house.* In 1825, Birkbeck Hill records, half of them were sold by Dr. Scholl (to whom Beckford eventually gave them) to Mr. Halliday, an Englishman, *who lived in a tower near Orbe.* The remainder were dispersed, some going to America, but many volumes were still in the possession of a resident of Geneva as lately as the year 1876, though I can find no record of them after that date.

Richard de Bury fulminates in a whole chapter of his *Philobiblon* against the careless abusers of books in his time: as a youthful student lounging over his studies, *when the winter's frost is sharp, his nose running from the nipping cold* and dripping down and unwiped until *he has bedewed the book before him with ugly moisture;* another marks passages with the fetid *black filth of his nails,* and *distributing straws* between the pages so that *the halm may remind him of what his memory cannot retain,* thus distending the book from its *wonted closing.* Such abusers, he says, do not fear to eat fruit or cheese over the open pages, or to carry a cup to their mouths over them, dropping into the book crumbs and spots of liquid. They wet the pages with *spluttering showers* from their lips as they dispute with their companions, and when they pause in their studies to take a nap they fold their arms and sleep upon the book, crumpling the leaves, and then seek to mend them, to their further damage, by folding them back. When the rain is over and gone, and the flowers appear on the earth, they will sally forth and stuff their volumes *with violets, and primroses, with roses and quatrefoil.* They will use wet and perspiring hands to turn over pages; thumb white vellum with gloves covered with dirt: *with fingers clad in long-used leather will hunt line by line through the pages;* throw them aside unclosed so that they get full of dust; make notes and other inky exercises in their margins.

In those times also there was a *class of thieves* who shamefully mutilated books by cutting away the margins and endpapers to use the materials for letters, *a kind of sacrilege,* he well says, *which should be prohibited by the threat of anathema.* As a preventative of some of these evils he puts out that no student should go to his books after meals without washing his hands. No grease-stained fingers should unfasten the clasps, or turn the leaves of a book; no crying child should be let admire the capital letters lest he soil the parchment, *for a child instantly touches what he sees.* And, finally, *let the clerk,* he advises, *take care also that the smutty scullion reeking from his stewpots does not touch the lily leaves of books, all unwashed.*

Many bookmen might I reckon up who have used books scurvily, tearing their leaves open with a finger or blunt instrument instead of using a paperknife of ivory or bone. James Thompson, the poet of *The Seasons,* did not scruple to attempt this delicate operation with his *candle-snuffers. To introduce Wordsworth into one's library,* Southey tells De Quincey, *is like letting a bear into a tulip garden;* he had no mercy on his own or other people's books, and once at tea-time De Quincey observed him take up a butter-knife to open the pages of a volume of *Burke: he tore his way into the heart of the volume with this knife, that left its greasy honours behind it on every page.* De Quincey was not shocked at this proceeding, he was surprised only that Wordsworth should have been so precipitate in his vandalism, as a more appropriate book-knife could easily have been discovered; he was even inclined to extenuate the act because the book was a common one. *Had the book been an old black-letter book, having a value from its rarity,* he would *have been disturbed in an indescribable degree; but simply,* he is quick to add, lest perchance he be convicted of bibliophily, *with reference to the utter impossibility of reproducing that mode of value.* As for the *Burke,* he himself *had bought the book, with many others, at the sale of Sir Cecil Wray's library, for about two-thirds of the selling price.* He only mentions *the case to illustrate the excess of Wordsworth's outrages on books, which made him, in Southey's eyes, a mere monster; for Southey's library was his estate; and this difference of habits would alone have sufficed to alienate him from Wordsworth.*

Others, as Richard de Bury observes, use books as receptacles for papers and other objects, thus straining their covers beyond bearing point. A clumsy offender was Selden, who would *buy his spectacles by the gross,* using them to mark the place in a book where he happened to leave off reading. *It was quite a common thing, soon after his library came to the Bodleian, for spectacles to drop out of the books as they were taken incautiously from the shelves. It has been my custom,* Medwell, the American Grangeriser, ingeniously confesses, *for over forty years to insert articles, from magazines and newspapers, pertinent to the subjects, in my books; many of them are so full as nearly to burst their covers, and some I have been obliged to have rebound to save them;* and like damage is done by botanists, who look upon a book as nothing more than a press for plants and flowers: a vestibule to the herbarium.

When Dr. Johnson was engaged upon his edition of *Shakespeare,* David Garrick refused to lend him copies of the old plays in his collection, *knowing that he treated books with a roughness ill-suited to their constitution,* and he thought that he had gone quite far enough *by asking Johnson to come to his library.* The great man took his revenge by saying nothing of Garrick in his Preface. That Dr. Johnson was rough on books I have sufficiently noticed, but I cannot ignore another piece of evidence from his *Life of Young,* where after commending the keenness bestowed by the poet upon the perusal of books, he proceeds to describe Young's crude method of marking pages, with evident approval: *When any passage pleased him, he appears to have folded down the leaf,* so that many of the books, which the Doctor had seen, *are by these notes of approbation so swelled beyond their real bulk, that they will not shut.*

Several learned men have not scrupled to treat books as though they were newspapers by tearing or cutting out extracts to save themselves the trouble of copying them. I have already noticed Edward FitzGerald's habit of pollarding literature by cutting out of his books the sections which gave him no pleasure and binding up only those which were to his taste, and in order to show that such habits are not unusual among scholarly men, I shall cite a few further instances. Charles Darwin had no respect for books, *but merely considered them as tools to be worked with;* when they fell to pieces with rough use he held them together with metal clips; *he would cut a heavy book in half to make it more convenient to hold,* and he *would tear out, for the sake of saving room,* all the pages of pamphlets *except the one that interested him.* Dr. Hughlings Jackson, founder of the science of neurology, had the same bad habit: *he had no compunction about tearing out any portion which interested him, and would frequently send to a friend a few leaves torn out of a book dealing with any subject in which he knew the friend to be interested.* His library was thus a collection of mutilated volumes. On purchasing a novel at a railway bookstall, which he often did, his first act was to rip off the covers, then to *tear the book in two, putting one half in one pocket and the other in the other.* On one such occasion the clerk at the stall stared at the performance of this sacrilegious act with such obvious amazement that Jackson, observing him, remarked: *You think I am mad, my boy, but it's the people who don't do this who are really mad.* But no more fantastic desecration is recorded than that of Shelley, who had a passion for making and sailing paper boats. He could not resist the temptation to pursue these nautical adventures whenever he came to a pond, and any paper which came to his hand was requisitioned for this miniature shipbuilding. If he had stopped at letters and newspapers, or even those banknotes which are said to have augmented his curious purpose, he would not have figured in my black-list, but when all other raw material of the craft failed, he did not shrink from turning to one *of the portable volumes which were the companions of his rambles.* He applied their fly-leaves *as our ancestor Noah applied Gopher wood; but,* Hogg explains, *learning was so sacred in his eyes that he never trespassed further on the integrity of the copy.*

Scholars do not hesitate to mix books with eating apparatus. *I have sometimes heard of an* Iliad *in a nutshell,* says Swift, *but it has been my fortune to have much oftener seen a nutshell in an* Iliad. Madan recalls Dean Burgon's study table in Oriel with *forgotten teacups at various elevations, on jutting promontories of the alpine "massif" of books, once stately and fragrant,* show the results of unfair usage, and that in his various movings from one place to another *more than one has been foully injured by a great nail driven into a packing-case.* In such misfortunes he felt no regret, for so long as a volume held together he was not troubled by its outward show.

How readers of the commoner kind will wet their fingers to expedite the turning of pages is well known. But this naughty habit is not confined to rude fellows of the baser sort, for not so long ago a *learned vandal* was observed in the University Library at Cambridge in the act of *wetting his forefinger* for this same purpose. He was nicely rebuked by Jenkinson, the librarian, who *silently caught his hand and laid it on the table.* Well may Madan disapprove of giving scholars permission to rove freely round the shelves of Bodley's Library. *The great men of literature,* he says, *are often the very persons* who could be least trusted in those rich store-rooms; and he goes on to recount their depredation, as pulling books out by the top of their backs, fingering them, turning leaves by *the application of moisture,* and holding them open on a table by *putting other volumes on them;* finally, *they seldom know how or where to put a volume back,* as he well remembers upon a sight of the Douce Romm MSS, after a visit from Robinson Ellis or the Malone room after Swinburne had been allowed to sample it. *We have societies for the prevention of cruelty to children and other animals,* observes Walter Jerrold, *why have we no society for the prevention of cruelty to books?* A favourable answer might have been more necessary in olden times, but even in our day there are not wanting those ingrates who misuse books and treat them with neglect, for I find so experienced a witness as Dr. Hagberg Wright holding up the ancients as examples to some readers of our time. In bygone times readers, he says, *were counted by tens, but they loved the books they read, and handled them with reverence and care.* Nowadays readers have *deteriorated;* they do not love their books as their ancestors loved them. *Too often,* he says, *they handle them as bricks and buy them as furniture; they even mutilate them,* and if, as he believes, *book-lovers always remain lovers of books* though *some of them have degenerated into bibliomaniacs,* many of them are rough wooers, if we may judge by the treatment of books in our lending libraries. One such library mentioned by Alexander Smith was no better than a *Greenwich Hospital for disabled novels and romances; each book had been in the wars,* and *the tears of three generations* had *fallen upon their dusty pages.*

In conclusion I must set out a few words on the perils of bookbinding, for although these dangers may be avoided by careful attention, the binder is still often a biblioclast by accident, stupidity, or ignorance. In my chapter of first editions I have said something about "condition," and how modern collectors demand their specimens in "mint state," so here will do no more than commend a fashion which is both scientific and protective. Had it always prevailed, mutilated copies of rare books would not have been so common. Even so recently as the year 1881 Andrew Lang was not a fully convinced opponent of cut margins, for although he knew that *once the binder begins to clip he is unable to resist the seductive joy, and cuts the paper to the quick, even into the printed matter,* he was only *almost tempted to say that margins should always be left untouched.* There is now no doubt. Margins should never be cut. All books should appear intonsis capillis, *with locks unshorn, as Motteley the old dealer used to say, an* Elzevir *in its paper wrapper may be worth more than the same tome in morocco, stamped with Longepierre's fleece of gold.* No collector of our time would commit such an error as to rebind a fair copy, still less allow his binder to cut the margins of any book. The biblioclastic bookbinder is, however, still a menace, and Blades is so incensed against him that he is encouraged by memories of how Dante in his Inferno *deals out to the lost souls tortures suited with dramatic fitness to the past crimes of the victims,* to imagine that had he *to execute judgment on the criminal binders of certain precious volumes* he has seen, *where the untouched maiden sheets entrusted to their care have, by barbarous treatment, lost dignity, beauty and value,* he *would collect the paper shavings so ruthlessly shorn off, and roast the perpetrator of the outrage over their slow combustion.* He justifies this drastic punishment on the ground that, however much the plea of ignorance may have been justified in the past, there is no such excuse in these times, *when the historical and antiquarian value of old books is freely acknowledged,* Quarter should not be given.

On Reading and Collecting

BY HERBERT FAULKNER WEST

This essay is from West's The Mind on the Wing, *his 1947 sequel to the landmark book* Modern Book Collecting for the Impecunious Amateur. *West was a professor of comparative literature at Dartmouth and a promoter of nature writing. This essay is an excellent summary of the ins and outs of collecting and caring for books.*

I hope the report recently announced by the National Opinion Research Center of Denver, in which 41 percent of those questioned said they preferred reading to all other forms of recreation, is true. I happen to prefer it also, and I write these chapters primarily for fellow readers and collectors who buy books not for speculation but because they want to read them. The fact that a book you buy may rise in value is fine, but it should be secondary to the fact that you have bought it because you want to read it and have it on your own shelves.

Many strange and interesting characters who have the urge to collect are known to all booksellers. Many of them usually know nothing of literature, but the urge to collect (the acquisitive instinct we share with squirrels) is irresistible. One bookseller friend of mine told me some of his clients are taxi drivers and letter carriers, and one, a house painter, has a good library but has never read a book.

Collectors who are simply speculators hurt the book market and make things difficult for the honest collector, and, as one bookseller told me recently, they tempt booksellers to evil deeds. John Hersey's *A Bell for Adano,* 1944, a much overrated book, through speculators rose to $20 or $25 for the first edition, but it wasn't long before it dropped to where it belonged in the first place—at about its published price. The moral here is not to be stampeded by ballyhoo but calmly and critically to judge the book for yourself.

The collecting instinct is deeply rooted in all men, women, and children. I read not long ago of one Sergeant Spann who collected 3,000 war souvenirs in less than two years overseas. He had sent home, so the article stated, copies of *Mein Kampf,* Bibles in four languages, German weapons, clocks, beer steins, pipes, and even a couple of wedding rings. Spann started, so the Associated Press dispatch stated, collecting cigar bands when he was two years old, then turned to match folders, chewing-gum wrappers, marbles, and snakeskins. I have a lot of sympathy for Sergeant Spann, as I have for collectors of *Aspidistra lurida,* bottlecaps, upholstered carpet tacks, dust wrappers, trade cards, dog collars, stuffed birds, stuffed shirts, whisky bottles, Heinz labels, preserved chutney, theater programs, bus tickets, comic valentines, pressed ferns, birds' eggs, old nails, horseshoes, locks of hair, prints and etchings, snuffboxes, Sandwich glass, nasturtium seeds, empty cartridge cases, beds Washington slept in, cigarette cases, diamonds, champagne corks, copies of the *National Geographic,* stocks and bonds, human skulls, knives, Philippine bolos, ichneumons (the Egyptian mongoose), meerkats (suricates), Krugeriana, playing cards, and photographs of Hollywood dream boys and girls. Still, all in all, I prefer books to all of these, and even to beautiful postage stamps.

The sale in 1946 of the Franklin Delano Roosevelt stamp collection proved the vitality of philately. Jacob Blanck in the February 23, 1946, issue of *Publishers Weekly* sounded a rather plaintive note. "To become a book collector requires," he asserted, "a degree of lettering greater than that possessed by the average schoolboy," who collects stamps. "Now this, we must admit," he goes on to say, "may sound somewhat ludicrous to the comparative few who think only in terms of First Folios (Shakespeare's invariably), Fanshawe, Tamerlane, or the bibelot issued by Eugene Field back in his Denver days. But the fact is that book collecting *need not be, and is not,* necessarily so expensive as the deluxe purveyors would wittingly, or otherwise, have the public believe. Unfortunately the stories of the small and sometimes remarkably fine specialized collections that cost but the fraction of an inscribed *Moby-Dick* never reach the headlines."

A decade ago I wrote a book showing reasonably conclusively that the impecunious amateur can, without going into bankruptcy or losing his wife's affection, build up a fine library of modern first editions. I know quite a few men of modest means who have made author collections, so complete and so fine that they were worthy of presentation to great libraries, of such writers as Richard Jefferies, Edward Thomas, T. F. Powys, Roy Campbell, Stephen Spender, W. H. Auden, R. B. Cunninghame Graham, Aldous Huxley, H. L. Mencken, C. M. Doughty, H. M. Tomlinson, Katherine Mansfield, Katherine Anne Porter, Edward Garnett, Wilfrid Scawen Blunt, Norman Douglas, Henry Williamson, Michael Fairless, W. H. Hudson, Howard Fast, and many others.

Book collecting can be the most rewarding of interests for the collector who reads the books he collects, and who buys only the books he wants to read. I was once moved by a Chinese student some years before the war who actually cut down on his meals so that he could buy a new fine edition of Shelley (Scribner's) and certain Nonesuch Press books that he loved and desired in a beautiful format. Of that particular year he is the only student I can vividly recall.

Reading develops the critical faculty and what Pascal called *esprit de finesse* (good taste and judgment) more rapidly than any other interest I can think of, and these are qualities that we do not have in America in any overwhelming abundance. Travel, one hears, broadens the mind, but I've known people who have been around the world who returned as empty-headed as when they left, though they did bring back a few souvenirs made in Birmingham. It is not long before the persistent reader may differentiate between the quality of one writer as compared with another. From Kipling to Chaucer is quite a gap, but it is one that, in time, may be bridged by any intelligent reader.

The number of friends one makes through book collecting may also be prodigious, and such friendships are among the most rewarding I have. Not only does the constant reader feel a kinship with a favorite author, living or long dead, but also one makes friends with booksellers, generally a fine lot, with critics, writers, and fellow book collectors. I have corresponded for years on the friendliest of terms with men I have never seen who shared with me their interests in certain authors together with their knowledge of books and collecting. The late Paul Lemperly of Cleveland, Ohio, I never saw, but for years his letters to me were so charming and so full of his genuine and enthusiastic love for books, and packed so full of unusual bibliographic lore, that after his death I deposited his letters in the Dartmouth College Library.

Alumni tell me constantly their sense of loss and regret that after leaving college they don't read anymore. If they had, while in college, developed the habit of building up a personal library, they wouldn't feel this as acutely as many of them do. It is often pathetic to see the great number of men and women who appear to have no inner resources whatever, who are afraid to be alone, who play bridge hour after hour with an almost sinister desperation, and who pursue themselves in circles in a desperate effort to "kill" time. They make a lot of psychiatrists rich.

Fortunate indeed was the late Sir William Osler, and others like him, who early in life developed a love for reading that greatly enriched his life as long as he lived; made him, in fact, a better, more enlightened, more human physician.

Best-sellers, written often with Hollywood in mind, and ballyhooed by the bright advertising boys, the book societies, and the newspaper reviewers who discover masterpieces ten times a week, seldom have lasting merit. One exception was Charles Jackson's honest study of an alcoholic, *The Lost Weekend,* 1944, which deserved all that was said about it, but even this fine novel sold only a fraction of the number of copies sold of *Forever Amber,* a trashy book that will be forgotten as soon as it is screened. The finest novel I read in 1945 was William Maxwell's *The Folded Leaf,* and if it was a bestseller I'll be surprised. Who now reads *The Winning of Barbara Worth, Lavender and Old Lace, The Trail of the Lonesome Pine, The Girl of the Limberlost,* or *The Inside of the Cup?*

My friend George Matthew Adams of New York is a book collector of note, with a highly developed critical sense, and he is one *who reads the books he collects.* He feels something like this about them:

For many years [he writes] I have been a modest collector of first editions of books that have especially interested me. There was a time when I smiled at first-edition collectors. I do it no more. I crave their association. I learn something new from them all. I wrote to an old friend of mine and told her of my beautiful collection of first editions and asked her to come and see them. Her reply was: "I thought books were to be read." Well, great books are to be read, and should be, but when they are great books, they are also to be loved.

Adams then goes on to say that Hilaire Belloc, a highly civilized writer, once said that after he had read a great book in its first edition, all other editions were spoiled for him.

I can understand [Adams writes]; a first edition, especially of a really good book, represents so much of the dreams, the struggles, and the anticipation of the author. Often it has meant his hunger in its creation. . . . George Gissing had to borrow money to get his first book, *The Workers in the Dawn,* into print, as no publisher would assume the risk. Stephen Crane had to do the same when he had his *Maggie: A Girl of the Streets* published. And so few people were interested that only a few hundred copies of each were ever sold. Today a first edition of either is costly, and *Maggie* once brought $3,700 at a sale. There is something of the soul of an author in the first edition of his books, and especially of his first book.

Curiously enough, the discriminating reader who buys first editions of books he wants to read often does make a very sound investment. Suppose, for instance, that a collector had bought Mary Webb's books as they appeared, had kept them in the dust wrapper, and put them on his shelves. He would have made, had he chosen to sell them some *decades* later, several thousand percent on his investment. Robert Frost's *A Boy's Will,* 1913, now brings $100 for a first issue; it could have been bought for a few shillings in 1913. In 1855 when Whitman's *Leaves of Grass* appeared no copies sold in Brooklyn or in New York. A fine copy today is worth $1,000, and in the early thirties I saw a copy at Rosenbach's in Philadelphia for $4,000. Poe could scarcely give away *Tamerlane,* but the last auction price was $15,000 in the book market. I don't know, or care, what Van Wyck Brooks's *The Flowering of New England,* 1936, is worth mint today, but I paid $4 for my copy, which is still pristine in its rather unimaginative dust wrapper.

All of which leads me to the advice given by one of America's premier booksellers, the late James F. Drake. His three "Don'ts on Book Collecting," which still are sound advice, are:

1. Don't buy a book unless you like it. (In other words, don't buy a book just because someone says it is a book you ought to have.)
2. Don't buy a book unless it is a first edition, and if there is a point of issue, the first issue.
3. Don't buy a book unless it is in the best possible condition.

His son, Colonel Marston E. Drake, adds: Don't buy a book just for an investment. Investment should be in negotiable securities so that proceeds can be immediately realized on them by calling a broker and telling him to sell them. If one will, however, buy the books he likes, observing the three don'ts, he is backing his judgment against the world's—if people agree with him, more will want those books and they will be bound to go up in value; if they don't agree with him, what difference does it make anyway? He has the books he *likes.*

I was once told that the values of the late A. E. Newton's books held up better when the crash came in 1929 than did many of his securities. The fluctuation in price for a good copy of the *Kilmarnock Burns,* for instance, is very slight: it will always bring around $3,000, the price depending, of course, on its condition.

In a quarter of a century of collecting I have learned a few things that will almost certainly be of value to the beginner, and even, in some instances, to the experienced collector. These points follow:

1. In the first place, an "edition" may be defined as including all copies of a book printed from *one* setting of type. If the type is "reset," then a second edition appears.

The *Shorter Oxford English Dictionary* defines "edition" as "the whole number of copies printed from the same set of types and issued at one time," and it defines "first" as "that is before all others in time; earliest."

A great English collector defined correctly, I think, what a first edition is. Viscount Esher: "The first edition of a book is its first appearance in print, wherever it may have been published."

In spite of the literalness and exactness of the above definitions, most collectors, curiously enough, deviate considerably from them because of the "following the flag" theory.

This, in brief, means that if one collects an American author, he buys the American edition even though the book may have been published first in England or in Timbuktu; or if an English author, he buys the first English edition even though the book may have been first published in Carmel or in Hong Kong.

John Galsworthy's *The Forsyte Saga,* 1922, was first published in the United States, but most collectors want the first English edition, which came out after the American one. Mark Twain's *The Adventures of Huckleberry Finn* came out in England first, in December 1884, and the American edition came out somewhat later, postdated 1885, but collectors of Mark Twain buy the American edition and they pay a lot more for it. Perfectionists will probably want both editions.

On the other hand, collectors pay $100 for a copy of the American Robert Frost's *A Boy's Will,* in the English edition, and the American edition of the same book can be bought for one tenth of this amount. "Consistency," after all, as Emerson reminded us, "is the hobgoblin of little minds."

2. Printings from the same type at different times are differentiated by calling each printing a "new impression" of the edition. The "first edition" naturally means the first impression of the edition, and this is the one collectors ought to have.

3. The word "issue" is often confusing to the beginner in collecting. Occasion sometimes arises, after a certain number of copies of a book have been sent out from the publisher's warehouses, to alter the makeup or textual content for some error of fact, for a mistake in typesetting, or for some indiscretion of phrase or sentiment, or just because the censor has demanded the excision of a certain passage. The word "issue" is used to differentiate between the first group of the first edition and the second group (slightly altered in one way or another) of the first edition. An "issue" may thus be defined as all copies of an edition that are put on the market at one time, if differentiated by some substituted, added, or subtracted matter from those copies of the same setting of the type that were put on the market at other times. Copies must actually have been "issued" before the word can be used.

Another example may be cited. Say a book has a first printing of one thousand copies. Five hundred of these are bound up for sale, while the remainder is held in unbound sheets until the first five hundred are sold. The first five hundred constitute the *first issue of the first edition.* Then say another two hundred copies are bound possibly in wrappers, or in a different-colored cloth or buckram, or in cloth with a slightly different weave, or perhaps in the same cloth, with or without blind lines or publisher's device, as the case may be. Even if the first binding is duplicated exactly, which, in fact, is nearly impossible, these copies are the *second issue of the first edition.*

Henry David Thoreau's *A Week on the Concord and Merrimack Rivers* was printed in an edition of a thousand copies in 1849. A few less than three hundred were sold. These copies are the first issue of the first edition. Thoreau bought back the remainder (he paid for the printing in the first place) and put them in his attic. After his death these were reissued with a new title page dated 1862, and they constitute the second issue of the first edition. A copy is worth considerably less than one of the first issue, in spite of the slight association value it has. Who knows if Thoreau didn't actually handle my copy, for which I paid only $20 in the early thirties? I like to think so.

A catalogue description may be helpful at this point:

A Boy's Will. Robert Frost. New York: Henry Holt, 1915. 12mo, original cloth.

First American Edition. First Issue with the misprint "Aind" for "And" in the last line on p. 14. Backstrip slightly dull; otherwise fine.

This description implies that a certain number of copies of the Holt edition were actually sold by the publisher before the misprint was corrected. After the mistake was changed a second issue went forth.

4. The word "state" is often seen in book catalogues. This may be explained by quoting an example from David A. Randall's *New Paths in Book-Collecting,* 1934. Writing of Robert Frost's *Mountain Interval,* 1916, he says it exists in three "states." "In the first, on page 88, line 6 was omitted and line 7 duplicated, so both lines 6 and 7 read, 'You're further under the snow—that's all.' In the second the error was corrected, line 6 reading as it should, 'Sounds further off, it's not because it's dying,' and a cancel leaf was inserted. The third is like the second except that that leaf is an integral part of the signature." The use of the word "state" here instead of "issue" means that the copies with duplicate lines were corrected before the book was issued

by the publishers and that all three "states" were issued at the same time. Had some copies of the book been issued before the remaining copies were corrected as he describes, and then issued at a later date, the word "issue" and not "state" would be correct.

5. The term "cancel leaf" refers to the occasional practice of cutting out a certain leaf of a book that has been printed and bound, and of pasting on the stub thus left another leaf with different wordings. Cancellations are done by publishers to save expense. If some copies go out *before* a cancellation is made, these copies constitute the first issue, but if all copies are published after cancellation, then no "issue" is involved.

6. The word "signature" is the binder's term for a folded sheet. It was the practice some years ago to print a small letter or figure in the margin at the foot of the first page of a sheet, to guide the binder in folding, but this practice has been carried out less and less in recent years in the United States.

7. A general ruling regarding printer's errors might be formulated as follows: Printer's errors are *unimportant* so far as values and "points" go. One of Conrad's bibliographers points out that the first edition of his *The Arrow of Gold*, 1919, lacks the letter "A" from the title heading on page 67 (which reads, "The rrow of Gold"), and concludes that the second issue has the omission rectified. This is silly, as most hair-splitting generally is, for in this instance during the process of printing the sheets the letter on the press wore away; the printer realized this and, after inserting a new letter A, started the press again. Both copies, with the A or without it, are the first issue.

8. A good general rule to follow in the case of advertisements in the back of a book in deciding an "issue" is that the dates of advertisements at the end of a book are often misleading and do not, with any degree of certainty, designate priority of issue.

9. Collectors will be wise to buy books when possible with the dust wrapper preserved, for then they will be more certain of getting a cleaner copy and one less shopworn. In ninety-nine cases out of a hundred, however, a dust wrapper has little or nothing to do with

priority of issue, and if it should have, how are you going to be sure that you have the original wrapper that the book had when issued? A dust wrapper is important mainly because it helps keep a book in pristine condition.

Collectors are advised to retain the dust wrappers on their books. Personally I find they give variety and color to the walls of my library, and they do protect the books from dirt and the bindings from fading. If one is forced to sell a book he will get more for it if it has the dust wrapper than if it is missing, since most collectors desire immaculate "mint" copies if such exist, and dust wrappers help keep a book in fine condition.

10. A misunderstanding exists even among experienced collectors, I am told by bookseller friends, concerning the meaning of the words "uncut" and "unopened." *Uncut* means that the pages of a book have not been trimmed by the knife of a binder, or since it left the printing press. *Unopened* means that the pages, folded in the printing and binding process, have not been cut or "opened" by a paper knife to enable one to read the book. I always cut the pages as I want to read them, but there are many collectors who will pay much more for an unopened copy than for one with the leaves cut, and they leave them unopened on their shelves.

11. The collector may be warned about the flossy type of so-called deluxe editions that are made-to-order rarities, and fly-by-night private press books. These badly printed productions are not to be confused with the fine press books issued by top-notch printers such as the Limited Editions Club, the Heritage Press (as a rule), the Spiral Press, the Grabhorn Press, the Yale University Press, the Nonesuch Press, the Overbrook Press, the Southworth-Anthoensen Press, the Peter Pauper Press, the Colt Press, the Trovillion Press, and other fine presses.

12. There is a difference, also, in "presentation" copies. A real presentation copy will generally carry the author's presentation inscription to a friend with his signature, and this type of book does have association and sentimental value as well as a higher commercial value than copies that contain only the author's signature, often

practically forced, or done in a shop window or in a department store, to sell the book.

Beware, too, of forgeries, as there have been many instances of "forged" presentation copies. I recommend to the reader a most interesting book called *The Shelley Legend,* by Robert Metcalf Smith, New York, Charles Scribner's Sons, 1945, which gives a clear account of some famous literary forgeries. Lady Shelley said: "I have seen letters of Shelley's that have been forged so exactly that no man could possibly have detected them who did not possess the originals." The Shelley forger was self-styled "Major George Gordon Byron" and claimed to be Byron's son by a Spanish lady (his real name was probably De Gibler). He made his living for some years selling autograph letters, Byron presentation inscriptions in countless volumes, forged Shelley and Keats letters, and other literary documents he wrote himself.

13. Do not bind your first editions, but if they are rare enough, or if you can afford it, it would be fine to have slipcases made for your valuable and treasured books. If you do have a book rebound, the binder should be warned *not* to trim the edges, *not* to cut out inscriptions or advertisements. Bind as is.

In France books are generally issued in paper wrappers so that the owner can bind them to suit his or her taste, but contemporary books lose a large percentage of their value so far as collectors are concerned if they are rebound.

14. Condition *is* of utmost importance to the collector unless the book is a great rarity or is a presentation copy or has some association value. Never buy less than a "fine" copy if a "fine" copy of the book exists.

Edwin B. Hill, the dean of private printers in this country, for many years a resident of Ysleta, Texas, whence he issued his pamphlets to those fortunate enough to get them, and now of Tempe, Arizona, is a book collector and reader of his books. His attitude is typical of that of many book lovers, so I quote from a recent letter:

> In my sixty-odd years of serious garnering of books, I have placed *first* the book itself. Then, condition. Of course, I would possess a

book in immaculate condition—but, not being financially oppor-
tune, I have chosen the best I could (not!) afford.

I've chosen books from libraries of importance when they were
to be acquired—private collections; books with inscriptions;
books from libraries of persons of whom I have knowledge.

Condition? I picked up a first edition of one of Emerson's
scarcer books—not a great rarity—for a dime. It was in the Salva-
tion Army store in El Paso. It had been damp stained and the
cover is loose. It could be expertly repaired—but I have preferred
to add other books to my holdings for the sum the repairs would
cost. So this ruin is one of the "as is" brand.

The few books I have left from the Charles Lamb library are of
course in sad condition. You remember what Crabb Robinson
said of Lamb's library—the finest collection of books in the worst
possible condition he had ever seen? Lamb went the step further.
He chose books in wretched condition for the reason that he
could afford them. While I have not tried to out-Lamb Saint
Charles, I've certain books in that category. After all, the book's
the thing.

I'd never pass a bargain in a wanted book, however badly damaged it might be, hoping someday to replace it with a perfect or at
least a better copy. But that is of other days: Now I buy not at all,
for the burden of living in this mad-money age precludes this one
necessity: for it *isn't* a luxury.

All collectors own "reading" copies, and in the following chapters
many books mentioned are not available to anybody in first editions. Reading is the important thing; collecting first editions is only
a means to that end.

15. Another fairly good rule to follow is never to buy just because,
for the moment, the author brings fancy prices. Popularity is not
usually permanent. This is especially true of modern writers such as
William Faulkner, James Branch Cabell, John Steinbeck, G. B.
Shaw, John Galsworthy, William Saroyan, and others.

The books of real merit are best, and the decision must be left to
one's own judgment, but on the whole, as regards fiction, at least,
the best are the books that depict character. These are the ones that
endure. Becky Sharp, Sam Weller, Pickwick, Sherlock Holmes, Tom
Sawyer, Huck Finn, Tom Jones, are everlasting and so are the novels
in which they appear.

Collect to read and not to be in style. A collector should follow his own hunches or be guided by the best critics.

16. In the book market there are frequent changes in values. A book by a forgotten author will suddenly attract new collectors, and one of the pleasures of collecting is in rediscovering a forgotten author of genuine merit. Alexander Smith's *Dreamthorp,* 1863, has recently had a revival; and when is *Kilvert's Diary,* London, Jonathan Cape, three volumes, 1938–1939–1940, going to be recognized for the fine book it is?

17. There is danger in collecting all the books, pamphlets, and ephemera of an author since if and when the collection is sold a few good things will go at fancy prices and the balance for almost nothing. It is better, many collectors think, to collect several authors rather than just one. It is needless to collect every book by a favorite, though that has been my practice. It is better to collect the best of several of many writers, and that has been my practice, too.

A fascinating chapter in modern book collecting was revealed after a magnificent feat of modern detection by John Carter and Graham Pollard in their book *An Enquiry into the Nature of Certain Nineteenth Century Pamphlets,* 1934 (London: Constable & Co., Ltd.; New York: Charles Scribner's Sons). This is a fully documented exposure of a group of more than fifty "first editions" of such eminent authors as Wordsworth, Tennyson, Dickens, Thackeray, the Brownings, Swinburne, George Eliot, William Morris, R. L. Stevenson, and Rudyard Kipling, consisting mostly of "privately printed" or "pre-first" pamphlets. These appeared in all the standard bibliographies and were generally accepted for upward of three decades until the publication of the above book. Even now a few die-hards refuse to believe that Thomas J. Wise, M. A. Oxon., premier bibliographer in England in our time, was the forger of these pamphlets, aided and abetted, innocently or not, by H. Buxton Forman and the late Edmund Gosse.

The exposure of the real character of these books, as Carter and Pollard said, introduced scientific methods that were never before applied to bibliographical problems. The paper used in the printing was analyzed under the microscope, and its evidence assessed in the light of some original research into the history of paper manufacture. The peculiarities of type were traced to the printer, and the involved story of the establishment of these books in bibliographies and in the rare-book market is patiently unraveled.

Long before this book was written it was felt "that the privately printed first edition of Mrs. Browning's *Sonnets from the Portuguese* (*Sonnets by E. R. B.,* Reading, 1847) was not all that it should be."

Actually the *Sonnets* were first published to the world in the second edition of her collected *Poems* (two volumes, Chapman & Hall, 1850), but in 1894 Edmund Gosse told for the first time a story of their original printing in 1847. T. J. Wise, who had printed them, and Forman corroborated Gosse.

The 1847 issue of the *Sonnets,* condemned by their paper and their type, is unquestionably a forgery. The evidence is so overwhelming that there "can be no possible doubt whatever." They are still collectors' items, but as literary curiosities and not as the real thing.

Before 1861 rag paper was the only material used for the printing of books. Straw began to be used in 1861, and then ten years later esparto grass (an Iona coarse grass that grows in Spain and the north of Africa) was used, and any paper using esparto must have been made after 1861. Analysis showed that the paper in the 1847 edition of the *Sonnets* was made from a chemical wood and esparto. This was very careless of the forgers, who should have used rag paper.

Whether the forgeries began as a joke and succeeded so well in fooling collectors that it was impossible to turn back, we will never know. Certainly Wise sold his reputation cheaply.

All collectors are urged to read Carter and Pollard's book, for it throws a lot of light on the length that certain bookmen will go to bilk collectors. On the whole, however, I know of no friendlier or more honest group than booksellers, either in England or in the United States. They are helpful, friendly, courteous, honest, and generally lovers of books themselves. It is a wise book collector who numbers among his close friends several book dealers.

It was not very long ago that Oscar Lion of New York City, who has what must be the finest privately owned Whitman collection in America, was approached by a man who wanted to sell him a first edition of *Leaves of Grass.* It didn't require much acumen to detect the fraud, as fraud it was, for Mr. Lion knew of the facsimile edition of the thin, green 1855 edition printed by Mosher in Portland, Maine. The volume had been "worked over" to make it appear old, but such was Lion's sense of humor that he bought it anyway for a nominal sum, and it is now one of the items in his collection.

A friend whose opinion on books I respect wrote to me with suggestions for some new paths in collecting. In general the collector will find prices cheap in such collecting, for it is demand that raises the price of books as it does everything else. He suggests American poetry before 1850 as a field of real interest. Many of the poets are obscure, but a collection would be worthwhile as the collector could contribute to our body of knowledge concerning American literature. Rarely are there more than one small edition of each, which makes the task a little easier. A collection of American plays could be made; not of the very early rarities, but all plays written by Americans during a stated period. Another field for the collector might be illustrated American books other than those by the much collected Frederic Remington and Howard Pyle; books with woodcuts, steel engravings, or lithographs; American bindings in leather and cloth that would throw light on the history of American binding and show how bindings have changed; a collection of old parlor table books; books by writers for girls and boys, not the rare paper juveniles, but the books by Oliver Optic, Horatio Alger, G. A. Henty, Edward Eggleston, Edward Stratemeyer, and so on. These are seldom reprinted and are vanishing fast. One could collect books with unusual inscriptions by former collectors, with considerable amusement and profit.

Many collectors know that their greatest pleasure came from the search for and purchase of their books. Only recently a sprightly old gentleman of eighty-four voiced these sentiments. My happiest recollections of London are centered around my book hunting there, and I await the time when I can go hunting there again.

It is also fun to collect single authors. Other paths suggest themselves: regional collections (a friend of mine has a magnificent collection of Vermontiana, which he plans to leave to the Vermont Historical Society); juvenile books; books on mountain climbing; war books; nature books; fishing books; modern poetry; books on painting and architecture; state guides (I have all the W.P.A. guides, some of which are getting increasingly difficult to procure); the best novels of various authors, one for each (such as Arnold Bennett's *The*

Old Wives' Tale, Somerset Maugham's *Of Human Bondage,* John Galsworthy's *The Forsyte Saga,* Theodore Dreiser's *An American Tragedy*); privately printed material; finely printed books; books illustrated by such men as Edward A. Wilson, Hugh Thompson, Arthur Rackham, Robert Gibbings, and Claire Leighton; military history; and many others. The number of paths possible for a collector to blaze are really unending.

I consider the following modern English writers well worth reading and collecting: H. E. Bates, Sean O'Faolain, Mary Webb, Stephen Spender, W. H. Auden, C. Day Lewis, Christopher Isherwood, Evelyn Waugh, David Garnett, C. E. Montague, H. M. Tomlinson, Katherine Mansfield, Angela Thirkell, Joseph Conrad, W. H. Hudson, R. B. Cunninghame Graham, Wilfrid Scawen Blunt, Freya Stark, Gertrude Bell, Edward Garnett, A. Conan Doyle, John Galsworthy, H. St. John Philby, C. M. Doughty, T. E. Lawrence, D. H. Lawrence, James Joyce, Thomas Hardy, A. E. Housman, Llewelyn Powys, Richard Jefferies, Theodore Powys, Siegfried Sassoon, Norman Douglas, Edward Thomas, Edmund Blunden, Sean O'Casey, J. M. Synge, Henry Williamson, Neil Gunn, Neil Munro, Herbert Read, and Robert Graves. Others I leave for your discretion.

American writers that I read and collect include William McFee, Henry Miller, Anaïs Nin, Katherine Anne Porter, Kay Boyle, Hervey Allen, Stephen Vincent Benet, Thomas Boyd, Kenneth Roberts, Eudora Welty, Edgar Lee Masters, Theodore Dreiser, Carl Sandburg, Ring Lardner, H. L. Mencken, Robert Frost, Edna St. Vincent Millay, George Santayana, T. S. Eliot, Henry James, Logan Pearsall Smith, Willa Cather, John Burroughs, Rowland E. Robinson, William Beebe, D. C. Peattie (who writes too many books to maintain the standard he set with *An Almanac for Moderns*), John Muir, Ernest Hemingway, and of course others. I personally have a blind spot in the case of John Steinbeck and Saroyan, both of whom have innumerable followers.

Good hunting!

How to Care for Books

ESTELLE ELLIS AND
CAROLINE SEEBOHM

An interesting volume for book lovers—and a delightful hit in book-stores—was the lavishly illustrated 1995 volume At Home with Books, *in which the libraries of the rich and famous were pictured, along with wonderful pieces on books and book care. The following essay is the authors' summary of the current state of book care.*

In 1880 William Blades wrote his comprehensive *The Enemies of Books.* This classic, though filled with stern admonitions, is as relevant today as it was a century ago. Blades's work speaks to those who are building or restoring a library, starting a special collection, or those simply interested in preserving the books they read in their youth for their children and grandchildren. Just as people often think to create a protected environment for paintings or photographs, so should they for their books.

1 Fire

> There are many of the forces of Nature which tend to injure books; but among them all not one has been half as destructive as fire.

> —W.B.

Blades calculates that not only is fire the most destructive of all enemies of books, but that only one-thousandth of the books that once
existed still exist, thanks to what he calls the "fire-king."

Good housekeeping, according to the National Fire Protection
Association, is the number one way to prevent a fire. As in a forest
deprived of rain, overly dry conditions are conducive to fire. Climate
control through central air-conditioning can guard against the drying and dust-promoting nature of heat. Some collectors use fireproof walls or containers and choose nonflammable or fire retardant
material for library curtains.

Smoking is as bad for books as it is for people. Not only does it increase the chances of fire because of a dropped ash or fallen match,
but smoke can work its way into the pages of books and leave a smell
behind. If you smoke, or have guests who do, be especially alert
when you're in the library.

After studying the effects of a serious fire that caused considerable
damage due to heat, Don Etherington, former conservator of the
Harry Ransom Humanities Research Center, found that books that
had been oiled resisted heat better than those that had not been
treated. The smaller the book, the greater the damage. Leather bindings and labels, including those in glass-fronted cases, frizzled or
looked bubbled, particularly those on upper shelves where heat was
most intense. Rapid decrease in humidity may be the reason for this.
Leather bindings should be put on lower shelves even in glass-
fronted cases where they are, in general, better protected. Polyester
dust jackets are also a good book saver.

If fire or smoke does damage to your books, there are materials
that can help you repair them. Jane Greenfield, author of *The Care
of Books,* finds that Pink Pearl erasers work better than any other material for removing scorch marks. Damp sponges work best on
smooth cloth but do not work well on paper. Extra-fine steel wool
will take soot off leather bindings and leave them intact. However,
she says, "Beware of chemical sponges which leave residual film. To
get rid of any lingering smell after a fire, thoroughly air books out on
a slightly breezy day. Stand books, fanned out, on a table in the
shade, but do not leave them overnight. Some damage restoration
firms can also provide equipment to dissipate residual odor." To find
such a firm in your area, check the Yellow Pages under "Fire and
Water Damage Restoration."

2 Water

Next to Fire we must rank Water in its two forms, liquid and vapour, as the greatest destroyer of books.

—W.B.

Aside from flooding through natural disaster or otherwise, water vapor or general dampness can lead to mold and disfigured books. As Blades describes it, "Outside it fosters the growth of a white mould or fungus which vegetates upon the edges of the leaves, upon the sides, and in the joints of the binding."

Doris Hamburg, in *Caring for Your Collections,* notes the warning signs of dampness and methods of treatment. A musty smell and the appearance of fuzzy spores are the tip-offs. If mold develops, as it is prone to do in seaside houses or in basements, remove the affected books and place them in a dry area. Then, on a sunny day, take the books outside and lightly brush the mold with a soft camel-hair brush to remove the spores. Dabbing, but not rubbing, with a kneaded eraser will show whether the material is too delicate to be brushed. If so, or if in doubt, bring the books to a professional conservator.

Mold develops because of poor air circulation and too much humidity. So if you're keeping books in glass-fronted bookcases, make sure that you open them periodically to provide essential ventilation. Mold grows at 70 degrees Fahrenheit and 65 percent relative humidity in stagnant air. It can be prevented or controlled by maintaining a library temperature below 70 degrees Fahrenheit and by allowing relative humidity to climb no higher than 60 percent, preferably keeping it closer to 50 percent. Air-conditioning and fans can be used for climate control. Dehumidifiers help through the warmer seasons. Humidifiers should be used in winter when a well-heated library also means too little humidity, which can dry out books and increase the risk of fire.

If you live in a house that tends to flood, keep your bookshelves at least twelve inches from the floor. Collector Timothy Mawson recalls the morning he came into his New York shop after such in-house flooding. "A water pipe broke in the men's room above and totally flooded everything. We used waxed paper between the pages of the books so they would not stick together and worked at it for nearly forty-eight hours, saving an enormous number of books."

If your books get wet, those that are not absolutely saturated can be dried by fan. Stand the books on several layers of paper towels or unprinted newspaper (available at art supply stores) and let one or two fans blow on them if possible; use a piece of Styrofoam under the opened book for support. Books can also be dried by placing paper towels or unprinted newspaper within the book, one every fifty pages or so. (Newspaper is a good absorber, but because of its acidic content it should not be left inside a book for too long.) The towels and/or newspaper should be changed often—a time-consuming operation. When books are almost dry (slightly cool to the cheek), close them and finish the drying under light weights. Softcover books can be dried this way or hung on a clothesline. (If your collection is seriously damaged by water, remind your insurance company that the longer wet books sit and mold forms, the higher the cost of restoration; this may hasten an appraisal.)

For books with coated paper, such as most illustrated books, freeze or vacuum drying is recommended. (This paper tends to stick together when wet and then dried by the usual method.) Wrap your books in freezer paper and pack them tightly in plastic milk crates. While taking books to a rapid-freezing facility is best, a home freezer can be used. After the books are frozen, they should be kept at −15 to 20 degrees Fahrenheit until a vacuum-drying facility can take them to be dried. (In vacuum drying, water goes straight from ice to vapor.)

Very few facilities offer these techniques of freezing and vacuum drying. For addresses to those in your area, contact WEL T'O Associates, P.O. Drawer 40, 21750 Main Street, Unit 27, Matteson, IL 60443; (312) 747-6660. Also check the Yellow Pages under "Fire and Water Damage Restoration."

3 Gas and Heat

Treat books as you should your own children, who are sure to sicken if confined in an atmosphere which is impure, too hot, too cold, too damp, or too dry.

—W.B.

Blades, writing about the twin dangers of gas and heat, had witnessed the damaging effect his gas lamps had on books stored on upper shelves. The sulphur in the gas fumes had turned them into the consistency "of scotch snuff." Today, air-conditioning and protective cases are the best guards against chemical threats.

Though chemicals such as sulphur dioxide and other air pollutants are a potent danger to books, heat alone can damage books by drying out and destroying their bindings. Heat, Jane Greenfield says, increases the deconstructive power of acid that may be lurking within a book's paper or ink, and causes a lowering of relative humidity.

Designer Jack Lenor Larsen recalls visiting an elegant library years ago and being told that four maids would apply Vaseline to all the leather bindings twice a year to prevent them from drying out. For those without four maids or a lot of free time, the best preventative to heat damage is to maintain a library temperature of between 60 and 70 degrees Fahrenheit, preferably at the lower end of the scale, and to keep books away from radiator and other heat sources.

4 Light

> *The electric light has been in use in the Reading Room of the British Museum, and is a great boon to the readers. However, you must choose particular positions if you want to work happily. There is a great objection too in the humming fizz which accompanies it . . . and there is still greater objection when small pieces of hot chalk fall on your head.*
>
> —W.B.

Though Blades foresaw the downside of electric lighting for the reader, he did not foresee its particular dangers to the books themselves. "Light," Dorris Hamburg writes, "causes changes in the paper structure itself as well as leading to bleaching, fading, darkening, and/or embrittlement." The ultraviolet rays in fluorescent lights can be damaging, explains Elaine Haas, president of TALAS, a professional resource center for libraries. If you have very valuable books, she suggests you slip special ultraviolet absorbent material over the fluorescent tubes.

But in addition to artificial light sources, sunlight can be equally or more damaging. Even indirect sunlight can lead to fading. An unpopular but simple way to protect your collection is to draw the blinds in your library. Food book collector Richmond Ellis uses window shades on the bookshelves themselves.

5 Dust and Neglect

> *Dust upon Books to any extent points to Neglect, and Neglect means more or less slow Decay.*

> —W.B.

For those who hate to dust, there are storage options to avoid the problem. Jack Lenor Larsen adopted Japanese design practices and found that "if fabrics are hung up from the ceiling to cover the books, I don't have to look at a lot of stuff all the time. It also reduces dust and therefore cleaning and breakage." Window shades can also protect books from dust and other pollutants. Make sure any material you use is acid-free. Protective book boxes can preserve rare books from dust or pollution.

There is no formula for how often a library must be dusted; it depends on the environment. Anthony Trollope dusted his library twice a year. Frequent vacuuming and/or sweeping will reduce dust buildup. A feather duster is the classic implement for removing dust, but a vacuum cleaner is better. A portable mini-vac, or Dustbuster, though less powerful, may be easier to use in the small spaces between books. Barbara Kirschenblatt-Gimblett uses something in between—a Service Vacuum Cleaner she ordered through Contact East, Inc., North Andover, Massachusetts. Designed for cleaning delicate office equipment like computers, disk drives, and printers, this vacuum is portable and relatively light, weighing a total of nine pounds.

Regardless of the method you choose, Jane Greenfield recommends you begin by cleaning the top edge of the book. Dust and vacuum away from the spine and hold the book tightly so the dust does not work its way down into the pages. You can use saddle soap on leather bindings to remove dust, dirt, and grime, but not on gold tooling or turn-ins (leather-bound books whose binding extends within the inside edges of the covers and spine). Any moisture can cause blackening and cracking of deteriorating leather, so clean them only if you have to. If you decide to clean your leather bindings, form a lather with the saddle soap and rub the lather into the leather. Wipe off the excess with a clean, damp sponge, drying the binding with a lint-free cloth. Let the book dry completely before putting it back. For cloth bindings, you can use Bookleen Gel, available from library resources. For rare paper bindings, expert help may be required, such as described in Anne F. Clapp's book, *Curatorial Care of Works of Art on Paper: Basic Procedures for Paper Preservation.*

6 Ignorance

> *Ten years ago, when turning out an old closet in the Mazarine Library, of which I am librarian, I discovered at the bottom, under a lot of old rags, a large volume. It had no cover nor title-page, and had been used to light the fires of librarians.*

—W.B.

Even the best-educated bibliophiles, like author and journalist Roger Rosenblatt, are torn between their respect for books and their desire to enjoy them to their fullest, for instance, by engaging with the text through scrawled commentary. "It's shameful to admit: I deface books all the time," he says, referring to his penciled scribbles. "And I enjoy seeing the scribbling of others. There is a communicative and emotional value in a record of another human being's thoughts and feelings left for future readers to happen upon. Of course, though this harms a book, if the scribbler happens to have been Henry James or James Joyce, the book becomes much more valuable."

Books can also be damaged by people's well-meaning efforts to repair them, particularly by using nonrestoration-quality material such as transparent or duct tape to repair torn pages or bindings. Bookbinders have to use Unseal Adhesive Releasing Solvent to remove such tape from books. If you do not wish to take a damaged book to a professional restorer, binders Wilton Wiggins and Douglas Lee advise you to wrap the book in acid-free paper and tie it up with library tape, a flat cotton string that can be used to hold the book together if the spine or binding is loose. There are also special tapes available in a first-aid kit from TALAS in New York and other resources.

7 The Bookworm (and Other Vermin)

> *There is a sort of busy worm*
> *That will the fairest books deform,*
> *By gnawing holes throughout them.*
> *Alike, through every leaf they go,*
> *Yet of its merit nought they know,*
> *Nor care they aught about them.*
>
> *Their tasteless tooth will tear and taint*
> *The Poet, Patriot, Sage, or Saint,*
> *Nor sparing wit nor learning.*
> *Now, if you'd know the reason why,*
> *The best of reasons I'll supply:*
> *'Tis bread to the poor vermin.*

—J. DORASTON (QUOTED BY WILLIAM BLADES)

Worms, beetles, and creepy-crawlies of all kinds can chomp through your precious volumes and turn them into fodder—and birthing places for larvae. "If," Jane Greenfield says, "you have termites in your bookshelves, or if you are stacking books from suspect areas, like barns, cellars and attics, you should freeze the collection before placing it in your library." She reports that a simple at-home method was developed by Yale University biology professor Charles Remington: Make sure the books are completely dry, thereby preventing the formation of ice crystals. Seal books or wrap them well in plastic bags, preferably made of polyethylene, and freeze them at 6 degrees Fahrenheit in a domestic freezer. (At Yale, books are frozen at −20 degrees Fahrenheit for seventy-two hours.) This will kill all beetles and insects at all stages of development.

Fifteen Books We Would Memorize If We Were the "Living Books" Characters in Ray Bradbury's Novel Fahrenheit 451

BY THE EDITORS

In 1953 Ray Bradbury's futuristic novel, Fahrenheit 451, *was published. It was about a world in which books have been outlawed and the government employs "firemen" to burn libraries and destroy all books (which catch fire at a temperature of 451 degrees Fahrenheit). The solution of those few insurgents devoted to books was to memorize and actually become the classics they wished to preserve, retelling them verbatim to others. The vision was profoundly disturbing to all book lovers (Bradbury delights in doing that), but it set the editors to thinking: Which books would they want to become? These books are not presented as the most important, or the most influential, or the greatest—or any such noble description. They are the books that we feel have become so much a part of us that if we ever found ourselves forced to, we could memorize them in order to preserve them.*

1. *The Sun Also Rises* by Ernest Hemingway
2. *Catch-22* by Joseph Heller
3. *Night* by Elie Wiesel
4. *1984* by George Orwell
5. *The Sound and the Fury* by William Faulkner

 6. *Atlas Shrugged* by Ayn Rand
 7. *April Morning* by Howard Fast
 8. *The Great Gatsby* by F. Scott Fitzgerald
 9. *Catcher in the Rye* by J. D. Salinger
10. *A Separate Peace* by John Knowles
11. *Demian* by Hermann Hesse
12. *Cat's Cradle* by Kurt Vonnegut, Jr.
13. *To Kill a Mockingbird* by Harper Lee
14. *Portrait of the Artist as a Young Man* by James Joyce
15. *Time and Again* by Jack Finney

> *Some books are to be tasted, others to be swallowed, and some few to be chewed and digested; that is, some books are to be read only in parts; others to be read but not curiously; and some few to be read wholly, and with diligence and attention.*
>
> —FRANCIS BACON, "OF STUDIES," *ESSAYS* (1625)

"Nothing thanks. I don't *read* books,
I just like to be in their presence occasionally."

The "100" Game

The people who reacted negatively to the Modern Library list issued in 1998 seemed to be unaware that such lists have a long and distinguished history. Here are two lists of 100 greatest books selected seventy years apart—one from A. Edward Newton's 1928 book, This Book-Collecting Game, *and the other from the Modern Library.*

100 Greatest Novels in the English Language

BY   A.   EDWARD   NEWTON

"You seem to get a lot of pleasure out of book-collecting. I am a man" (or woman) "of some little means and ordinary intelligence; I have always been fond of books and reading. Can you give me any suggestion as to what to collect?"

Having received hundreds of letters of this general tenor, after due consideration I venture to suggest the collection of good novels. The novels I recommend must be written in English; they should have a certain bibliographical interest, and for the most part be fairly accessible in first editions; they must be readable today, and if they were once popular—so much the better.

I have been told and I have reluctantly come to believe that the greatest novels have been written in the Russian language. I admit their greatness, but I do not much care for them: they are immense canvases—like Tintoretto's—and they are almost certainly gloomy, when they are not tragic. But, however great, foreign novels have no place either in my life or in my list.

I shall not attempt to make any distinction between a novel and a romance. Someone has said that a story filled with tea fights is a novel, while if it is filled with sea fights it is a romance; this distinction will serve as well as any other. We all know what we mean when we use the word "novel": it is the literary form that today makes the widest appeal the world over. People can and do read novels who read little else; they are suited to every taste and age, and, speaking generally, they are read and forgotten.

Anticipating the further question, "What novels shall I collect?" I have with the advice of several eminent writers of fiction, and with the suggestions of many friends and the aid of a bookseller or two, prepared my list of

ONE HUNDRED GOOD NOVELS

1. *Adam Bede*	Eliot
2. *Adventures of Sherlock Holmes, The*	Doyle
3. *Alice in Wonderland*	Carroll
4. *Babbitt*	Lewis
5. *Barchester Towers*	Trollope
6. *Ben-Hur*	Wallace
7. *Caleb Williams*	Godwin
8. *Captains Courageous*	Kipling
9. *Cashel Byron's Profession*	Shaw
10. *Casuals of the Sea*	McFee
11. *Children of the Mist*	Phillpotts
12. *Cloister and the Hearth, The*	Reade
13. *Colonel Carter of Cartersville*	Smith
14. *Conqueror, The*	Atherton
15. *Conrad in Quest of His Youth*	Merrick
16. *Cranford*	Gaskell
17. *Crisis, The*	Churchill
18. *Crock of Gold, A*	Stephens
19. *Cruise of the "Catchalot," The*	Bullen
20. *Damnation of Theron Ware, The*	Frederic
21. *David Copperfield*	Dickens
22. *Democracy*	Adams
23. *East Lynne*	Wood
24. *Emma*	Austen
25. *Esther Waters*	Moore
26. *Ethan Frome*	Wharton
27. *Evelina*	Burney
28. *Sir Richard Calmady*	Mallet
	(Mary St. L. Harrison)

29. *Frankenstein* — Shelley, Mrs.
30. *Green Mansions* — Hudson
31. *Handy Andy* — Lover
32. *Heart of Midlothian, The* — Scott
33. *Henrietta Temple* — Disraeli
34. *History of Sandford and Merton, The* — Day
35. *Honorable Peter Sterling, The* — Ford
36. *Honour of the Clintons, The* — Marshall
37. *Huckleberry Finn* — Mark Twain
38. *Humphrey Clinker* — Smollett
39. *Jane Eyre* — Brontë (C.)
40. *Joanna Godden* — Kate-Smith
41. *John Halifax, Gentleman* — Mulock
42. *Joseph Vance* — De Morgan
43. *Lady Audley's Secret* — Braddon
44. *Last Days of Pompeii* — Bulwer-Lytton
45. *Last of the Mohicans, The* — Cooper
46. *Lavenger* — Borrow
47. *Life and Adventures of Peter Wilkins, The* — Paltock
48. *Life and Opinions of Tristam Shandy, Gent, The* — Sterne
49. *Little Minister, The* — Barrie
50. *Little Women* — Alcott
51. *Lorna Doone* — Blackmore
52. *Luck of Roaring Camp, The* — Harte
53. *Man of Property* — Galsworthy
54. *McTeague* — Norris
55. *Moby-Dick* — Melville
56. *Monsieur Beaucaire* — Tarkington
57. *Moonstone, The* — Collins
58. *Mr. Midshipman Easy* — Marryat
59. *Mr. Facey Romford's Hounds* — Surtees
60. *New Grub Street* — Gissing
61. *Mr. Britling Sees It Through* — Wells
62. *Nigger of the Narcissus, The* — Conrad
63. *Nightmare Abbey* — Peacock
64. *Of Human Bondage* — Maugham
65. *Old Wives' Tale, The* — Bennett
66. *Ordeal of Richard Feverel, The* — Meredith
67. *Pamela* — Richardson

68.	*Parnassus on Wheels*	Morley
69.	*Peter Ibbetson*	Du Maurier
70.	*Picture of Dorian Gray, The*	Wilde
71.	*Portrait of a Lady*	James
72.	*Prisoner of Zenda, The*	Hawkins
73.	*Rasselas*	Johnson
74.	*Red Badge of Courage, The*	Crane
75.	*Rise of Silas Lapham, The*	Howells
76.	*Robert Elsmere*	Ward
77.	*Robbery Under Arms*	Bolderwood
78.	*Romantic Comedians, The*	Glasgow
79.	*Scarlett Letter, The*	Hawthorne
80.	*Story of a Bad Boy*	Aldrich
81.	*Story of Kennett, The*	Taylor
82.	*Ten Thousand a Year*	Warren
83.	*Tess of the d'Urbervilles*	Hardy
84.	*Thaddeus of Warsaw*	Porter
85.	*Three Black Pennys, The*	Hergesheimer
86.	*Tom Brown's School-Days*	Hughes
87.	*Tom Burke of Ours*	Lever
88.	*Tom Cringle's Log*	Scott
89.	*Tom Jones*	Fielding
90.	*Treasure Island*	Stevenson
91.	*Two Years Before the Mast*	Dana
92.	*Uncle Remus*	Harris
93.	*Uncle Tom's Cabin*	Stowe
94.	*Vanity Fair*	Thackeray
95.	*Vicar of Wakefield, The*	Goldsmith
96.	*Virginian, The*	Wister
97.	*Way of All Flesh, The*	Butler
98.	*Westward Ho!*	Kingsley
99.	*Wuthering Heights*	Brontë (E.)
100.	*Zuleika Dobson*	Beerbohm

I could say why I admit a certain author or a certain book and exclude another, but I do not wish to be asked to give my reasons. I suggest that every collector make his own list.

Let it be understood that by collecting novels, I mean collecting the books in first editions, as they were originally published, whether in calf, boards, parts, or cloth, and in good condition. Good is a relative term: it will be practically impossible to find an old and popular novel in fine condition. Books which have passed into and out of "lending libraries," or books which have been read by a whole generation of readers, invariably show grievous signs of wear. Every collector will decide for himself whether he will take on a poor copy of a book, hoping to get a better one later, or wait until a good copy turns up. I recommend both courses.

It was an easy matter to select sixty volumes for my list: there could be little or no disagreement as to the best sixty novels. The next twenty occasioned difficulty and much discussion, but it was carried on without undue acrimony: "It's your list, not mine," a man would say. The last twenty brought about a pitched battle: "No sane man would omit Marie Corelli and Ouida and include Tarkington and Owen Wister, and why in heaven's name do you omit *Pickwick*?" My first thought was to place an asterisk (*), à la Baedecker, after the title of the sixty novels about which there was no question; a question mark (?) after the title of the next twenty—the doubtful titles; and an exclamation point (!) after the last twenty—"which no sane man would think of." But why deprive my reader of the pleasant feeling of superiority which he might have in himself appraising the comparative value of all the books in my list? It seemed that a pleasant hour might be passed in placing here a star, there a question mark, and elsewhere an exclamation point. Then it occurred to me that my reader might not be provided with sixty stars, twenty question marks, and twenty exclamation points. Whereupon, taking a leaf out of the eccentric Lord Timothy Dexter's famous book—in which he massed the punctuation marks on one page, that his readers might pepper and salt his work as they pleased—I secured from my publisher the space necessary to provide the given number of "points," and here they are, very much at my reader's service.

```
   *    *    *    *    *    *    *    *    *    *
   *    *    *    *    *    *    *    *    *    *
   *    *    *    *    *    *    *    *    *    *
   *    *    *    *    *    *    *    *    *    *
   *    *    *    *    *    *    *    *    *    *
   *    *    *    *    *    *    *    *    *    *
```

?   ?   ?   ?   ?   ?   ?   ?   ?   ?
?   ?   ?   ?   ?   ?   ?   ?   ?   ?
!   !   !   !   !   !   !   !   !   !
!   !   !   !   !   !   !   !   !   !

The novels I have selected have at one time or another enjoyed great popularity or had some special significance. I include *Uncle Tom's Cabin* and omit *Old Town Folks,* which is a better novel. The thoughtful reader will soon discover why I have included Conan Doyle and Joel Chandler Harris, and omitted Poe and O. Henry.

It is hardly worthwhile recommending a book which in first edition is practically nonexistent, like *Pamela,* but it can be had, at a price, and as it is the cornerstone or capstone of any collection of modern English novels, I have included it in my list. Some very rare books can be had cheaply—with luck. An excellent copy of *Lady Audley's Secret* was sold for almost nothing not long ago; and a correspondent writes me that he recently bought a first edition of *Moby-Dick* for ten cents and sold it to a bookseller for sixty dollars; he asked me what I thought of the transaction. I told him that I should have respected him more if he had doubled both his buying and his selling price.

My list is designed to suggest the collection of other books by the same author, or similar books by various authors. *Zuleika Dobson* never had the success of *David Harum,* but it will be read when *David Harum* is forgotten, on account of its enduring fantastic charm; and if Beerbohm's novel leads the reader to collect Max, it will have earned its place in this list. It will be observed that only one book by each author is indicated: a better and less interesting list could be made if some authors were permitted two or more books. There are one hundred great novels in the English language, but there are not a hundred great novelists—not by any means.

If I were asked how these novels can be obtained, and how one is to tell a first from a second or twenty-second edition, I should reply: Consult the booksellers' catalogues. It won't be long before the arrival of a catalogue will mean a pleasant thrill, especially if the catalogue has been compiled with care. The secondhand booksellers of London and the English provinces will be found the cheapest, but one may read many catalogues before coming across a book which he will care much to own, and by the time the order is received on the other side the item will almost certainly have been sold. On the other hand, not only are most of the catalogues published in this country well printed, but they are mines of bibliographical information: they may, indeed, be regarded as textbooks of literature, and as such they may be profitably studied. Even with good catalogues, you will make mistakes at first: we all do, but keep right on, studying as you go.

I put Dickens at the top of my list of novelists, but for steady reading Trollope gives me more pleasure. With no single masterpiece to his credit, he has written a greater number of thoroughly readable novels than any other English author.

I do not undervalue humor; it is only too rare. It is easy to be tragic; tragedy lives just around the corner from most of us. I am, with Sterne, "firmly persuaded that every time a man smiles—but much more so when he laughs—it adds something to this fragment of life."

It is very sad to think that, out of our population of over one hundred and ten million people, it has been estimated that only about two hundred thousand are consistent book-buyers. Too few people understand the joy of buying books, and too few people know how to sell them. People are taught to sell bonds and automobiles and washing machines, but books are supposed to sell themselves. Bessie Graham should be teaching the art of bookselling, not to fifty people, but to five thousand. A correspondence course could be instituted: let the publishers club together and establish a School of Bookselling.

Too many people believe that it is an extravagance to buy books. "He has a book; in fact, several": well, the more he has the more he wants, usually. Too much that has been written about books is very "high hat" indeed. "A book is a window through which the world looks out": such a statement only bewilders the average man. Lord Gregory of Fallodon voices my opinion very simply. "Books are the greatest and most satisfactory of recreations. I mean the use of books for pleasure: without having acquired the habit of reading for pleasure, none of us can be independent."

As life tends to become more and more distracting, let us firmly hold on to books. We move to the country to escape interruptions of the city, and the damned telephone keeps ringing all the time, and now the radio has added to its distractions. For myself, I have no desire to hear a political speech, a concert, a sermon, some cheap jokes, and a lot of "static," all in one evening—or, indeed, any of them in any evening. I prefer to live behind the times with a good book—not too far from a wood fire in winter, in the shade of a tree in summer; but it is difficult to read out-of-doors: Nature, in her quiet way, has a way of interrupting us.

To come back to my list of novels. I have changed it again and again; it is not right now and never will be. There are fashions in novels as there are in plays; a twenty-year-old play is rather silly: "it dates," we say, meaning thereby that its machinery creaks. At a recent revival of *The Two Orphans,* girls whose knees were "overexposed" as the photographers say; with bobbed hair, and whose skirts were a mere flounce, laughed at scenes which had caused their mothers to weep copiously—mothers whose crowning glory was their hair and who wore bustles to make their skirts "hang"—who upon leaving the theatre covered their red and swollen eyes with a veil, that no one should suspect how thoroughly they had been enjoying themselves.

Old Father Time, with his scythe and his whiskers, has seen so many things come and go that he is reluctant to express an opinion as to what is permanent. The novel of today is gone tomorrow: at the moment it is the fashion to praise *The Bridge of San Luis Rey;* where will it be in six months? I should have found a place in my list for a novel by Ouida; for *All Sorts and Conditions of Men,* by Besant; for *The Manxman,* by Hall Caine; for *John Inglesant,* by Shorthouse . . . There are certainly forty novels just as good as those to which the reader will append a question mark or an exclamation point.

One final word to collectors: Avoid artificial rarities, most private press books, masterpieces of printing, reprints of famous books in expensive and limited editions. Stick to first editions; don't be afraid to pay a good price, a high price, for a fine copy of any important book, but be sure that it is important. The better the book, the higher the price, the better the bargain. And a good rule for a beginner is to read every book he buys: this will slow down his purchases somewhat but will make him a better collector in the end.

Books are intended to be read; the collecting
of them is only an incident in their
lives as it is in ours,
saying which,
in the words of William Blake,
"The Scribe of Pennsylvania casts his pen
upon the earth."

Top 100 English-Language Novels of the Twentieth Century

BY THE EDITORS OF
THE MODERN LIBRARY

1. *Ulysses,* James Joyce
2. *The Great Gatsby,* F. Scott Fitzgerald
3. *A Portrait of the Artist as a Young Man,* James Joyce
4. *Lolita,* Vladimir Nabokov
5. *Brave New World,* Aldous Huxley
6. *The Sound and the Fury,* William Faulkner
7. *Catch-22,* Joseph Heller
8. *Darkness at Noon,* Arthur Koestler
9. *Sons and Lovers,* D. H. Lawrence
10. *The Grapes of Wrath,* John Steinbeck
11. *Under the Volcano,* Malcolm Lowry
12. *The Way of All Flesh,* Samuel Butler
13. *1984,* George Orwell
14. *I, Claudius,* Robert Graves
15. *To the Lighthouse,* Virginia Woolf
16. *An American Tragedy,* Theodore Dreiser
17. *The Heart Is a Lonely Hunter,* Carson McCullers
18. *Slaughterhouse Five,* Kurt Vonnegut, Jr.
19. *Invisible Man,* Ralph Ellison
20. *Native Son,* Richard Wright
21. *Henderson the Rain King,* Saul Bellow
22. *Appointment in Samarra,* John O'Hara

23. *U.S.A.* (trilogy), John Dos Passos
24. *Winesburg, Ohio,* Sherwood Anderson
25. *A Passage to India,* E. M. Forster
26. *The Wings of the Dove,* Henry James
27. *The Ambassadors,* Henry James
28. *Tender Is the Night,* F. Scott Fitzgerald
29. *The Studs Lonigan Trilogy,* James T. Farrell
30. *The Good Soldier,* Ford Maddox Ford
31. *Animal Farm,* George Orwell
32. *The Golden Bowl,* Henry James
33. *Sister Carrie,* Theodore Dreiser
34. *A Handful of Dust,* Evelyn Waugh
35. *As I Lay Dying,* William Faulkner
36. *All the King's Men,* Robert Penn Warren
37. *The Bridge of San Luis Rey,* Thornton Wilder
38. *Howards End,* E. M. Forster
39. *Go Tell It on the Mountain,* James Baldwin
40. *The Heart of the Matter,* Graham Greene
41. *Lord of the Flies,* William Golding
42. *Deliverance,* James Dickey
43. *A Dance to the Music of Time* (series), Anthony Powell
44. *Point Counter Point,* Aldous Huxley
45. *The Sun Also Rises,* Ernest Hemingway
46. *The Secret Agent,* Joseph Conrad
47. *Nostromo,* Joseph Conrad
48. *The Rainbow,* D. H. Lawrence
49. *Women in Love,* D. H. Lawrence
50. *Tropic of Cancer,* Henry Miller
51. *The Naked and the Dead,* Norman Mailer
52. *Portnoy's Complaint,* Philip Roth
53. *Pale Fire,* Vladimir Nabokov
54. *Light in August,* William Faulkner
55. *On the Road,* Jack Kerouac
56. *The Maltese Falcon,* Dashiell Hammett
57. *Parade's End,* Ford Maddox Ford
58. *The Age of Innocence,* Edith Wharton
59. *Zuleika Dobson,* Max Beerbohm
60. *The Moviegoer,* Walker Percy
61. *Death Comes to the Archbishop,* Willa Cather

62. *From Here to Eternity*, James Jones
63. *The Wapshot Chronicles*, John Cheever
64. *The Catcher in the Rye*, J. D. Salinger
65. *A Clockwork Orange*, Anthony Burgess
66. *Of Human Bondage*, W. Somerset Maugham
67. *Heart of Darkness*, Joseph Conrad
68. *Main Street*, Sinclair Lewis
69. *The House of Mirth*, Edith Wharton
70. *The Alexandria Quartet*, Lawrence Durrell
71. *A High Wind in Jamaica*, Richard Hughes
72. *A House for Mr. Biswas*, V. S. Naipaul
73. *The Day of the Locust*, Nathanael West
74. *A Farewell to Arms*, Ernest Hemingway
75. *Scoop*, Evelyn Waugh
76. *The Prime of Miss Jean Brodie*, Muriel Spark
77. *Finnegans Wake*, James Joyce
78. *Kim*, Rudyard Kipling
79. *A Room with a View*, E. M. Forster
80. *Brideshead Revisited*, Evelyn Waugh
81. *The Adventures of Augie March*, Saul Bellow
82. *Angle of Repose*, Wallace Stegner
83. *A Bend in the River*, V. S. Naipaul
84. *The Death of the Heart*, Elizabeth Bowen
85. *Lord Jim*, Joseph Conrad
86. *Ragtime*, E. L. Doctorow
87. *The Old Wives' Tale*, Arnold Bennett
88. *The Call of the Wild*, Jack London
89. *Loving*, Henry Green
90. *Midnight's Children*, Salman Rushdie
91. *Tobacco Road*, Erskine Caldwell
92. *Ironweed*, William Kennedy
93. *The Magus*, John Fowles
94. *Wide Sargasso Sea*, Jean Rhys
95. *Under the Net*, Iris Murdoch
96. *Sophie's Choice*, William Styron
97. *The Sheltering Sky*, Paul Bowles
98. *The Postman Always Rings Twice*, James M. Cain
99. *The Ginger Man*, J. P. Donleavy
100. *The Magnificent Ambersons*, Booth Tarkington

91 Chambers Street

BY EDWARD ROBB ELLIS
(MAP OF FOURTH AVENUE BROADWAY
BOOKSELLERS BY MAHLON BLAINE)

Ellis began writing his diary at the age of sixteen in his native Illinois, and continued to his death in 1998, creating a diary that wound up in the Guinness Book of Records *as America's largest. As an active journalist for, among others, the* New York World-Telegram, *Ellis was a keen observer of the times and an honest chronicler of this world. In this entry from his 1995 collection,* A Diary of the Century, *Ellis captures the atmosphere of a used-book shop, one of many that flourished (or floundered) in lower Manhattan in the 1950s. How many booksellers? In the middle of the entry we've placed Mahlon Blaine's 1958 map, a promotional piece for the "Fourth Ave. Broadway Booksellers' Association," identifying nineteen shops (in an area that also included a dozen non-members). Steve Seskin's bookshop on Chambers St. was a few blocks south of the area covered on this map.*

THURSDAY, MAY 15, 1958

Steve Seskin and I were alone in his book shop at 91 Chambers St. The front door was open invitingly, almost beseechingly, so I kept within my trenchcoat against the chill gusts prowling this gray day. A moment after I entered, [my wife] Ruthie phoned Steve to order a book for her boss, and my eyes met his laughingly. After hanging up

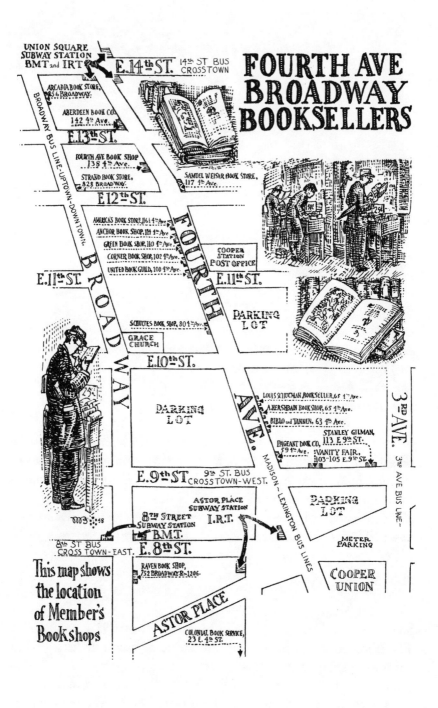

UNION SQUARE
SUBWAY STATION
BMT and IRT

E. 14th ST.   14th ST BUS
CROSSTOWN

FOURTH AVE BROADWAY BOOKSELLERS

ARCADIA BOOK STORE,
856 BROADWAY.

ABERDEEN BOOK CO.
142 4th AVE.

E. 13th ST.

FOURTH AVE BOOK SHOP
138 4th AVE.

STRAND BOOK STORE,
828 BROADWAY.

SAMUEL WEISER BOOK STORE,
117 4th AVE.

E. 12th ST.

AMERICA'S BOOK STORE, 116 4th Ave.

ANCHOR BOOK SHOP, 114 4th Ave.

GREEN BOOK SHOP, 110 4th Ave.

CORNER BOOK SHOP, 102 4th Ave.

UNITED BOOK GUILD, 100 4th Ave.

COOPER
STATION
POST OFFICE

E. 11th ST.   E. 11th ST.

BROADWAY BUS LINE—UPTOWN—DOWNTOWN.

BROADWAY

FOURTH

PARKING LOT

SCHULTES BOOK SHOP, 80 4th Ave.

GRACE CHURCH

E. 10th ST.

PARKING LOT

LOUIS SCHUCMAN BOOKSELLER, 65 4th Ave.

A. HERSHBAIN BOOK SHOP, 65 4th Ave.

BIBLO and TANNEN, 63 4th Ave.

STANLEY GILMAN,
113 E. 9th ST.

PAGEANT BOOK CO,
59 4th Ave.   VANITY FAIR,
103-105 E. 9th ST.

AVE.

3RD AVE.   3RD AVE BUS LINE—

MADISON~LEXINGTON BUS LINES

E. 9th ST   9th ST. BUS
CROSSTOWN-WEST.

PARKING LOT

METER PARKING

ASTOR PLACE
SUBWAY STATION
I.R.T.

8TH STREET
SUBWAY STATION
B.M.T.

8th ST BUS
CROSSTOWN-EAST.

E. 8th ST.

COOPER UNION

This map shows the location of Member's Bookshops

RAVEN BOOK SHOP,
752 BROADWAY R. 1206.

ASTOR PLACE

COLONIAL BOOK SERVICE,
23 E. 4th ST.

the phone, Steve turned to me. The laughter had drained from his brown eyes and his face became cloud-gathered.

"Eddie," said Steve, "I've come to a decision."

I waited, my eyes on his.

"I've decided to sell out. I'm putting an ad in the Sunday paper."

The moment I had dreaded was upon me. Turning on my heel, I muttered "Jesus Christ!" and strode away, walked several paces away with my face averted, snorted "Jesus Christ!" and stalked back, wheeled again to pace and pace and heavily breathe. "Jesus Christ!"

Finally, drawing up in front of Steve, I stopped and faced him. Steve fumbled with lean fingers in his tobacco pouch.

"I'm defeated," he said. "I've had it. I've come to the end of my tether."

The words I spoke seemed forced through my pores: "What do you plan to do, Steve?"

"Oh, teach school, I guess." I knew that he had a master's degree. "Guess I'll get a job as a high school teacher—that is, if they'll have me now.

"You know, Eddie, everything I've done seems wrong. This business is a failure. I'm a failure—"

"Goddamnit!" I interrupted. "Now, none of that! You're not a failure, Steve. Don't ever let yourself think that."

"And why the hell not?"

I said: "Look: So you've been in the book business twenty-five years and so you haven't made any money. This doesn't mean there's anything wrong with you. It's just that your values don't happen to be the standard values of this particular civilization—the goddamn businessman's civilization!"

As though not hearing me, Steve spoke, his saddle-brown eyes vacant: "The truth of the matter is, Eddie, I'm suffering from a deep malaise. You know what this means. Here in this shop I tried to create a little cultural center, you might say. I threw out all the goddamn cheap paperback novels of crime and lust so that I might give the public the worthwhile books. I didn't want to cheapen myself by handling that kind of trash. Culture? There is no culture in America! I don't know why I should be so proud as to try to sell the books I have here. The hell with it. Better yet I should turn this into a schlock house and sell whatever goddamn trash the people want."

"You couldn't," I said.

"I know I couldn't," he said hopelessly. "But the fact remains, Eddie, that I'm a failure."

"Like hell you're a failure!" I snorted, glaring at him. "Now, I know this won't solve your problems or put any money in your pockets, but some day you may remember this: You may remember that one day a guy named Eddie Ellis looked you in the eye to say: Steve Seskin, you're one helluva nice guy!"

From a pocket, Steve extracted a Kleenex and put it to his nose.

"So I'm a nice guy," he said in a hollow voice, and his cheeks appeared even more sunken.

"Yes, you're a nice guy," I repeated.

"This malaise . . ." Steve mumbled.

"You tried," I said, and the words sounded like mockery in my own ears.

By this time, to get off my broken foot, I had taken that chair I often use in Steve's store. He stood behind his counter, a man of forty-six, middling height, lean, his hair whitening, dapper moustache, neat in appearance, a victim of America's bitch goddess Success, his heart laid open on her altar, the red oozing out in a meaningless sacrifice.

"I wish I had words of wisdom," I tried again. "But I haven't. I can't be a Pollyanna." I sighed. "After all, Steve—it's all a lot of shit!"

He knew that by this I meant—Everything. "Yes," he nodded, animated for the first time, "it sure is all a lot of shit! You work and you plan—why, how long can I go without a vacation? In a one-man operation like this, I get up in the morning and I don't feel too well and then I worry about what happens if I can't get to the store, because there's only me. It's—Look: Twenty-five years in the book business, and now I come to this!"

The phone rang. As I later learned, it was Steve's sister, Selma. "Yes," he was saying, "I've decided to sell out. . . . Yes, I've talked it over with Helen . . ." He meant his wife.

I walked and cursed and cursed and walked, and with curses on my lips there was very little in my brain. After Steve got off the phone we spoke mostly in silences.

"Did I mention how much I'm asking?" Steve said.

"No. No, you didn't say."

"Well, I'm asking for only $15,000—although my stock alone is worth at least $20,000."

"What happens if you don't find a buyer?"

"Well, my lease has a year or so to go. Way I feel, maybe I'd do something unethical, really compromise. Such as, for instance, stop buying any more books, just sell what I have here, then get out."

"What's unethical about that?"

Steve hesitated. "There might be some creditors left."

"You owe some money, Steve?"

"Every businessman owes money."

Then he said: "If I can't win fighting fair, maybe I'll fight some other way."

"Hell," I snorted, "and have ulcers again in six months!"

"A man has to compromise."

"Sure," I agreed, "sure a man has to compromise—but within limits. I compromise every day and I hate it. But life is compromise. As I said, though—within limits."

"I'm tired," Steve said. "I'm tired of fighting. I can tell you, Eddie, but I couldn't even tell Helen or Selma: This malaise of mine . . . truly, it's a deep-seated thing."

"I know," I said, and I really did know. "I'm like you, Steve. I'm a confirmed pessimist. That's why we agree it's all shit."

For a while we didn't talk. Steve tamped his pipe and struck another match. Trenchcoated, I leaned my elbows on the counter. After long thought I raised my chin.

"Steve, if you're really going to sell out—all at once, to one man—which way would it help you more: If I bought some books from you, I mean if I came in with a check for $200 or $300 and bought some titles I've been wanting, or if this man, whoever he is, if he came in and bought it lock, stock, and barrel?"

"Why, by selling to you."

"It would be only a drop in the bucket."

Steve's cheeks seemed to flatten. "Now if you're doing this just to help me—" he began.

"Nuts! I buy books. If I can get a bit of a bargain from you, I'm helping little old Eddie Ellis. But if I can help you a little bit at the same time—well, Steve, it's a mutual sort of thing."

Steve thought a moment. "I'd sell 'em for what they cost me and just a little bit more."

"Naturally! You have to take a profit! But, Steve, I'm thinking of myself now—really. Still, I sort of feel like a vulture picking over bones."

"You don't have to feel that way."

"No, Steve, I guess I really don't. Of course, I'd have to get Ruthie's approval."

"Of course."

"What if I came in after work some day and picked out what I want?"

"Well . . . How about Saturday? That way, I could sell some things to you before I put in the ad, and so my conscience will be clear. Besides, I could bring the car down, and then I could tote the books up to your place."

"Ruthie will scream," I laughed. " 'Where'll we put them?' she'll ask." Steve laughed, too. "Yeah, I know."

"If it's okay with you then—"

"Sure," said Steve. "Saturday?"

"I'll check with Ruthie."

When I got back to the office, I called Ruthie. She gave her approval instantly.

"I'll stop buying dresses," she said.

"Like hell," I said.

"Oh," she said, "I can buy dresses any old time. But this—well, this is the chance of a lifetime!"

I agreed.

"Poor Steve," she said.

Bibliobibliography—
Books About Books: A Selection

Bibliophilia—if not bibliomania—is as old as books themselves. It is even older, in fact, than printed books—Richard de Bury's classic, The Philobiblon (The Love of Books), *was completed in 1345, more than a hundred years before Gutenberg printed his first Bible. So as long as there have been bibliophiles, there have been books for and about them. Thus, this bibliography, extensive as it is, represents only a small sample of books on the subject.*

*With only two exceptions—*The Philobiblon *and Flaubert's* Bibliomania*—all the books described in this bibliography are first editions, and all are available through antiquarian booksellers. In many cases, however, revised editions of these books are also available.*

Books from which selections in this book were made are noted by an asterisk.

Adams, J. Donald. *Speaking of Books—and Life.* New York: Holt, Rinehart & Winston, 1965.

Adams, Randolph G. *Three Americanists: Henry Harrisse, Bibliographer; George Brinley, Book Collector; Thomas Jefferson, Librarian.* Philadelphia: University of Pennsylvania Press, 1939.

Aldis, Harry G. *The Printed Book.* Cambridge: Cambridge University Press, 1941.

Altick, Richard D. *The Scholar Adventurers.* New York: Macmillan, 1950.

Andrews, William. *Literary Byways.* London: William Andrews & Co., 1898.

Basbanes, Nicholas A. *A Gentle Madness: Bibliophiles, Bibliomanes, and the Eternal Passion for Books.* New York: Henry Holt & Co., 1995.*

Bay, J. Christian. *The Fortune of Books: Essays, Memories and Prophecies of a Librarian.* Chicago: Walter M. Hill, 1941.

Benjamin, Walter. *Illuminations.* New York: Schocken Books, 1968.*

Bennett, Paul A. *Books and Printing: A Treasury for Typophiles.* Cleveland: World Publishing Co., 1951.

Bennett, Whitman. *A Practical Guide to American Book Collecting (1663–1940): With All Items Arranged in Sequence as a Chronological Panorama of American Authorship and with Each Subject Considered from Bibliographical, Biographical, and Analytical Aspects.* New York: Bennett Book Studios, 1949.

Beresford, James. *Bibliosophia, or Book Wisdom.* London: William Miller, 1810.

Bishop, William W. *The Backs of Books and Other Essays in Librarianship.* Baltimore: Williams & Wilkins Co., 1926.

Blades, William. *The Enemies of Books.* London: Trubner & Co., 1880.

———. *The Pentateuch of Printing.* Chicago: A. C. McClurg & Co., 1891.

Blumenthal, Walter Hart. *Bookmen's Bedlam: An Olio of Literary Oddities.* New Brunswick, N.J.: Rutgers University Press, 1955.

Book Arts Club. *About Books—A Gathering of Essays.* Berkeley: Book Arts Club of the University of California, 1941.

Bouchot, Henri. *The Book.* London: H. Grevel & Co., 1890.

Brent, Stuart. *The Seven Stairs.* Boston: Houghton Mifflin Co., 1962.*

Brewer, Reginald A. *The Delightful Diversion: The Why and Wherefores of Book Collecting.* New York: Macmillan, 1935.

Burns, Eric. *The Joy of Books: Confessions of a Lifelong Reader.* Amherst, N.Y.: Prometheus Books, 1995.

Burton, John Hill. *The Book Hunter.* New York: Sheldon & Co., 1863.

Carter, John. *ABC for Book Collectors.* New York: Alfred A. Knopf, 1952.

———. *Books and Book-Collectors.* Cleveland: World Publishing Co., 1957.

———. *Taste and Technique in Book-Collecting: A Study of Recent Developments in Great Britain and the United States.* Cambridge: Cambridge University Press, 1948.

Clark, John Willis. *The Care of Books.* Cambridge: Cambridge University Press, 1901.

Cobden-Sanderson, T. J. *The Journals of Thomas James Cobden-Sanderson (1879–1922)*. New York: Macmillan, 1926.

Collison, Robert L. *Book Collecting: An Introduction to Modern Methods of Literary and Bibliographical Detection*. London: Ernest Benn, 1957.

Crane, Walter. *Of the Decorative Illustrations of Books Old and New*. London: George Bell & Sons, 1896.

Currie, Barton. *Fishers of Books*. Boston: Little, Brown & Co., 1931.

Davies, Robertson. *Tempest-Tost*. Toronto: Clarke, Irwin & Co., 1951.

———. *The Enthusiasms of Robertson Davies*. Edited by Judith Skelton Grant. New York: Viking, 1990.*

de Bury, Richard. *The Philobiblon*. Berkeley: University of California Press, 1948.

de Ricci, Seymour. *The Book Collector's Guide: A Practical Handbook of British and American Bibliography*. Philadelphia: Rosenbach Co., 1921.

Dibdin, Thomas Frognall. *Bibliomania; or Book Madness*. London: Longman, Hurst, Rees & Orme, 1809.

Donaldson, Gerald. *Books: Their History, Art, Power, Glory, Infamy, and Suffering According to Their Creators, Friends and Enemies*. New York: Van Nostrand Reinhold Co., 1981.*

Downs, Robert B. *Books That Changed the World*. Chicago: American Library Association, 1956.

———. *Books That Changed America*. New York: Macmillan, 1970.*

Eco, Umberto. *How to Travel with a Salmon & Other Essays*. New York: Harcourt Brace & Co., 1994.*

Ellis, Estelle, Caroline Seebohm, and Christopher Simon Sykes. *At Home with Books: How Booklovers Live with and Care for Their Libraries*. New York: Carol Southern Books, 1995.*

Everitt, Charles P. *Adventures of a Treasure Hunter: A Rare Bookman in Search of American History*. Boston: Little, Brown & Co., 1951.

Fadiman, Clifton. *Party of One*. Cleveland: World Publishing Co., 1955.*

Fadiman, Clifton, and John S. Majors. *The New Lifetime Reading Plan*. New York: HarperCollins, 1997.*

Field, Eugene. *The Love Affairs of a Bibliomaniac*. New York: Charles Scribner's Sons, 1896.

Fitch, George Hamlin. *Comfort Found in Good Old Books*. San Francisco: Paul Elder & Co., 1911.*

Flaubert, Gustave. *Bibliomania: A Tale*. London: Rodale Press, 1954.*

Furman, Laura, and Elinore Standard. *Bookworms: Great Writers and Readers Celebrate Reading*. New York: Carroll & Graf, 1997.

Gilbar, Steven, ed. *Reading in Bed: Personal Essays on the Glories of Reading.* Boston: David R. Godine, 1995.*

———. *The Book Book.* New York: St. Martin's Press, 1981.*

Goldstone, Lawrence, and Nancy Goldstone. *Used and Rare: Travels in the Book World.* New York: St. Martin's Press, 1997.

Goodspeed, Charles J. *Yankee Bookseller.* Boston: Houghton Mifflin Co., 1937.

Graffagnino, J. Kevin. *Only in Books: Writers, Readers, & Bibliophiles on Their Passion.* Madison, Wisc.: Madison House, 1996.

Grannis, Chandler B. *What Happens in Book Publishing.* New York: Columbia University Press, 1957.

Harrison, Frederick. *A Book about Books.* London: John Murray, 1943.

Hearn, Lafcadio. *Books and Habits.* Edited by John Erskine. New York: Dodd, Mead & Co., 1921.

———. *Talks to Writers.* New York: Dodd, Mead & Co., 1920.

Hendrickson, Robert. *The Literary Life and Other Curiosities.* New York: Viking, 1981.*

Highet, Gilbert. *People, Places, and Books.* New York: Oxford University Press, 1953.

Ireland, Alexander. *The Booklover's Enchiridion.* London: Simpkin, Marshall & Co., 1888.

Jackson, Holbrook. *Bookman's Pleasure.* New York: Farrar, Straus & Co., 1947.

———. *The Anatomy of Bibliomania.* London: Soncino Press, 1930.*

———. *The Fear of Books.* London: Soncino Press, 1932.

Johnson, Merle. *American First Editions.* New York: R. R. Bowker Co., 1929.

Jordan-Smith, Paul. *For the Love of Books: The Adventures of an Impecunious Collector.* New York: Oxford University Press, 1934.

Lang, Andrew. *Books and Bookmen.* London: George J. Coombs, 1886.

Lewis, Wilmarth S. *Collector's Progress.* New York: Alfred A. Knopf, 1951.

Madan, Falconer. *Books in Manuscript: A Short Introduction to Their Study and Use.* London: Kegan Paul, Trench, Trubner & Co., 1893.

Manguel, Alberto. *A History of Reading.* New York: Viking, 1996.

McMurtrie, Douglas C. *The Book: The Story of Printing and Bookmaking.* New York: Covici, Friede, 1937.

———. *The Golden Book: The Story of Fine Books and Bookmaking—Past & Present.* Chicago: Pascal Covici, 1927.

Merryweather, F. Somner. *Bibliomania in the Middle Ages; or, Sketches of Bookworms, Collectors, Bible Students, Scribes, and Illuminators.* London: Merryweather, 1849.

Michell, John. *Eccentric Lives and Peculiar Notions.* San Diego: Harcourt Brace Jovanovich, 1984.*

Miller, Henry. *The Books in My Life.* Norfolk, Conn.: New Directions, 1952.

Muir, Percy H. *Book Collecting as a Hobby: In a Series of Letters to Everyman.* New York: Alfred A. Knopf, 1947.

Newton, A. Edward. *The Amenities of Book-Collecting and Kindred Affections.* Boston: Atlantic Monthly Press, 1918.

———. *A Magnificent Farce and Other Diversions of a Book-Collector.* Boston: Atlantic Monthly Press, 1921.*

———. *The Greatest Book in the World and Other Papers.* Boston: Little, Brown & Co., 1925.*

———. *The Book-Collecting Game.* Boston: Little, Brown & Co., 1928.*

O'Connor, J. F. X. *Facts about Bookworms—Their History in Literature and Work in Libraries.* New York: Francis P. Harper, 1898.

Orcutt, William Dana. *The Kingdom of Books.* Boston: Little, Brown & Co., 1927.

———. *The Magic of the Book: More Reminiscences and Adventures of a Bookman.* Boston: Little, Brown & Co., 1930.

Oswald, John Clyde. *A History of Printing.* New York: D. Appleton & Co., 1928.

Perrin, Noel. *Dr. Bowdler's Legacy.* New York: Atheneum, 1969.

Powell, Lawrence C. *Books in My Baggage: Adventures in Reading and Collecting.* Cleveland: World Publishing Co., 1960.

Power, John. *A Handy-Book about Books—for Book-Lovers, Book-Buyers, and Book-Sellers.* London: John Wilson, 1870.

Pritchard, Francis Henry. *Books and Readers.* London: George G. Harrap, 1931.

Proust, Marcel. *On Reading.* New York: Macmillan, 1971.

Quindlen, Anna. *How Reading Changed My Life.* New York: Library of Contemporary Thought, 1998.*

Raabe, Tom. *Biblioholism: The Literary Addiction.* Golden, Colo.: Fulcrum Publishing, 1990.

Rees, Rogers. *The Diversions of a Bookworm.* London: Elliot Stock, 1886.

Rosenbach, A. S. W. *Books and Bidders: The Adventures of a Bibliophile.* Boston: Little, Brown & Co., 1927.*

———. *A Book Hunter's Holiday: Adventures with Books and Manuscripts.* Boston: Houghton Mifflin Co., 1936.

Rostenberg, Leona, and Madeleine B. Stern. *Old Books in the Old World: Reminiscences of Book Buying Abroad.* New Castle, Del.: Oak Knoll Books, 1996.

————. *Old Books, Rare Friends: Two Literary Sleuths and Their Shared Passion.* New York: Doubleday, 1997.

Saunders, Frederick. *The Story of Some Famous Books.* London: Elliot Stock, 1887.

Sawyer, Charles J., and F. J. H. Darton. *English Books 1475–1900: A Signpost for Collectors.* Westminster, England: Chas. J. Sawyer Ltd., 1927.

Schwartz, Lynne Sharon. *Ruined by Reading: A Life in Books.* Boston: Beacon Press, 1996.

Silverman, Al, ed. *The Book of the Month: Sixty Years of Books in American Life.* Boston: Little, Brown & Co., 1986.*

Starrett, Vincent. *Books Alive: A Profane Chronicle of Literary Endeavor and Literary Misdemeanor.* New York: Random House, 1940.

Storm, Colton, and Howard Peckham. *Invitation to Book Collecting: Its Pleasures and Practices with Kindred Discussions of Manuscripts, Maps, and Prints.* New York: R. R. Bowker Co., 1947.

Targ, William. *Carrousel for Bibliophiles: A Treasury of Tales, Narratives, Songs, Epigrams and Sundry Curious Studies Relating to a Noble Theme.* New York: Philip C. Duschnes, 1947.*

————, ed. *Bouillabaisse for Bibliophiles: A Treasury of Bookish Lore, Wit & Wisdom, Tales, Poetry & Narratives & Certain Curious Studies of Interest to Bookmen & Collectors.* Cleveland: World Publishing Co., 1955.*

————. *Indecent Pleasures.* New York: Macmillan Publishing Co., 1975.*

Tebbel, John. *Between Covers: The Rise and Transformation of Book Publishing in America.* New York: Oxford University Press, 1987.

Thomas, G. Alan. *Great Books and Book Collectors.* New York: G. P. Putnam's Sons, 1975.

Thompson, James Westfall. *Byways in Bookland.* Berkeley: Book Arts Club of the University of California, 1935.

Thompson, Lawrence S. *Bibliologia Comica, or Humorous Aspects of the Caparisoning and Conservation of Books.* Hamden, Conn.: Archon Books, 1968.

Uhlan, Edward. *The Rogue of Publisher's Row: Confessions of a Publisher.* New York: Exposition Press, 1956.

Van Dyke, J. C. *Books and How to Use Them.* New York: Fords, Howard & Hulbert, 1883.

Webber, Winslow Lewis. *Books about Books: A Bio-Bibliography for Collectors.* Boston: Hale, Cushman & Flint, 1937.

West, Herbert Faulkner. *Modern Book Collecting for the Impecunious Amateur.* Boston: Little, Brown & Co., 1936.

———. *The Mind on the Wing: A Book for Readers and Collectors.* New York: Coward-McCann, 1947.*

Winterich, John T. *Books and the Man.* New York: Greenberg, 1929.

Wroth, Lawrence C., ed. *A History of the Printed Book, Being the Third Number of the Dolphin.* New York: Limited Editions Club, 1938.

Permission Acknowledgments

Grateful acknowledgment is made to the following for permission to reprint previously published material:

Ballantine Books, a division of Random House, Inc.: Excerpt from *How Reading Changed My Life* by Anna Quindlen. Copyright © 1998 by Anna Quindlen. Reprinted by permission of Ballantine Books, a division of Random House, Inc.

Peter Benchley: "Why Does Nobody Collect Me?" by Peter Benchley. Reprinted by permission of the author.

Stuart Brent: Excerpt from "How to Get Started in the Book Business" from *The Seven Stairs* by Stuart Brent. Reprinted by permission of the author.

Crown Publishers, Inc.: Excerpt from *At Home with Books* by Estelle Ellis and Caroline Seebohm. Copyright © 1995 by Estelle Ellis and Caroline Seebohm. Reprinted by permission of Carol Southern Books, a division of Crown Publishers, Inc.

Farrar, Straus & Giroux, Inc.: "The Newark Public Library" from *Reading Myself and Others* by Philip Roth; Copyright © 1975 by Philip Roth; excerpts from *The Anatomy of Bibliomania* by Holbrook Jackson. Copyright © 1950 by Farrar, Straus and Company, now Farrar, Straus & Giroux, Inc. Reprinted by permission of Farrar, Straus & Giroux, Inc.

Harcourt, Inc.: "How to Justify a Private Library" and "How to Organize a Public Library" from *How to Travel with a Salmon and Other Essays* by Umberto Eco, copyright © Gruppo Editoriale Fabbri, Bompiani, Sonzogno, Etas S.p.A.; English translation copyright © 1994 by Harcourt Brace & Company, Inc.; "Unpacking My Library" from *Illuminations* by Walter Benjamin, copyright © 1955 by Suhrkamp Verlag, Frankfurt a.M., English translation by Harry Zohn copyright © 1968 and renewed 1996 by Harcourt Brace and Company, Inc. "Bibliomaniacs" from *Eccentric Lives and Peculiar Notions* by John Mitchell. Copyright © 1984 by Thames and Hudson, Ltd., London. All essays reprinted by permission of Harcourt, Inc.

HarperCollins Publishers, Inc.: Table of Contents from *The New Lifetime Reading Plan* by Clifton Fadiman and John S. Major. Copyright © 1997 by Clifton Fadiman and John S. Major. Reprinted by permission of HarperCollins Publishers, Inc.

Henry Holt and Company, Inc.: Pages 58–82 from *A Gentle Madness* by Nicholas A. Basbanes. Copyright © 1995 by Nicholas A. Basbanes. Reprinted by permission of Henry Holt and Company, Inc.

Alfred A. Knopf, Inc.: "Invasion of the Book Envelopes" from *Hugging the Shore* by John Updike. Copyright © 1983 by John Updike. Reprinted by permission of Alfred A. Knopf, Inc.

Kodansha America, Inc.: Pages 206–226 from *Light One Candle* by Solly Ganor. Copyright © 1995 by Solly Ganor; pages 255–259 from *A Diary of the Century* by Edward Robb Ellis. Copyright © 1995 by Edward Robb Ellis. Reprinted by permission of Kodansha America, Inc.

Lescher and Lescher, Ltd.: "Pillow Books" by Clifton Fadiman. Copyright © 1951, 1955 by Clifton Fadiman. Reprinted by permission of Lescher and Lescher, Ltd.

Little, Brown and Company: Pages 3–34 from *Books and Bidders* by A.S.W. Rosenbach. Copyright © 1927 by A.S.W. Rosenbach; pages 69–96, 97–125, and 382–392 from *The Book-Collecting Game* by A. Edward Norton. Copyright © 1926, 1927, 1928 by A. Edward Norton; pages ix–xxiii from *The Book of the Month* by Al Silverman. Copyright © 1986 by Book-of-the-Month-Club, Inc. All excerpts reprinted by permission of Little, Brown and Company.

The New York Times: "Lending Books" by Anatole Broyard (6/28/91). Copyright © 1981 by The New York Times. Reprinted by permission of *The New York Times.*

Penguin Putnam Inc.: Pages 316–323 from *The Enthusiasms of Robertson Davies* by Judith Skelton Grant. Copyright © 1990 by Judith Skelton Grant. Reprinted by permission of Viking Penguin, a division of Penguin Putnam Inc. Excerpt from *The Mind on the Wing* by Herbert Faulkner West. Copyright © 1947 by Herbert Faulkner West. Reprinted by permission of Coward-McCann, Inc., a division of Penguin Putnam, Inc.

The Reader's Catalog: "Norman Mailer's Ten Favorite American Novels" from *The Reader's Catalog,* First Edition. Copyright © 1989 RC Publications, L.P. Reprinted by permission.

Rosten Heirs c/o Madeline Lee: "Potch" from *People I Have Loved, Known or Admired* by Leo Rosten. Copyright © 1970 by Leo Rosten. Reprinted by permission of Madeline Lee for the Rosten Heirs.

The Rowfant Club: "The Bible Through the Ages" by Ben D. Zevin, a paper read before The Rowfant Club on October 21, 1955. Used by permission of The Rowfant Club, Cleveland, Ohio.

Roslyn Targ Literary Agency: Excerpt from *Indecent Pleasures* by William Targ. Copyright © 1976 by William Targ. Published by Macmillan Publishing Co., Inc. Reprinted by permission of the Rosyln Targ Literary Agency.

Simon & Schuster, Inc.: Excerpt from *Books That Changed America* by Robert B. Downs. Copyright © 1970 by Robert B. Downs. Reprinted by permission of Simon & Schuster, Inc.

Watkins/Loomis Agency, Inc.: Excerpt from *Bibliomania* by Roger Rosenblatt. Copyright © 1998 by Roger Rosenblatt. Reprinted by permission of Roger Rosenblatt and the Watkins/Loomis Agency, Inc.

Jonathan Yardley: "Ten Books That Shaped the American Character" by Jonathan Yardley (*American Heritage* magazine, April/May 1985, Volume 36, #3). Reprinted by permission of Jonathan Yardley.

About the Authors

HAROLD RABINOWITZ is the director of The Reference Works and has served as executive editor of the *McGraw-Hill Encyclopedia of Science & Technology* and science editor of the *Encyclopedia Americana*. He is the author of books on the history of aviation, the old west, and Judaica. He and his family live in Riverdale, New York.

ROB KAPLAN has over twenty-five years experience in the book publishing industry. He has held senior-level editorial positions with several major New York–based publishing houses and currently heads his own literary services firm, Rob Kaplan Associates, which he founded in 1998. He lives with his wife, two children, two cats, and more than 4,000 books in Cortlandt Manor, New York.